Cognitive Foundations of Calculated Speech

SUNY Series in Human Communication
Donald Cushman and Lawrence Kincaid, Editors

Cognitive Foundations of Calculated Speech

Controlling Understandings in Conversation and Persuasion

ROBERT E. SANDERS

State University of New York Press

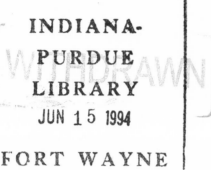

Published by
State University of New York Press, Albany

For information, address State University of New York Press, State University Plaza, Albany, N.Y., 12246

Library of Congress Cataloging-in-Publication Data

Sanders, Robert, 1944-
Cognitive foundations of calculated speech.

(SUNY series in human communication processes)
Includes index.
1. Communication—Philosophy. 2. Speech acts (Linguistics) 3. Communicative competence. 4. Conversation. 5. Persuasion (Rhetoric) I. Title. II. Series.
P91.S28 1986 401′.9 86-5869
ISBN 0-88706-350-0
ISBN 0-88706-351-9 (pbk.)

10 9 8 7 6 5 4 3 2 1

Contents

Preface vii

Glossary of Symbols xi

Part I. Toward an Adequate Theory of Strategic Communication: Conceptual and Metatheoretical Foundations 1

Chapter 1 Strategic Communication: Controlling Understandings 3

Chapter 2 Requirements for an Adequate Theory of Strategic Communication 23

Part II. Utterance Meanings and Specific Interpretations: Controlling Understandings in Discourses and Dialogues 43

Chapter 3 Types of Utterance Meaning: Propositional Content, Implicature and Illocutionary Act 47

Chapter 4 The Relevance of Utterances: Warrants for Specific Interpretations 79

Chapter 5 Laboratory Studies of the Specific Interpretation of Utterances 101

Part III. Controlling Understandings in Different Media and in Different Cultures 127

Chapter 6 The Specific Interpretation of Nonverbal Displays in Different Media, Alone and in Combination with Utterances 129

Chapter 7 Universals of Communication Competence: On Understanding and Being Understood by Foreigners 153

Part IV. A Theory of Strategic Communication and Its Application in Studies of Conversation and Persuasion 173

Chapter 8 The Strategic Formulation of Utterances and Nonverbals: Projecting Possible and Probable Consequences 175

Chapter 9 Orderliness, Disorder and Strategy in Ordinary Conversation 207

Chapter 10 Persuasion: Constraining Individuals and Changing Social Aggregates 229

Endword 247

References 253

Subject Index 267

Index of Proper Names 271

Preface

Communication is a problem for most people, at least occasionally. The problem usually makes itself felt in particular instances as uncertainty about what to say or do, or as anxiety about the way others will react, or as surprise at the way one's utterances and nonverbal displays were understood. Sometimes the problem is consciously anticipated, and an active effort made to solve it beforehand by arraying and evaluating different options of what to communicate, and how to communicate it.

Why should this be? Individuals generally know what they want or need to communicate. They have beliefs, attitudes, roles and responsibilities, and social purposes that generally dispose them in any instance to communicate certain thoughts or feelings to certain people.

Nor should it be any problem knowing how to express the thoughts or feelings one wants or needs to—at least not within one's own language community. As a species, people have a uniquely broad, open-ended capacity for expression and comprehension.

But the reason that communication problems arise nonetheless is that people often have other purposes when they communicate than simply to express their salient thoughts and feelings. On at least some occasions, people communicate to affect others—to exercise control over the understandings others form of the communicator, the situation, their interpersonal relationship, the task at hand, etc., thereby to make different actions and reactions more or less likely.

It happens that to be understood as one intends, and thus to promote or discourage certain (re)actions, it is not enough to form utterances and nonverbal displays according to rules of language, conventions of utterance, and conventions of nonverbal meaning and nonverbal display.

This is because one's utterances and nonverbal displays are

understood in terms of meanings that make them relevant—that contribute to the coherence and progress of the unfolding discourse or dialogue. That is the pivotal thesis of this book. The corollary is that others cannot reliably form an understanding of one's utterances and nonverbal displays if their contribution to the unfolding discourse or dialogue is unapparent. This entails that at any juncture of a discourse or dialogue, only some of the things a person is capable of saying and doing would contribute at all, and thus reliably communicate anything. Even fewer utterances and nonverbal displays would contribute so as to warrant being understood in the intended way, or at least a desirable way.

This creates a constant potential for conflict between what one is disposed to say or do, and the way that would be understood at that point in the discourse or dialogue. This is why it is occasionally problematic whether to communicate what one wants or needs to, and if so, how to communicate it so that it contributes to the discourse or dialogue in a way that diminishes the chances of undesired understandings.

On the other hand, there is a strategic benefit in this. One's respondents are also subject to these constraints. In that case, one can promote or discourage particular (re)actions by communicating at the present juncture so as to affect what those responses would contribute subsequently. This would influence the interpretation, and thereby the desirability and likelihood, of those responses.

The focus of this book on controlling understandings remedies some basic oversights in the way we have studied and theorized about communication. We have given little attention to the activity of communicating itself, and as a result we have relatively little understanding of the problematic and strategic aspects of formulating utterances and nonverbal displays. Instead, we have studied how and why communication plays the roles it does in various social practices and institutions. This overlooks the fact that whether social purposes are served or impeded depends on the constraints that emerge from the way the discourse or dialogue is made to unfold. The role of communication in social practices and institutions is thus variable and contingent on individuals' abilities to recognize and solve communication problems.

The following text is divided into four parts. Part I (Chapters 1–2) summarizes the substantive foundations of the thesis that the interpretation of what is said and done depends on how they contribute to the unfolding discourse or dialogue. Attention is also given to the metatheoretic consequences of accounting for what people communicate, and how they communicate it, in terms of constraints that emerge from projected interpretive consequences, apart from any psychological and social forces on the communicator.

Part II (Chapters 3–5) shows that the way utterances are understood is a function of principles by which an utterance is relevant to antecedent and subsequent constituents of discourses and dialogues. This includes making those principles explicit and providing empirical support for them, in addition to substantiating the claim that the way utterances are understood in particular instances cannot be explained in terms of rules of language and conventions of utterance alone.

Part III (Chapters 6–7) makes explicit principles of relevance in terms of which nonverbal displays are understood in particular instances, alone and in conjunction with utterances. This enables detailing the influence that interpreted nonverbals exert on the interpretation of utterances, and vice–versa. The interconnection between utterances and nonverbal displays is applied to distinguishing among communication media in terms of the resources each provides for controlling understandings. It is also applied to an explanation of how people can make themselves understood despite barriers posed by cultural and linguistic differences.

Finally, in Part IV (Chapters 8–10), those principles of relevance are transformed into forecasting principles within a decision-theoretic account of strategic communication. The utility of this account is then shown with reference to studies of conversation and studies of persuasion, respectively.

ACKNOWLEDGMENTS

The burdens put upon the families of academics who get caught up in a project like this are legend. Sharon and David made the sacrifices necessary to keep the household intact despite my frequent disappearances and unpredictable states of mind. On top of that Sharon did her best to get me to untangle my syntax, and to be less circuitous in my arguments.

Substantive reactions from Don Cushman and Bill Gudykunst while I was drafting the manuscript have been a considerable help. And a careful review of the finished manuscript by Dell Hymes gave me a chance to catch and repair important oversights at the eleventh hour.

Finally, I am greatly indebted to Virginia Apuzzo, Dan Bradley, Jerry Falwell, and Cal Thomas for generously giving me permission to quote from the transcript of a *Donahue* show on which they appeared. I have also received permission from Multimedia Program Productions, Inc. to quote from the transcript. And I am grateful to Joseph DeVito for permission to use his script of a family conflict from *The Interpersonal Communication Book.*

Glossary of Symbols

In this book, the formal representation of relationships and principles underlying strategic communication combines notations that are conventional in set theory and in first-order propositional logic. The glossary below is provided to acquaint readers with these notational conventions and to make explicit certain idiosyncratic usages.

[X]J	=	the object or set of objects, J, that is an extension or realization of the properties of some entity, X.
G:H	=	the qualities or conditions, G, that are manifested by the influence they exert on the state or parameters of H.
(f)P	=	the object or set of objects that derives from the entity P as a function of some operation on P.
K^{-1}	=	the logical or conventional reciprocal of the entity K.
$\{z \mid \alpha z\}$	=	the set of objects z such that z satisfies some condition α.
$E \cap F$	=	intersection: an operation on two sets, E and F, that derives the set of all objects contained in both E and F.
$D \varepsilon F$	=	set membership: D is a member of the set F.
$A \rightarrow B$	=	logical implication: if A, then B.
$A \leftrightarrow B$	=	logical entailment: B if and only if A.
$\Gamma \Rightarrow \Sigma$	=	pragmatic implication of one condition, Σ, by another, Γ. This notation is reserved to represent the conditional on which strategic judgments are predicated, and can be paraphrased: "insofar as Γ is true, it is warranted to conclude that Σ is true."

Part I

Toward an Adequate Theory of Strategic Communication: Conceptual and Metatheoretical Foundations

The following two chapters present, respectively, the conceptual and metatheoretical underpinnings of this book. The first part of Chapter 1 is a summary of the conceptual foundations and implications of the postulate that people are constrained with respect both to what they communicate, and when and how they do so, by the interpretive consequences they project.

In the second part of Chapter 1 there is an analysis of a recorded conversation that illustrates and substantiates this postulate. The conversation is between two undergraduate women who were asked to exchange and resolve any complaints they had about each other as dormitory suitemates. However, on an entirely unrelated topic early in the conversation, student F disclosed her anxieties about negative feedback. That created interpretive consequences of directing subsequent complaints at F that student E evidently found undesirable. E first changed the topic away from that disclosure, then later tried to get F to retract or qualify her disclosure of insecurity, and failing that, introduced the idea that complaining is cathartic (thus warranting a more desirable interpretation of complaining). Those and other features of the conversation can be accounted for as attempts by E to manage its development in order to change the projected interpretive consequences of directing complaints at F.

Chapter 2 is about the consequences for theory and research of accounting for utterances and nonverbal displays in terms of constraints resulting from projected interpretive consequences. Such an account would predict the relative probabilities of possible utterances and nonverbal displays, but not any occurrences. This is because utterances and nonverbal displays would have to be represented in theory as strategic options that are more or less probable at each juncture of a discourse or dialogue, and not as occurrences that follow necessarily from the exertion of sufficient psychological or social force. This gives empirical studies a more complex and indirect role. A theory that predicts relative probabilities rather than events cannot be founded just on regularities in observed events, nor can empirical studies directly falsify such a theory. Empirical studies cannot play a significant role in the development of theoretical formulations of this kind, and function to test them only indirectly, by developing a corpus of circumstantial evidence that cumulatively either substantiates or casts doubt on the validity of particular formulations.

CHAPTER 1

Strategic Communication: Controlling Understandings

STRATEGIC COMMUNICATION

Utterances and nonverbal displays are STRATEGIC when they are formulated in a particular way because it is projected that that will have social utility. An account of strategic communication must therefore make explicit the basis for such projections.

The social utility of utterances and nonverbal displays is contingent first of all on how they are interpreted—i.e., on the understandings they foster about objects and events in the environment, about the speaker's traits and intentions, and about the situation. In addition, the social utility of utterances and nonverbal displays is contingent on how they affect subsequent speech and behavior.

Projecting Interpretations

The logically first problem in strategic communication is to control as much as possible how one's utterances and nonverbal displays are understood. Being understood in the desired way minimizes the chances of provoking unintended responses. Failing this, what a person says and does cannot reliably serve his/her personal or social purposes.

The most that communicators can do to control understandings is to formulate their utterances and nonverbal displays according to the rules, conventions and principles shared with the audience, in such a way as to maximize the chances of being interpreted in the intended way (or to minimize the chances of unintended interpretations). This necessitates projecting the INTERPRETIVE CONSEQUENCES of taking one or another of the communicator's perceived options of content, style and delivery.

It might seem that the bases for such projections would have to be the rules of language and conventions of utterance in the community, and conventions of nonverbal meaning and nonverbal display. However, these rules and conventions are not sufficiently powerful to project the SPECIFIC INTERPRETATION that contemplated utterances and nonverbals will likely receive in a given instance. Rather, those rules and conventions of expression entail only an array of POSSIBLE INTERPRETATIONS, any one of which may be focused on and responded to in a given instance.

> The possible ways of interpreting an utterance or nonverbal display in a given physical or social environment will be referred to here as its "meanings" in that environment. Generally, the rules and conventions of expression specify that an utterance or nonverbal display has some meaning(s) if it has certain features and occurs in an environment with certain features.

For most utterances in a given environment, the rules of language and conventions of utterance collectively entail that each utterance has at least one each of two—and often three—types of meaning: PROPOSITIONAL CONTENT, ILLOCUTIONARY ACT and often IMPLICATURE. Correspondingly, most nonverbals can signal any of several distinct interior states and/or institutional events or acts.

However, utterances and nonverbal displays occur not only within a given physical or social environment, but at particular junctures of unfolding discourses and dialogues. (The term DISCOURSE is used here to denote a sequence of expressions that a single 'author' has produced and brought to a conclusion. The term DIALOGUE is used here to denote a sequence of expressions produced alternately by two or more authors that is concluded when there is either mutual consent or unilateral withdrawal.) Despite the various meanings an utterance or nonverbal display has in a given environment, only one of those meanings—i.e., the specific interpretation—is typically focused on and responded to at each juncture of the discourse or dialogue in which it is entered.

> The specific interpretation of an utterance or nonverbal display is that meaning that it is WARRANTED to focus on and respond to at a particular juncture of a discourse or dialogue. The principal hypothesis here is that a specific interpretation is the product of a judgment that it is the meaning by which the utterance or nonverbal display is relevant—i.e., contributes to the progress and coherence of the unfolding discourse or dialogue.

The distinction between *meaning* and *specific interpretation* entails that the problem of controlling understandings cannot be solved simply by formulating utterances and nonverbal displays according to the rules and conventions of expression. That can only ensure that the desired interpretation is included among several possible meanings. The strategic problem is to exercise as much control as possible over what specific interpretation one's utterances and nonverbal displays will receive.

The principles formulated here by which verbal and nonverbal entries in discourses and dialogues are judged relevant and receive specific interpretations provide a sufficiently powerful basis for projecting the interpretive consequences of different ways of formulating an entry. The primary goal here is thus to make explicit those principles and their application to strategic communication.

Projecting Effects on Subsequent Social Conduct

The second aspect of the social utility of utterances and nonverbal displays is the effect they have on what the author or the audience subsequently says and does. However, projecting the behavioral consequences of contemplated utterances and nonverbals involves the same set of principles as the one involved in projecting their interpretive consequences.

Given that the specific interpretation of an utterance or nonverbal is contingent on the way it is relevant to its antecedents, then the entries that the author of a discourse makes at a given juncture will limit both what he/she can subsequently say and do that is relevant and what the specific interpretation of particular subsequent entries would likely be. An author's current entry in a discourse thus affects the relative probabilities of his/her own subsequent entries.

Hence, one can project from the relationship of an author's current entry to its antecedents what he/she will likely say and do subsequently (or at least what he/she will likely not say or do subsequently).

Similarly, insofar as the author's respondents are also strategic because they have a vested interest in the social utility of what they say and do, then they too have as their logically first consideration how their contemplated utterances and nonverbal displays will be interpreted. That is of course a function of whether those utterances and nonverbal displays are relevant, and in what way, to the communicator's present entry. In that case, the behavioral consequences of the communicator's entry depend on how it has limited what is subsequently relevant. This means that the strategic problem is to formulate entries so that they affect the interpretive consequences of particular responses in ways likely to dispose respondents towards desired ones or away from undesired ones.

Calculations of what to say and do in order to increase the likelihood of the desired utterances or nonverbal displays therefore depend on precisely the same principles by which one calculates the specific interpretation that one's own present utterances and behaviors will likely receive.

Work on the meanings of utterances and nonverbals has generally been segregated from work on message strategies and message effects. This has obscured the interrelationship between communicating so as to make oneself understood in the desired way and communicating so as to affect what is subsequently said and done. A summary of this connection will therefore be useful. This is given in the chain of propositions below:

1. The way others understand us is a function of the way our utterances and behaviors affect the progress and coherence of the unfolding discourse or dialogue.
2. In order to avoid undesired understandings, we must formulate our entries so as to contribute (or not contribute) in certain ways to the progress and coherence of the discourse or dialogue. Thus, at any given juncture there are constraints on what to communicate and how to communicate it.
3. The constraints on our utterances and behaviors that result from efforts to control their meanings and specific interpretation may interfere with what has to be said or done to achieve some social goal. This will foster

either a change in what we communicate and how we communicate it to achieve the goal, or revision or abandonment of the goal.

4. The public effects of messages are registered as their uptake in subsequent speech and behavior. Therefore, uptake also is constrained by its projected interpretive consequences. This can be exploited by communicators seeking to achieve some particular resolution of a discourse or dialogue if they devise their messages in such a way as to affect the interpretive consequences of—and thus promote or inhibit—certain subsequent entries (in the discourse) or certain responses (in the dialogue).
5. Communicators can calculate what to communicate, and how and when to communicate it, in order to promote the desired uptake by projecting the interpretive consequences of each possible subsequent entry of interest, as they follow from each contemplated way of formulating the present entry.

The central purpose of this book is to support these propositions, and its organization parallels their development above. Following the two introductory chapters, Chapters 3–5 make explicit the basis people have for judging the meanings and specific interpretations of utterances. Chapter 6 extends that to nonverbals, alone and in conjunction with utterances. Chapter 7 gives reason to treat as universals of communication competence the principles of specific interpretation formulated in Chapters 4 and 6. In Chapter 8, those interpretive principles are transformed into heuristic principles for projecting the way that contemplated utterances and behavior will affect constraints on subsequent entries in the discourse or dialogue. Chapters 9 and 10 utilize the preceding formulations to account for messages in conversation and in persuasion as the product of calculations of what to communicate, and how to communicate it, to achieve (or avoid) certain outcomes.

ACHIEVING COHERENCE AND PROGRESS IN DISCOURSES AND DIALOGUES

The main concern in this book is the cognitive basis for formulating entries in discourses and dialogues so as to exercise control over the way one is understood, and over the subsequent progress of unfolding discourses and dialogues. But this broad concern arose from work on a much narrower problem (Sanders, 1980, 1981). Semantic and pragmatic theories taken collectively indicate that several distinct types of meaning (propositional content, illocutionary act and implicature) can be assigned equally well to an uttered expression of language in most instances (see, e.g., Austin, 1962; Grice, 1967; Searle, 1969; Kempson, 1977; Gazdar, 1979; Cole, 1981; Levinson, 1983). That raises the question of how interpreters decide in each instance which meaning, or type of meaning, among those alternatives an utterance should be (was intended to be) focused on.

One basis interpreters have for deciding on the (type of) meaning to focus on would be any privileged knowledge they have of the communicator that enables a construal of which focus was intended. But such privileged knowledge is uneven and unreliable. Any general and systematic basis for deciding what (type of) meaning to focus on must therefore involve just what can be known from the PUBLIC RECORD.

The public record comprises just the antecedents of the utterance in question and its consequents. But that is a sufficient basis for deciding what (type of) meaning to focus on. Each type of meaning is distinguished both in terms of the features that interpreted antecedents must have for that particular type of meaning to follow (i.e., be relevant), and in terms of features that interpreted consequents must have to follow from that type of meaning. In that case, the type of meaning that should be (was intended to be) focused on in a given instance can be judged as being the one that is relevant to those features that COHERE (i.e., are the common denominator among) at least some interpreted antecedents or consequents in the discourse or dialogue (see Chapter 4). A comparable problem and a parallel solution also arise with regard to nonverbals (Sanders, 1985; see especially Chapter 6). This leads to the first of two key postulates below:

First Postulate. To achieve a desired understanding, or at least to avoid undesired ones, communicators are constrained at each juncture regarding the content and style of their entries so that the entry will be relevant to antecedents (or to intended subsequent entries) in a way that warrants focusing on the intended meaning, or at least not on any undesired ones.

Note, however, that if the specific interpretation of an utterance is contingent on the way its interpreted antecedents and/or its interpreted consequents are cohered, then specific interpretations are FLUID (i.e., subject to revision over time). When a new entry in a discourse or dialogue is made, it may or may not have a meaning that is relevant to the features that have cohered its interpreted antecedents. If it does, then of course it is warranted to focus on that (type of) meaning, and the warrant for subsequently focusing on that (type of) meaning will be incrementally strengthened. However, if a new entry is made that does not have a meaning relevant to the features that have cohered its interpreted antecedents, the interpreter can either conclude that that entry is tangential or incoherent, or that (at least some of) its antecedents were interpreted and cohered incorrectly. It is an empirical question how interpreters proceed in such cases, but it is likely that at least sometimes they will reinterpret and reintegrate the antecedents. This likely depends on the relative ease of discovering an alternate way of cohering those antecedents, and on the strength of the presumption that the new entries in question are not tangential or incoherent. Hence, there is a second postulate below:

> **Second Postulate.** As new entries are made in discourses and dialogues, they can warrant retrospective changes in the specific interpretation of some antecedents. Conversely, new entries can change what the interpretive consequences would be of subsequently taking particular options of content, style, and delivery.

Applications to Studies of Discourse and Dialogue

The notion that entries are constrained so that they will contribute in some particular way to the coherence and progress of discourses and dialogues makes it possible to account for the functional differences among stylistic variants (e.g., Sanders, 1984). The particular way an utterance is formed and phrased makes its relevance to particular antecedents more or less explicit, and thus increases or diminishes the likelihood of its receiving a given specific interpretation. Further, the way an utterance is formed and phrased narrows or broadens what can relevantly be said and done subsequently.

In addition, the notion that entries are constrained so as to contribute in some particular way to coherence and progress provides a solution to a nagging problem in studies of discourse and dialogue. While there seem to be organizing principles in discourses and dialogues by which the individual parts are integrated into coherent wholes, the specific nature of these principles has been elusive.

In one way or another, however, the presumption in most attempts to isolate these organizing principles is that they are a product of structural relations between formal components of discourses and dialogues (e.g., van Dijk, 1972, 1977; Rumelhart, 1975; Schegloff, Jefferson and Sacks, 1977; Edmondson, 1981; Longacre, 1983). But that need not be so. It is equally possible that discourses and dialogues are organized entirely in terms of meaning relations among their individual constitutents. This would explain the elusiveness of organizing principles within particular discourses and dialogues, let alone across them. The meanings and specific interpretations of entries often have to be adjusted against each other as the discourse or dialogue unfolds, in order that in the end both the specific interpretation of a given entry is relevant to its interpreted antecedents and the specific interpretations of its consequents are relevant to it. In that case, the organizing logic of any given discourse or dialogue is fluid, depending on how its constituent entries are interpreted and cohered.

Applications to Studies of Message Construction and Message Effects

The most central aspect of strategic communication—the basis for taking particular options of content, style, delivery, and timing as a discourse or dialogue unfolds—has been the most elusive. It has not been clear how to account for the particular ways in which utterances and nonverbals are formulated except with reference to the communicator's knowledge of the subject matter, what the communicator is disposed to communicate because of his/her attitudes and personality, the sociology of his/her relations to the audience, and the conventions of speech in his/her community.

However, the theoretical importance of a communicator's cognitions, and psychological and social dispositions decreases when it is taken into account that communicators are constrained at each juncture so that their utterances and behaviors will contribute in a particular way to coherence and progress. For strategic purposes, the disposition to say or do something in particular is a secondary consideration to the following ones: (1) whether that utterance or nonverbal display can relevantly be entered in the discourse or dialogue at that juncture, and (2) which outcomes become possible (i.e., relevant) and which do not if contemplated utterances and nonverbal displays are entered at that juncture. With these considerations in mind, the primary component of an account of strategic communication must be the principles by which communicators project the interpretive consequences of different options of content and style, not dispositional factors.

This makes the strategic formulation of entries in a discourse or dialogue analogous to the selection of lexical entries in producing an utterance. To a considerable degree, the lexical item inserted at a given juncture can be accounted for in terms of syntactic and semantic constraints created by what was inserted antecedently. The particular goals of the speaker, which can be described in terms of qualities that the speaker desires the unfolding utterance to have (e.g., grammaticality, concreteness or abstractness, truth or falsity, newsworthiness, etc.), account only for the selection of lexical items within those constraints.

Let us apply this analogy to the formulation of entries in a discourse. As the discourse unfolds, the meaning relations among its components—and the requirements they engender for progress and coherence—will increasingly constrain what the author can add subsequently (and increasingly create expectations in the interpreter about what will follow). Like the author of a single utterance, the authors of discourses control each entry and thus the constraints that emerge as the discourse unfolds. Authors therefore have erred if they find themselves unable to finish the discourse as they had intended because key entries would be incoherent or receive undesired interpretations. When the authors of discourses do become tangled up in that way, it is probably because of inattentiveness, the complexity of the discourse, or because they attached an intrinsic value to certain previous entries and overlooked their negative utility.

The same analogy extends to the formulation of entries in dialogues, but in a more complicated way. Having a dialogue with others is analogous to collaborating with them in the composition of an utterance, with each permitted to add only one word at a time, having to take turns with each other, and not necessarily seeking the same outcome. This makes it difficult to ensure that the final product will correspond to what any of the participants originally intended. Participants in dialogues make separate decisions about what to say or do, thus making it possible that their respective entries will cohere in ways that produce unintended and undesired constraints. If this occurs and interferes with making entries that participants want or need to, or with achieving the goal they intended, there are three possible remedies. They can either return the dialogue to an earlier juncture and replace the entries there with alternatives calculated to void those unintended constraints, or one or more participants can adopt different goals, or the dialogue can be brought to a premature end.

Note that on this analogy, there is no difference between communicating to obtain a response or to make one. It is the same intellectual problem in either case: to calculate how to move the discourse or dialogue toward (or away from) certain outcomes within the constraints that have emerged up to the given juncture.

Accordingly, when the participants in dialogues have shared interests and common goals, the entries of each are likely to constrain the other in ways wholly compatible with the goals they both have. This predicts that in such cases, dialogues can progress rapidly and even be truncated unless (Hymes, personal communication) the participants draw them out for the sheer pleasure of it.

However, when participants are at cross-purposes, so that, e.g., as one participant makes entries designed to narrow the parameters of what can meaningfully follow and thus foster progress in the direction of certain outcomes, the interpretive consequences and constraints created by those entries will generally be undermined by the entries of others. Lewis (1979) has shown that there is the potential for such fluidity even in what seem like inherent features of sentence meaning.

This potential for fluidity in social interactions means that at an extreme they can take on a surreal aspect, like a game of chess played on a board that changes its contours and boundaries, with pieces that appear or disappear or change in power, as the result of each player's moves. If the participants in social interactions are not minimally committed to mutually reaching a conclusion, their entries need not be constrained as is needed for the sequence to cohere and progress. It is consistent with this generalization that psychotherapists generally insist that before treatment begins, their patients admit to having a problem and needing help. Otherwise, like any interactants at sufficiently great cross-purposes, they can be caught up then like characters in an absurdist drama intent on playing a game that is not only impossible to win, but cannot even progress.

AN ILLUSTRATIVE CASE

The way in which entries are constrained by their projected interpretive consequences, and the way such constraints can change as the discourse or dialogue unfolds, are exemplified in Conversation I (Wiemann, 1977; see the Appendix to this chapter for a transcript).

This conversation between "E" and "F" is one of several that were elicited from pairs of female undergraduates who shared rooms or suites at a large public university in the eastern U.S. Each pair was asked to engage in conversation, in the course of which they were to state and resolve any complaints they had about each other.

Like the other three pairs of women, E and F engage in routine chitchat for the greater part of the conversation and turn to the assigned task of exchanging complaints at the end. A synopsis of their conversation, with key excerpts, follows:

TURNS

1–29 F initiates topic (before the tape begins): *E's unhappiness about recent romantic difficulties and in particular with one man she dated who was insecure.*

30 F: . . . Yeah, Rich doesn't understand [how insecure people can be]. I was telling him . . . um . . . before the Senate elections that, if I lose, I am going to be really upset and it will be much worse to lose this year because I feel everybody . . . by my record they wouldn't think I did a good job this year or something. That'll really, really, you know, be really . . . low, and uh, he couldn't . . . uh . . . understand why my self-esteem was so dependent on this stupid little election.

31 E: Oh, come on.
32 F: And I was, uh, it was just a good thing I won. *(laughs)*
33 E: I guess so. *(laughs)*
34 F: So, you know, really, it's pretty good.

35–50 E initiates topic: *F's plans for housing in the coming school year, and related gossip about potential housemates.*

51 E: Do you honestly start feeling attacked when people, you know what I mean . . . like?
52 F: Yeah.
53 E: So, even if like . . .
54 F: Even if it's not like anything about my character or anything, but you know, you can tell me my handwriting's messy, you know and it . . .
55 E: That would bother you?
56 F: Pretty much. Well, it would depend on the mood I'm in.

57–61 E initiates topic: *the wisdom of airing irritations or dissatisfactions with others as preferable to suppressing them.*

62–end F initiates topic: *F over-interprets E's antecedent entry as a complaint and apologizes, creating a coordination problem on the assigned task of stating and resolving complaints.*

This conversation exhibits a progressive breakdown of topical orderliness and coordination from turn 51 to the end. The difficulties that emerge from turn 51 to the end can be accounted for with reference to F's disclosure at turn 30 that she is unable to handle negative feedback about herself. This disclosure was topically linked to E's prior talk about her problems with an insecure boyfriend, and there is no reason to suppose that F had any ulterior purpose for it. However, that disclosure also has the (apparently unintended) effect of creating an ad hoc interpretive rule that negative feedback addressed to F counts as a psychological assault on her. For E, this evidently created undesired interpretive consequences if she were to complain about anything that F did, thus interfering with E's ability to carry out the assigned task of stating and resolving complaints.

It is consistent with this construction that E's initial response to the disclosure is to say "Oh, come on" and then two turns later to introduce a wholly unconnected topic. It also follows that E subsequently brought the disclosure up again at turn 51 to confirm F's vulnerability to criticism. And given confirmation, it follows that E changed topic again at 57, this time to the introduction of an alternative ad hoc interpretive rule, where complaining counts as a catharsis and not an assault.

E evidently considered that her effort to introduce a substitute interpretive rule was prematurely cut off by F. Hence, the conversation ends with an extended "Alphonse-and-Gaston" routine. Both women are independently seeking to help the other escape the interpretive consequences of F's disclosure, and neither will defer on that point to the other. The trigger for this is F's abrupt apology at turn 62 for being untidy, predicated on the complaint E insinuates at turn 61 by citing their different attitudes towards keeping their room straightened up. (It can be speculated that F over-interpreted E's utterance and responded to it because she realized at that juncture what E's problem was, felt responsible, and tried to facilitate their performance of the task by taking the role of the wrongdoer). F subsequently reiterates the apology, refuses to comply with E's request that she reciprocate by counter-complaining, and asks E to complain further about her. E (evidently unconvinced that uttering criticisms had ceased being interpretable as hostile), talks at cross-purposes to F, trying to back away from the complaint F responded to and trying at least to get F to "retaliate" and even the score.

It fully supports this analysis, and the underlying conceptualization here, that all else having failed, E explicitly spoke to the interpretive issue in her three successive final turns: "I never meant it to be nasty" (turn 73); "when I say it, I don't mean it, so don't get mad" (turn 75); and finally, "So . . . but . . . you . . . you know what I mean" (turn 77).

A number of the specific contentions that were made above are exemplified in Conversation I. First, a communicator (in this case E), armed with something to communicate and the means of expressing it may nonetheless fail. E had good reason to doubt whether anything she did to express her complaints would have had either the meaning or the specific interpretation she intended.

Second, it is clear that entries in a discourse or dialogue affect the way subsequent utterances and behaviors will be interpreted. F's disclosure is by no means the only instance of this in the conversation, but it is by far the most visible.

Third, when participants work at cross-purposes to control the way a dialogue unfolds, the result is the sort of confusion and breakdown evident in Conversation I after turn 62.

Fourth, the formulating of utterances and behavior on the basis of projections of their interpretive consequences is evident from E's efforts to deal with the constraints produced by F's disclosure well in advance of undertaking the task of stating and resolving complaints.

Fifth, E's and F's conversation proceeds as it does precisely because of the fluidity of understandings possible in discourses and dialogues. E's goal subsequent to turn 51 is evidently to alter the way in which her intended complaint will be understood, and her problem following turn 61 is that she cannot be certain which of the possible ways of understanding that complaint is being focused on by F.

Finally, and most importantly, E's entries at several junctures must have been predicated on forecasts of the interpretive costs and benefits of key options at that juncture. It is difficult otherwise to explain E's initial reaction to F's disclosure at turn 30, and especially the effort to establish alternative "rules" for interpreting complaints in turns 57–61.

In addition, there are a number of facts about Conversation I that can most parsimoniously be accounted for by presuming that entries in discourses and dialogues are constrained with regard to the interpretive consequences of what is entered. First, it is only with reference to the postulate that subsequent interpretations are influenced by the antecedent sequence that—in light of the stipulated objective of the conversation (to state and resolve complaints)—F's disclosure acquires the functional status of a problem (possibly accounting for E's topic change away from it at first, and certainly accounting for the topic change back to it later).

Second, E's exhibition of anxiety after turn 62 (her back-pedaling, efforts to elicit complaints from F, overt mentions of her concern about interpretive consequences) is only explicable with reference to the interruption of her efforts in turns 57 and 61 to establish alternative meanings for stating complaints; those efforts in turn are only identifiable as such with reference to the status of F's disclosure as a problem.

Third, there are at least two solutions to the interpretive problem

F created (either F takes the initiative and volunteers herself as the recipient of complaint, or E establishes the alternative rule for interpreting complaints). It is only with reference to such alternative solutions that it is possible to explain the pattern of confusion after turn 61 as a result of the women working at cross-purposes, even while they are working jointly on the surface to fulfill the request to state and resolve complaints.

Controlling Understandings and Strategic Communication

Conversation I exemplifies that what is necessary to continue the progress and further the coherence of a conversation may interfere with making entries that are called for by the social purposes of the conversants. The theoretical utility of principles by which entries to discourses and dialogues contribute to their progress and coherence thus goes beyond their importance in accounting for the specific interpretations that are focused on and responded to at particular junctures. They enable communicators to calculate the interpretive consequences of their own entries, and the interpretive consequences of their own subsequent entries or the subsequent entries of the respondent(s). Thus, principles of specific interpretation are the basis of an account of the strategic formulation of what to communicate, and how to communicate it, at particular junctures.

APPENDIX: CONVERSATION I

(Simultaneous speech is marked by double slashes (//) and underlining)

1. E: It's sorta depressing. Why is she coming to you? Why doesn't she come to me? It kills me.
2. F: I don't know. Everyone is coming to me, saying you are depressed.
3. E: What did you say? *(laughs)* That cracks me up.
4. F: I . . . I hadn't noticed. I've been like so off in my own world the past couple of days. Because I've been so like with the chem testing and the play, and being so nervous about all those things that I didn't even have a chance to notice how you were. Uh, I . . . I never seem to notice how people are acting that much. //<u>But that's</u>
5. E: <u>Uh, uh.</u>

6. F: . . . that's happened to me several times before, not just–
7. E: And they came //to you.
8. F: Yes, they do and I say, gee, I didn't notice; I didn't know, and I start wondering *(laughs)* well, gee, should I act like–
9. E: Nah, it kills me. Because, uh, you of all people. I mean, you know, I'm surprised she didn't come see me. Because she usually comes and says, you know. "Come on, what's the matter?" You know.
10. F: I don't know. I think she likes to confirm her suspicions, before she . . .
11. E: *(laughs)*
12. F: No . . . she thinks . . . if she thinks she was the only person who thought you were depressed maybe it was her own perception //but uh . . .
13. E: No.
14. F: Uh, other people thought you were depressed too.
15. E: No, I wasn't.
16. F: Was it about Dave, though?
17. E: Yeah. *(laughs)*
18. F: Ah, well, I mean it's a normal reason to be depressed. Like . . . if you were kind of depressed for no reason, then I would be //you know
19. E: Yeah, well I–
20. F: I understand why you feel depressed //but, it's just . . .
21. E: No, I just feel–
22. F: I see no reason why you should really be worried.
23. E: Aw, come on. I mean, come on. This is Dave, this is Jeff, this is Sam and . . .
24. F: Sam?
25. E: Aw, come on, I told you about that. I'm not going to tell you about it now, but I told you //about it.
26. F: When he told you . . . ?
27. E: Oh, no, no, no; this is just when a lot of things . . . his whole attitude //[garbled]
28. F: uh huh, uh huh. Oh, okay. //Would he be criticized?
29. E: Oh, god. Oh, uh. //[garbled] oh, he's
30. F: Once he stops crying. Yeah, Rich doesn't understand that. I was telling him . . . um . . . before the Senate election that, if I lose, I am going to be really upset and it will be

much worse to lose this year because I feel everybody . . . by my record they wouldn't think I did a good job this year or something. That'll really, really, you know, be really . . . low, and uh, he couldn't . . . uh . . . uh . . . understand why my self-esteem was so dependent on this stupid little election.

31. E: Oh, come on.
32. F: And I was, uh, it was just a good thing I won. *(laughs)*
33. E: I guess so. *(laughs)*
34. F: So you know, really, it's pretty good.
35. E: Yeah, commuter—that cracks me up, to think of you like that. I'm not sure I'll be a commuter yet. I do not know where I will be living next year, but . . . That's [?] You didn't take rooms just in case //did you?
36. F: Yeah, I did.
37. E: Oh, you did? Where's yours?
38. F: Over on State 24.
39. E: Is that Bear's house?
40. F: No, it's the one with blue carpet.
41. E: Oh, I don't know anything about those houses. Which one's hers?
42. F: 826. 'Cause she told us to take rooms there just in case, uh, mostly because she wants, when we decide to move on campus . . . and she doesn't know what to do . . . she'll move freshmen.
43. E: Yeah, you can do that without any problem.
44. F: But we'd better get accepted though, because Cheryl wouldn't like Nan.
45. E: Oh *(laughs)*, oh, uh, yeah, I kinda knew that.
46. F: And Nan's very nervous about Cheryl. Well, a lot of people are.
47. E: Yeah, well . . .
48. F: Nan's very nervous, but doesn't care what Cheryl thinks. But she comes in a room to see if I am there . . . and um–
49. E: Cheryl says she's feeling strange . . .
50. F: Well, if I'm not there and Cheryl's there, she doesn't know what to say.
51. E: Do you honestly start feeling attacked when people, you know what I mean . . . like?
52. F: Yeah.
53. E: So, even if like . . .
54. F: Even if it's not like anything about my character or anything, but you know, you can tell me my handwriting's messy, you know, and it . . .
55. E: That would bother you?
56. F: Pretty much. Well, it would depend on the mood I'm in.
57. E: Oh, well, I . . . if there is something wrong with me, and I told

this to my roommate last year . . . if you've got a complaint about me, you know, just tell me. You know, like, I mean, how am I supposed to know? Right? And if I have a complaint about someone, I should tell them too. Only sometimes I can't. *(laughs)*

58. F: Yeah, I have trouble with that, too. *(both laugh)*
59. E: Yeah, um //I mean
60. F: At least it's best to let them come out in the open because if you just sit and let them grow you get angrier and angrier about little things that aren't necessarily all that important, but . . .
61. E: That's what happened last year with Lucy. I didn't tell her my problems. Instead, I did silly things like keep them in . . . you know, because it's ridiculous about me getting upset with things like, you know, it's just how I am about neatness. You know. Well, you don't feel the same way, right? [pause] *(both laugh)*
62. F: That's true. I'm . . . I'm sorry. I think things have been really busy lately.
63. E: Yeah.
64. F: And I haven't had time to clean up. I'll really try.
65. E: Oh, no, the problem, you know . . . just . . . like I'm sure there are things about me that really bother you, too. [long pause] Come on. Well, I'm not perfect—sometimes.
66. F: Well, uh . . . [long pause]
67. E: Come on; it's all right.
68. F: Let me think about it for awhile, Okay? It's . . . it's not the kind of thing I could, could come up with off the top of my head. I want time to think about it first.
69. E: Okay, good; I'm always ready to listen. Always.
70. F: Is . . . is there anything else besides the room being messy? 'Cause I will . . . I will really try with that. But when it gets bad and I don't notice, just tell me 'cause it's the sorta thing I might forget, so just //you know.
71. E: Is [garbled]
72. F: If there's a lot of shit on the floor, just kind of drop a subtle hint and say, "My God, look at that shit on the floor!"
73. E: But you know, like I never meant it to be nasty—never, like it's just something really petty that we shouldn't even worry about. We've got so much more bigger things to worry about than a messy room and me turning my alarm clock off every ten minutes in the morning. I mean, that's okay, no . . . like, we'll just . . .
74. F: *(laughs)*
75. E: Okay, but when I say it, I don't mean it, so don't get mad. I'm

not attacking you at all. Like I said, you know, I think that being roommates is a really difficult situation because you take two people from two different backgrounds, and stick them together and expect them to coexist peacefully in one room. Yeah, come on, you can't have it all the time.

76. F: I can't coexist peacefully with myself in one room.
77. E: Yeah, look at me. So . . . but . . . you . . . you know what I mean.
78. F: Yeah, no problem.

CHAPTER 2

Requirements for an Adequate Theory of Strategic Communication

It was postulated in Chapter 1 that the content and style of strategic utterances and behaviors are constrained so that they will contribute to the coherence and progress of a discourse or dialogue. It was also postulated that the contribution of an entry to coherence and progress is contingent and probabilistic, a function of what has preceded it in the discourse or dialogue, and what is entered subsequently. The minimal requirement for a theory of strategic communication is that it logically implies those two postulates. For this, the theory has to have certain substantive and formal features.

SUBSTANTIVE FEATURES OF A THEORY OF STRATEGIC COMMUNICATION

Constraints on Utterances and Behaviors

Inasmuch as both of the key postulates here are about constraints on the content and style of entries in discourses and dialogues, it is obviously important that the notion of a CONSTRAINT ON EVENTS be made explicit.

It is first necessary to make explicit the notion *event.* Let it be said that any event has the following components: an entity, E; a passage of time from T_1 to T_2; an initial equilibrium state of E, $[E]S_1$; a final equilibrium state, $[E]S_2$; and a force exerted on E, F:E. An event can then be formally defined as change in an entity over time following the exertion of some force, from an initial equilibrium state to a final equilibrium state:

[1] EVENT $=_{dfn}[(T_1)(([E]S_1) \cdot (F{:}E)) \cdot (T_2)([E]S_2)]$

Let it further be said that different forces can be exerted on E, with some having a greater probability of changing E's equilibrium state than others. When the probability is 1.0 of some change in the state of E subsequent to the exertion of F:E, then F:E is a necessary and sufficient determinant of that event.

Now consider that an entity can acquire properties or exist under conditions that alter the probabilities of certain changes in the state of E upon the exertion of F:E. Such properties or conditions are CONSTRAINTS on the behavior of E. For example, adding alcohol to water changes the probability that the water will boil when heated to 100° C. Lashing a boat to a pier changes the probabilities of different motions under certain conditions of wind and current. A child's acquisition of a grammar changes the probability that its vocalizations will be unorganized and unstructured under conditions of psychological drive. In each case, a change in E's equilibrium state, [E]ΔS, occurs with a certain probability, p_1, unless E acquires certain properties or conditions, λ, which change the probability to p_2 that [λE]ΔS will result from the exertion of F:λE:

[2] CONSTRAINT (λ) $=_{dfn}[(F{:}E \rightarrow (p_1)[E]\Delta S) \cdot (F{:}\lambda E \rightarrow (p_2)[\lambda E]\Delta S)]$

The first postulate in Chapter 1 is that the content and style of entries in discourses and dialogues is constrained by their projected effect on coherence and progress. In light of [2], this postulate can be restated as follows: the effects on coherence and progress that a communicator projects an entry with a certain content and style will have are an acquired cognitive property that alters the relative probabilities of different ways of formulating and producing utterances or nonverbal displays under the exertion of particular social and psychological forces.

It follows that a theory of strategic communication that rests on this notion of constraint will not predict what communicators say and do under some set of initial conditions. Rather, such a theory will predict the relative probabilities of entries at given junctures with different possible features of content and style. Suppose we then take as given that an entry influences uptake by affecting its interpretive consequences (as in Chapter 1). In that case basing a theory of strategic communication on the notion of constraint entails that *what we say and do alters the probabilities that certain utterances or nonverbals will subsequently be produced, but does not itself "cause" anything to be said or done.*

This necessitates that an account of strategic communication be subdivided. One part of such an account is as above, a specification of the principles by which entries in discourses and dialogues are constrained. But this cannot explain what individuals actually say or do, or even that they communicate at all. For that, there has to be a separate but complementary specification of the range of effects that psychological, social and cultural forces have on what is communicated and how and when it is communicated.

Changes in Constraints over Time

The specific interpretation that an utterance or behavior would receive if entered at one juncture may be different from its specific interpretation if entered at another, given that its antecedents will differ and so might the meaning relations among them. Similarly, specific interpretations of entries in discourses and dialogues can be changed in retrospect if subsequent entries foster changes in the meaning relations among their antecedents. The constraining properties of discourses and dialogues can thus change as they unfold over time.

There are of course a variety of methodologies for describing systems where there is change over time (e.g., stochastic modeling, time-series analyses), but they uniformly make an assumption that fails in this case. They assume a process or changes that range over a fixed set of primitive states. However, the 'states' of discourses and dialogues that change over time are the specific interpretations of their component utterances and behaviors. Specific interpretations are not primitive states, nor is there is reason to think that the set of such interpretations is finite.

The Content of an Adequate Theory

If entries in discourses and dialogues are constrained by their antecedents, and those constraints are fluid (subject to change over time), then there cannot be any general principles such that under a given set of initial conditions, it is necessary that some particular entry be made, or an entry with certain properties. But if we cannot capture the systematic aspect of formulating entries by treating that activity as a mechanical or routinized one, then we have to treat formulating entries in discourses and dialogues as an INTELLIGENT ACTIVITY.

The systematic character of an intelligent activity does not derive from the physical (time-space) relationships and patterns in what actors specifically do, but from the "logic of the game" by which actors can conceptually organize and interrelate moves, and thus form and implement plans.

Let us characterize an intelligent activity as a methodical organization and utilization of resources to achieve some result, where the following criteria obtain:

1. There are constraints on what resources can be utilized and how they can be organized.
2. There are at least two possible ways of organizing and utilizing one's resources.
3. There is no certainty about the result of organizing and utilizing one's resources in a particular way, nor is it obligatory to adopt any particular method to bring about the intended result.
4. There are connections between one's resources and the results one intends that enable calculations of the possibility and probability of certain results from certain ways of organizing and utilizing one's resources.

A theory of such an activity must therefore have as a component a set of principles by which the available means are probabilistically linked to outcomes, principles that actors must in some sense 'know' to systematically undertake the achievement of their objectives. But of course, specifying such principles does not explain what actors specifically do to achieve some objective, or the fact that they do (or do not) make the effort at all.

This leads us, precisely as it did before, to the need for subdividing an account of strategic communication into two parts. One part must be a specification of the principles by which entries in discourses and dialogues affect the probability of certain consequences. It is these principles that enable communicators to project the (probable) social utility of contemplated utterances and behaviors.

The other part of the account must be a separate and complementary specification of the psychological, social, and cultural forces that result in the adoption of particular objectives and the undertaking of efforts to achieve them. This subdivision closely resembles Chomsky's (1965: 3–27) distinction between a theory of COMPETENCE and a theory of PERFORMANCE.

Competence and Performance

It is a radical departure from current trends in language studies, semiotics, and communication to make a competence/performance distinction. The most explicit objections to such a distinction have of course been made in language studies where the distinction originated and where it has had a profound impact on theory, methods and data.

From the way in which the Chomskyan competence/performance distinction materialized in linguistics, a rich corpus of empirical data about performance was made functionally (but not actually) peripheral, especially facts about individual and community differences in the way linguistic expressions are formed, articulated, and understood. Hymes (1964), Searle (1972), Kaufer (1979), Bradac et al. (1980), Bailey (1981), Kreckel (1981) and Taylor (1984) have collectively indicted the competence/performance distinction for the following:

1. Failing to take into account that speakers and hearers must know more than just grammatical rules and word meanings to speak and understand their language, but must also know when to speak and to whom, at what level of formality, in which among alternate possible dialects, etc.
2. Preventing serious attention in linguistic theory to the connection between cultures and the forms and lexicon of their languages, and to influences on change in forms and lexicon over time.
3. Focusing linguistic theory on a corpus of sentence forms and sentence meanings that have little correspondence to the sentences people actually produce and the understandings they have of them.
4. Substituting "intuitions" about grammaticality, sentence interrelationships and sentence meanings for empirical evidence about those matters.
5. Discounting any empirical counterevidence regarding a theory of competence by presuming that any and all behavioral "deviations" from the theory are a function of performance variables.

Some of these criticisms, particularly 1 and 2, reflect only the frustration of efforts to gain widespread recognition of the need for work on psychological, social, and cultural influences on linguistic behavior. Greater importance has for a considerable period been attributed to work on underlying principles. This involves the politics of research more than any defect in the competence/performance distinction.

However, the remaining criticisms, 3–5, reflect real abuses that have been spawned by the Chomskyan distinction. But these have not so much resulted from a defect in the distinction itself as from the methodological failures of its proponents. These failures in turn have been magnified by the philosophical prejudices of its critics.

Philosophical Prejudices

Studies of social conduct have generally had a positivistic orientation. This is (at least in part) to enforce as much objectivity as possible in the face of considerable potential for subjectivity. Only what is observed or measured counts as data, and only collations of regularities and generalizations in such data count as theory. In many cases, this orientation has fostered, and in turn been bolstered by, increasingly sophisticated methods of statistically analyzing the quantitative features of observed conduct. In this context, it is bound to be suspect and misunderstood to claim that the observation and measurement of at least some types of conduct cannot in itself result in adequate generalizations and explanations.

Nonetheless, without reference to the principles by which actors undertake to bring about certain results, the observation of an intelligent activity can only produce reliable generalizations about practices that have become routinized or customary. Worse, given generalizations and explanations based solely on observation, no theoretical distinction can be made between the occurrence of improbable conduct that is aberrant, and the occurrence of improbable conduct that is the product of systematic innovations by creative actors. This was Chomsky's (1957: 5) point in comparing the sequences *Colorless green ideas sleep furiously* and *Furiously sleep ideas green colorless,* both of which (at the time) were equally improbable but one of which is a well-formed innovation in English.

Methodological Problems

Much of the work being done on the organizing principles underlying linguistic behavior has become unsystematic and ad hoc, based entirely on introspection, but this was not always so. There was in fact an operating methodology in early Chomskyan linguistics, though it was more conventional than explicit. The method in brief involved checks and balances: intuitions about the form and substance of particular organizing principles were tested by the following: (1) whether they could be independently motivated and (2) whether they could be incorporated into the established formalism for representing such principles without adversely affecting its internal consistency. The established formalism for representing such principles was (to be) tested in turn by the following: (1) its internal consistency and completeness, and (2) its consistency with the formal relationships and hierarchies evident in the way children acquire their ability to speak and understand their native language.

However, the reliance on an established formalism against which to test intuitions about underlying principles rapidly eroded, largely as a result of an intensifying concern with pragmatic and social aspects of linguistic behavior that cannot be captured by any single, uniform set of principles for organizing such conduct. This erosion of reliance on an established formalism did not lead as it should have to a diminished reliance on introspection. As a result, the competence/performance distinction did (indirectly) foster a tolerance for ad hoc generalizations rooted largely in introspection. But this is not inevitable.

The Necessity of a Competence/Performance Distinction

In studies of certain types of behavior it is a practical necessity to distinguish theoretically between competence and performance, between the organizing logic of the activity and the determinants of actual conduct. Whenever a type of behavior is learned by internalizing a set of principles for constructing behaviors of that type—rather than learned by building a repertoire of specific behaviors—then it is possible for actors to make errors in applying those underlying principles. In that case, as already noted, generalizations based on observed regularities will be unreliable because the data will include both well-made and defective instances, with little basis for discriminating between them.

The study of behaviors of that type therefore has to be subdivided. One concern has to be to make explicit the underlying principles of organization from which well-made contributions follow, principles that actors must tacitly 'know' to engage in that type of behavior at all (a theory of competence). This is crucial if just for the sake of enabling theoretical distinctions between well-made and defective contributions. The other concern is to isolate the cognitive, affective, and social conditions that influence when and how people actually exhibit behaviors of that type (a theory of performance).

There are at least two empirical indexes of whether such a subdivision of theory is necessary in studying a given type of behavior. One is whether original and creative behaviors ever occur, whether actors are able at least sometimes to depart from habit and custom and act adaptively or, if necessary, innovatively, without substantial trial and error. Such creativity indicates that actors have acquired a mastery of principles for producing and understanding new behaviors of that type, rather than a fixed repertoire of specific behaviors.

The second index is whether actors and observers alike reliably discriminate between well-made behaviors and defective ones, and can repair defects. Such discrimination indicates the mastery of principles for organizing the behavior against which the 'correctness' of specific behaviors can be assessed. But more importantly, the occurrence of recognizable errors also indicates that those organizing principles are not the sole influence on the construction of actual behaviors of that type, so that making such principles explicit is necessary but not sufficient to explain what people are observed to do.

The formulation of entries in discourses and dialogues is an activity that displays both of these characteristics. Individuals are at least sometimes adaptive, and even innovative, in selecting among options of content and style in formulating entries. At the same time, individuals sometimes self-correct their contributions to discourses and dialogues so as to avoid creating undesired 'demands,' and are sometimes admonished by others for having made contributions that are (projected as) inadequate to foster the desired resolution or likely to foster an undesired one.

Thus, in making explicit the principles by which entries contribute to the progress and coherence of discourses and dialogues, and are interpreted accordingly, this book makes explicit what communicators have to 'know' to generally avoid strategic infelicities, and when they do occur, to detect and remedy them. This logically precedes and is distinct from an account of the cognitive, affective, social, and cultural forces on the formulation of entries in discourses and dialogues.

The Empirical Reality of Principles of Specific Interpretation

Because the principles of interest here are constraints on the specific interpretation of utterances, and not determinants of them, the empirical fact will not necessarily conform to the theory. It is possible in any given instance that interpreters will not focus on and/or respond to the type of interpretation that is warranted in principle. This obviously raises two serious concerns. First, what matters of fact do these principles account for? Second, in what ways can specific formulations of those principles be tested against the facts?

Matters of Fact Explained by Principles of Specific Interpretation

The principles of interest specify the relationship that entries with a specific interpretation must have to other interpreted entries to warrant focusing on that meaning. This entails that to exercise any control over how one is understood, one has to control what is added to the discourse or dialogue before or after the entry in question. This has effects that surface in the public record, as in Conversation I.

Generally, these principles create a potential for, and thus account for the fact that, there are problems at some junctures in dialogues in coordinating turns at speaking. These generally occur at junctures where it is critical for the sake of controlling specific interpretations to retain or obtain control of the floor to speak.

Second, these principles create a need for, and thus account for the fact of, entries in discourses and dialogues that do not contribute to completing the task or business at hand, but that create warrants for (or against) focusing on and/or responding to key meanings of subsequent entries. The fact that entries are made to create such warrants has been recognized but not adequately accounted for in Brown and Levinson's (1978) analysis of the social motivation for pre-requests and other such formulas, and Edmondson's (1981) identification of such structurally extraneous material as "disarmers," "expanders," and "grounders." The need for—and the content and style of—introductions and conclusions in extended discourses are similarly accounted for by the principles of specific interpretation. In addition, these principles account for entries in discourses and dialogues that explicitly react to or express frustration over chronic 'misinterpretations,' as when a response is predicated on an unwarranted interpretation so as to avoid being responsive to what the communicator evidently intended.

And finally, these principles account for less tangible but far more important facts about the everyday practice of communication. It is taken here as a matter of fact—about the cognitive basis of communication rather than about the skills of individuals—that people (at least sometimes) not only fail to achieve the outcomes they set out to achieve in discourses and dialogues, but may even fail to initiate any substantial progress towards them. It is taken as a corresponding fact that at particular junctures, individuals often experience as problematic the calculation of what to communicate and how to communicate it. The inability of people at times to make progress towards an intended outcome, and the problematic character of formulating entries, are both fostered, and thus accounted for, by principles of specific interpretation and the conflicts they engender between what has to be said and done to achieve that outcome, and what the interpretive consequences are projected as being.

It is also taken as a fact that is explained by principles of interpretation that individuals subjectively perceive themselves at some junctures as 'having no choice' about saying and doing certain things even though they would rather not, or as having to refrain from saying and doing certain things they want to. Of course, these 'reluctant' formulations of entries could be attributed in some cases to normative obligations rather than to purely interpretive considerations. However, there is no important difference: conforming to normative obligations results from placing the negative interpretive consequences of violating these obligations ahead of the practical disadvantages of conforming to them.

The Empirical Test of Principles of Interpretation

Despite there being certain tangible facts that are explained by these principles of interpretation, the principles do not predict any particular events (e.g., the content and style of particular entries in observed discourses and dialogues). Further, these principles cannot be falsified by the occurrence of 'deviant' events (e.g., if entries with a high relative probability are not made in a discourses or dialogue, and entries with low relative probabilities are). This is because it is fully consistent with these principles that respondents could make entries predicated on some other (type of) meaning from the one it was warranted to focus on, in order to avoid responding to the warranted (type of) meaning. For example, suppose that a communicator wants a favor from someone but does not want to explicitly ask, and so he/she implicates the request. The respondent may evade the request by not making his/her response relevant to the implicature, though that is warranted, but to the antecedent propositional content instead:

[3] S: Good morning, you're out bright and early.
H: My car won't start. You going to work soon?
S: I don't know. I've got flexible hours, so it's a new decision every day.
H: Well, what's today's decision?
S: I was thinking I'd just go with the flow.

The imperfect correspondence likely to exist between principles of specific interpretation and the actual behavior of communicators does not mean that the validity of these principles cannot be tested, nor does it mean that empirical data are irrelevant. It only means that empirical tests have to be indirect, and that the validity of these principles has to be contingent on the accumulated weight of the "circumstantial evidence" provided by a variety of independent tests, not on "crucial experiments."

The three most obvious ways of empirically testing these principles are as follows. First, these principles predict changes in specific interpretations as a consequence of varying certain features of the antecedent or subsequent sequence. Laboratory tests of this kind are reported in Chapter 5: they are sufficiently rigorous to have disconfirmed early formulations of these principles of specific interpretation (Sanders 1980, 1981), and to have confirmed the revised formulations given here in Chapter 4. Second, if specific interpretations are the meaning(s) of an entry that has features in common with the features of the specific interpretations of one or more antecedents and consequents, then in any instance it can at least be predicted which type of meaning, if not what particular meaning, will most probably be focused on. This is also done in two studies (the fifth and sixth) reported in Chapter 5.

Third, given the core premise here that entries are constrained by their projected interpretive consequences, these principles can be tested in terms of the effect of manipulating the antecedents of an entry on responses to it. More particularly, it can be observed whether such manipulations foster either: (1) changes in which next entries are preferred, or (2) changes in the relative probability of making certain possible entries next. However, tests along this line are easily contaminated. In the first study reported in Chapter 5, respondents were asked to specify and explain their preferences among alternative entries that could subsequently be made in test dialogues. Instead of explaining their preference in terms of its effect on the dialogue's coherence and progress, many respondents cited dispositional factors, such as what the normative obligations were in the situation, or what would be most true in regard to the topic of the dialogue.

The Content and Power of an Adequate Theory of Strategic Communication

An adequate account of the principles underlying strategic communication must satisfy the following requirements. First, such an account must support claims about the relative probability, as opposed to claims about the occurrence, of entries with certain features of content and style in discourses and dialogues. Second, such an account must not preclude an additional, separate concern with the forces on actors that result in the actual entries they make in discourses and dialogues.

These requirements are satisfied by a decision-theoretic explanation of strategic communication. Decision theories consist of principles that structure the connection between certain actions and subsequent actions and events (e.g., Radford, 1977; Holloway, 1979). This is precisely what follows from the principles by which entries in discourses and dialogues contribute to their coherence and progress.

A decision-theoretic account of strategic communication is consistent with the idea that individuals are able to organize and coordinate their social acts and understanding on the basis of shared cognitive schemata of specific types of situation and social undertaking (e.g., Wittgenstein, 1953; Goffman, 1959; Garfinkel, 1967; Pearce, 1976; Schank and Abelson, 1977; Abelson, 1981). However, the principles in this case conform more to the spirit than to the letter of that idea.

The departure here stems from the recurrent objections that representations of such schemata have been artificially narrow, too strong or too weak, or too vague. Winograd's (1980) critique of efforts to schematize the understanding of language is paradigmatic. His critique was that despite ingenious solutions to special problems, the general problem is how to simulate mechanically an activity that is judgmental and fluid. This is precisely the problem in making explicit the cognitive underpinnings of strategic communication.

The organizing principles utilized by communicators in formulating entries in discourses and dialogues, and by interpreters in processing them, cannot be represented by schemata of specified options at each given juncture in a 'pre-scripted' discourse or dialogue. First, that fails to capture a strategically critical aspect of dialogues and discourses: as they unfold, the constraints on next entries are altered by each present entry, so that they are fluid in regard to the outcomes that are achievable, the specific interpretations of particular entries, and the way in which their constituents cohere. Second, it fails to capture an essential aspect of any strategic conduct, that actors have the option of stepping outside the schematized parameters of an unfolding course of action, to alter, subvert, or terminate its progress.

Hence, fixed schemata are too weak to serve as adequate representations of the cognitive underpinnings of formulating entries in discourses and dialogues. Instead, the judgmental and fluid aspects of formulating entries strategically entail that the organizing principles that underlie strategic communication are heuristic for DERIVING AND REVISING ad hoc schemata that model the relationship between contemplated entries at a given juncture of the discourse or dialogue and their consequences. The principles by which utterances and behaviors contribute to the coherence and progress of discourses and dialogues are sufficient for that purpose.

Of course, one cannot disregard the key role of past experience and acquired social knowledge in projecting the consequences that are possible if entries are formulated in a particular way, and in assigning probabilities to those possible consequences. In fact, individuals are likely to take advantage of their past experience and acquired social knowledge, and tend towards 'satisficing' rather than being thorough and disciplined in practice about constructing and utilizing such models (Simon, 1965: 81–83). Nonetheless, to construct any such model at all there must be a systematic basis for arraying alternatives and linking them to outcomes. That is what is of interest here.

Projecting Interpretations of Contemplated Entries

First and most obviously, principles by which entries to discourses and dialogues contribute to their progress and coherence apply directly to projecting the interpretive consequences of making an entry at some juncture with the intended content, expressed (styled) in the intended way.

Projecting Interpretations of Entries Subsequent to the Contemplated One

Second, those principles apply to projecting how a contemplated entry (E_i) will affect the interpretation, and thus the likelihood, of a possible subsequent entry (E_j). E_i, as an addition to the unfolding discourse or dialogue, may promote an interpretation of E_j different from what some other present entry would. Such projections will enable estimates of the likelihood of E_j insofar as the communicator has cultural knowledge, and/or knowledge of the audience's specific dispositions, sufficient to estimate the attractiveness (or unattractiveness) of the projected interpretation of E_j subsequent to E_i. This is typified by a child who "blackmails" its parents into complying with a request by calculating how to set the stage for the request so that a refusal would be interpretable as some kind of hostile act—punitive, repressive, or uncaring.

Projecting Inferences about One's Own or Others' Character and Traits.

Finally, these principles by which entries in discourses and dialogues contribute to their progress and coherence enable inferences about the character and traits of their authors. (This account of inferences about the character and traits of individuals is consistent with most prevailing models of attribution and person perception, but improves upon them by being more explicit about the socially shared basis for selecting and processing data about others; cf. Schneider, Hastorf and Ellsworth, 1979).

Given that inferences about an actor consist of specifications of just those beliefs, values or traits that entail what the actor was observed to say and do, overt conduct in and of itself does not reveal much. Generally, an overt act follows equally well from diverse beliefs, values or traits.

Rather, publicly justifiable and useful inferences about individuals necessitate comparing their observed acts with at least some of the options that were available but that they functionally rejected. When an act is perceived as having been selected (whether actively or passively) from a known array of options, the inferential problem becomes this more structured and focused one: to construe beliefs, values or traits that are the 'common denominator' that entails both performing the overt act and rejecting the known options. For example, suppose that one observes a near-accident on an expressway when a speeding driver abruptly changes lanes just in front of an oncoming car:

1. It would likely be inferred that the driver is irresponsible and recklessly indifferent to others if he/she had been speeding directly towards slower-moving traffic, driving at speeds substantially in excess of the general flow of traffic, and ignoring openings in adjacent lanes that could previously have been entered safely in anticipation of reaching the slower-moving traffic.
2. It would likely be inferred that the driver is skillful, quick, and daring if a vehicle just ahead in his/her own lane had stalled and stopped

without warning, a truck had been passing in the far lane, and the only remaining option that would avoid a collision was to accelerate into a diminishing slot in the near lane.

3. It would be capricious to infer anything about the driver if no other cars than the one that was nearly hit were on the road, the weather and road conditions were optimal, and that maneuver was an isolated incident. The maneuver itself could then be attributed equally well to a momentary loss of control, inattention, sociopathic hostility, and so on.

The key to making inferences about individuals, then, is being able to gauge what their options were in a given instance. But the options are not often as physically and normatively explicit as in the case above. However, the options of content and expression that communicators functionally selected from can be gauged by reference to the principles by which entries to discourses and dialogues contribute to their progress and coherence. One basis for this is to reason backwards to alternatives of content and style that would (probably) receive the same specific interpretation that the actual entry got, but were functionally rejected. This can also be done by projecting the alternative meanings and specific interpretations that were functionally avoided by adopting certain details of content and style rather than others.

Hence, one can project what could be inferred about one's own character and traits from a contemplated entry. Similarly, one can project what could be inferred about the character and traits of one's respondent(s) from their projected entries. Given that such inferences can be valued as attractive or aversive (by community standards or some other criteria) these projected inferences are a further basis for calculating the costs and benefits of contemplated entries in discourses and dialogues.

In sum, the formulation of entries in discourses and dialogues so as to control the way they are understood, and to make progress toward the desired resolution (or away from undesired ones), has to be treated as a function of decision models that array the projected consequences of contemplated entries. As described above, projections of the consequences of formulating an entry in a certain way are a function of principles of specific interpretation. Those principles are thus the substance of a decision-theoretic account of strategic communication (see Chapter 8).

FORMAL FEATURES OF A THEORY OF STRATEGIC COMMUNICATION

The projected interpretive consequences of an utterance or non-verbal display are contingent on: (1) its content and style, and (2) what precedes it and what follows it in the unfolding discourse or dialogue. This entails that the projected interpretive consequences of an entry with certain properties can change as the sequence progresses. In that case, different possible consequences of formulating an entry in a particular way are more or less probable, with no one consequence being necessary except idiosyncratically (i.e., at a particular juncture with reference to the cognitions of a particular interpreter).

The General Form and Content of Theoretical Propositions

It follows that theoretical propositions here must be stated in a way that reflects the contingent and probabilistic nature of the interpretive consequences of formulating an entry in a certain way at a certain juncture in some sequence. This is accomplished by expressing theoretical propositions as conditional statements with the following general form and content:

> If an entry has certain features, and its antecedents or consequents have certain features, and those features are related in a particular way, then there is a *warrant*—whose strength may vary with the proximity and number of those antecedents or consequents—for *judging:*
>
> (1) that an entry has certain meaning(s) (see Chapter 3);
> (2) what specific interpretation of an entry to focus on (see Chapters 4 and 6);
> (3) that certain subsequent entries are possible, with a certain relative probability (see Chapter 8).

These conditionals differ from logical implications in two critical ways. First, the antecedent specifies initial conditions that justify or warrant the consequent but do not make its occurrence necessary. Second, these conditionals can include quantifiers that mark the degree to which those initial conditions warrant the consequent.

The power of those conditional statements is thus restricted in a way that captures the judgmental and fluid nature of projections of the consequences of contemplated entries in discourses and dialogues.

The warranting condition in some cases for the judgments 1–3 above are that a particular set theoretic relationship exists between features of the entry in question and features of some antecedent segment of the discourse or dialogue (e.g., intersection, or a member-set relation). In other cases, the warranting condition is that the entry in question has features such that the entry is an implicatum of the antecedent segment, or the antecedent segment has features that the entry in question presupposes. Such statements are formalized here in terms of both set theory and first-order predicate logic.

The Imperative to Utilize Formalisms

It is imperative to avoid stating theoretical propositions in ordinary language, even when there is only a weak motivation for adopting some formal system in particular. While this should not be controversial, some justification is called for nonetheless. Formalisms are not widely utilized in studies of social conduct, with work even in language studies relying on them increasingly less.

Achieving Explicitness

The terms and forms of ordinary language are so burdened with hidden presuppositions, connotations and associations, that using them to formulate abstract statements makes it virtually impossible to fully avoid some degree of vagueness and ambiguity.

Hofstadter (1979: 88–97) illustrates the concern here with the centuries of futile effort spent trying to prove the 'fifth' Euclidean postulate. The problem was that that postulate is contingent rather than necessary, but its limiting conditions were concealed by ordinary language. Euclid postulated that when any two straight lines, *L* and *L'*, both intersect some third line, and the inner angles of their intersection add up to less than 180°, there is some point where they intersect. The corollary is that given *L,* and some point, *A,* that is not on *L,* there is one line, *X,* and only *X* that can be drawn through *A* that will not intersect *L.* However, terms such as *straight line* in ordinary language were evidently so strongly associated with flat planes that it was overlooked that the notion of *straight line* can be applied to lines that lie on curved planes. For straight lines on certain curved planes, the 'fifth' postulate is false. For example, given a spherical plane with all straight lines on it running along an equator, there is no line that can be drawn through A which will not intersect L: given any two straight lines that run along an equator, there are two points at which the inner angles of their intersection with a third line sum to 180° and two points at which they intersect.

Testing Propositions

Terms in ordinary language that seem to correspond to formal logical operators actually have variable meanings (e.g., *and, not, either-or, if-then).* This makes it equivocal what relationship is being claimed between the parts of complex theoretical statements that incorporate such operators. This in turn obscures what would be sufficient to disconfirm such statements.

In addition, it is often equivocal whether the contrary of terms in ordinary language should be their explicit negative or a conventional antonym. For example, if it is predicted that people will greet each other under certain conditions, it makes a difference in testing the prediction whether the contrary of *greeting* is the negation *not greeting* (that only precludes certain messages), or it is the conventional antonym *disregarding* (that precludes communication altogether).

Capturing Generalizations

A further reason to formalize theoretical propositions is that it makes explicit any formal parallels between separate statements, and similarly any non-correspondences. Parallelisms in the relations among variables to each another can easily be obscured in ordinary language, because distinct terms have to be utilized in different statements to represent substantive differences in the variables involved.

Reducing the Chances of Ad Hoc Statements

Ad hoc theoretical propositions are ones that are developed in order to account for a particular body of data, without regard for their consistency with other pertinent data or the way they cohere with other theoretical propositions. Ad hoc theoretical propositions at bottom are symptomatic of theorists' lapses or a field's immaturity. They are thus never wholly preventable. But the chances of producing them, or at least the chances of overlooking that they are ad hoc, will decrease if some formal system has been adopted for expressing theoretical propositions. In that case, ad hoc propositions that are inconsistent with other data and/or other propositions will either not be expressible in the formal system that was adopted, or will have to be expressed in ways that contrast markedly with the expression of other propositions.

In satisfying the imperative to avoid stating theoretical propositions in ordinary language, the formal system here was adopted because it enables the statement of theoretical propositions in a way that captures the particular relationships of interest here, and has the appropriate power. There are no other reasons at this point to prefer this system to any other that equally well captures the judgmental and fluid nature of projecting the interpretive consequences of formulating an utterance or nonverbal display in some particular way.

Part II

Utterance Meanings and Specific Interpretations: Controlling Understandings in Discourses and Dialogues

Chapters 3–5 substantiate that the specific interpretations utterances receive in particular instances depend on what contribution they make to the coherence and progress of the unfolding discourse or dialogue. Suppose, for example, that a child who has misbehaved and is being threatened with punishment says to his parent: "You didn't punish Pat [sibling] when she broke the basement window." By the rules of language and conventions of utterance, this could be understood as implicating favoritism in the treatment Pat receives. Or it could be understood as a plea for mercy. Its specific interpretation in that instance is hypothesized to depend on which meaning is relevant to what was said and done previously and to what is said and done subsequently.

Chapter 3 shows that the three major types of utterance meaning—propositional content, illocutionary act, and conversational implicature—are distinct but non-exclusive. This entails that a focus on one or another (type of) meaning in any instance must be a function of principles distinct from, and operating in addition to, rules of language and conventions of utterance.

The distinctness of propositional content as a type of meaning has been undermined by claims that autonomous semantic theories are defective because they ignore pragmatic aspects of sentence meaning. Such claims are shown to rest on evidence that, on reanalysis, does not support them.

The claim here that propositional content and pragmatic meanings are non-exclusive is at odds with the working assumption in pragmatics that conversational implicatures are made and focused on just when propositional content is not 'cooperative.' However, this has not been grounded in explicit characterizations of implicated propositions, or of the basis for knowing what the content of an implicated proposition is. Hence, it is shown in Chapter 3 that implicated propositions have features unlike explicitly stated propositions, and thus are not simply alternative meanings. Further, an account is given of the principled basis for identifying breaches of conversational maxims, and construing from that and from the propositional content of the utterance what is implicated. By the principles involved, utterances may conversationally implicate some proposition without it necessarily being the case that the utterance's propositional content should or will be disregarded.

Finally, the claim that the different types of utterance meaning are distinct is contrary to Searle's view that propositional content and illocutionary force are non-detachable and interdependent components of meaning. Evidence is given that interpreters can focus on and respond to one of those types of utterance meaning in disregard of the other. In addition, principles are formulated that entail that the illocutionary act an utterance counts as depends only partly and contingently on its propositional content, and on related conditions specified in the constitutive rules of illocutionary acts. The illocutionary act that an utterance counts as arguably depends also on what act(s) would be consistent at the juncture with the structural requirements of the dialogue or discourse, and what act(s) would be consistent with the actor's evident dispositions.

In Chapter 4, principles are made explicit by which it is warranted to focus on and respond to some specific interpretation of an utterance among its various meanings. The warrant for focusing on a meaning of one type or another is that the utterance is relevant on that interpretation to antecedents or consequents in the discourse or dialogue. An utterance's relevance is operationalized as its contribution to the coherence and progress of the discourse or dialogue, with the requirements for making such contributions being different with respect to each type of utterance meaning. These principles are formulated in such a way that the strength of a warrant can vary, depending on the number of antecedents to which the utterance is relevant on a given interpretation, and on the utterance's psychological distance in the discourse or dialogue from these antecedents.

In Chapter 5, reports are given of six laboratory studies in which the independent variable comprised the antecedents of a test utterance, and the dependent variable was the interpretation of the test utterance preferred by respondents. The first four of these studies were tests of early theorizing that an utterance's specific interpretation is contingent on its relevance to a single antecedent, usually the immediate antecedent. This was consistently disconfirmed. The reformulated principles are those given in Chapter 4, and were directly tested in the fifth and sixth of these experiments. Overall, predictions of what (type of) meaning respondents would focus on, based on the principles in Chapter 4, were strongly confirmed.

CHAPTER 3

Types of Utterance Meaning: Propositional Content, Implicature and Illocutionary Act

The principal objective of this chapter is to rehearse and expand the foundational issue noted in Chapter 1. It was asserted that propositional content, illocutionary act, and conversational implicature are types of meaning that are NON-EXCLUSIVE (utterances have meanings of each type at the same time) but DISTINCT (relations between any two utterances such as equivalence or relevance will differ for each type of meaning).

However, the assertion that propositional content and conversational implicatures are non-exclusive departs from an assumption to the contrary in language pragmatics. The assertion that propositional content and illocutionary act are distinct types of meaning is a departure from the assumption in speech act theory that they are interdependent and non-detachable.

Justifying these departures requires reanalysis of each of those types of utterance meaning. Such an analysis is also needed to provide a foundation for the principles of specific interpretation detailed in Chapter 4.

THE RELATIONS AMONG TYPES OF UTTERANCE MEANING

The Relationship Between Illocutionary Force and Propositional Content

The connection here is widely considered one of interdependence, not distinctness, following Searle's (1969) treatment of features of propositional content as (weakly) constraining, but not determining, an utterance's force, and his characterization of illocutionary force in terms of a constraint on the use that (the speaker intends) the hearer makes of the utterance's propositional content. This implies that: (1) formulating an utterance so that it has a given content is not a separate problem from formulating it so it has a given illocutionary force, and (2) it is not optional for an interpreter to focus either on propositional content or on the act an utterance counts as.

However, as the social circumstances vary, utterances with different, even contradictory, content can count as the same illocutionary act and different illocutionary acts can be performed by uttering the same expression. For example, the same advice to exercise in a certain way could be given in one social circumstance by saying "You're not getting enough exercise," and in a different social circumstance by saying "You're exercising too strenuously." Similarly, saying "I'll be keeping an eye on you the whole time" could count as a warning in one social circumstance (an exam proctor speaking to an exam-taker), and as a promise in another (a coach to an athlete about to attempt a new and dangerous feat).

Further, the connection between the content of an utterance and its illocutionary force does not preclude focusing on one type of meaning in practical disregard of the other type. For example, if an utterance about the speaker's tight schedule has the illocutionary force of an excuse not to comply with the hearer's request, the hearer may focus on that utterance's content in disregard of its force as an excuse (e.g., asks what had caused the schedule to be so tight). Conversely, one can focus on the speaker's illocutionary act in disregard of propositional content, as when a speaker informs the hearer about how some task is performed, and the hearer focuses on what act the speaker performed (e.g., objects to being patronized by having been given that information) in disregard of the correctness and utility of the content involved.

The Relationship between Propositional Content and Conversational Implicature

The connection here is widely viewed to be dichotomous, not non-exclusive, given that Grice's (1975) starting point is that conversational implicatures are made if and only if the propositional content of an utterance somehow misses the point (fails to provide information as needed at that juncture in the conversation). Again contrary to the thesis here, this implies: (1) that formulating an utterance so that it has a certain content is not a separate problem from formulating it so that it implicates a certain proposition, and (2) that it is not optional for an interpreter to focus on one type of meaning or the other in a given instance.

However, utterances with different content can implicate approximately the same proposition. For example, in response to the question, "Is this your car?" one can implicate that it is by saying either "I have the keys" or by saying "No, I'm stealing it." Conversely, an utterance with a certain content will implicate different propositions in different circumstances. For example, when "Sally is an ardent vegetarian" is said in answer to "Let's invite Sally and Bill over for a barbecue," it implicates the speaker's disagreement that the proposed invitation should be made. In contrast, when "Sally is an ardent vegetarian" follows "I heard that Sally is having trouble finding an apartment mate," it implicates the speaker's belief that Sally's vegetarianism is a stumbling block for potential apartment mates.

Further, if the propositional content of an utterance is 'uncooperative,' so as to make a conversational implicature, it is nonetheless optional whether the interpreter focuses on and responds to the propositional content of the utterance instead of the implicature. Suppose for example that as two people step off an elevator person A says, "I'll see you later," and person B says, "I'm going that way too." B's reply is an irrelevancy that implicates B's disallowance of A's leave-taking. But it is optional (all other things being equal) whether person A focuses on and responds to the implicature (e.g., saying "But I'm going right in here to a meeting [indicating an adjacent door]"), or whether person A focuses on and responds to the propositional content (e.g., saying "I thought your office was over there [indicating the opposite direction]").

Possible and Specific Interpretations

Given that the rules of language and conventions of utterance collectively specify one or more meanings of at least two—and often three—types at the same time, the meaning specified by those rules and conventions are ones that it is possible for the interpreter to focus on.

But interpreters typically focus on and respond to one specific meaning, or at least one type of meaning, of an utterance among those possible (usually without awareness of the other possibilities). Because the rules of language and conventions of utterance cannot explain this, there must be an additional set of principles that does. These principles are made explicit in Chapter 4.

This distinction between *possible meanings* and *specific interpretations* is not, however, a distinction between competence and performance (between meanings that utterances have on formal grounds versus the ones that people are led psychologically and sociologically to actually focus on). Rather, the distinction here is between two sets of abstract principles by which interpretations are assigned, from either of which the performance of interpreters may deviate. The rules and conventions of language specify an utterance's possible meanings, but do not preclude other possible meanings that can result from the interpreter's errors or idiosyncracies. Similarly, the principles of coherence and progress in discourses and dialogues warrant focusing on a specific interpretation at a given juncture, but that does not preclude focusing on some other, unwarranted meaning because of error or idiosyncracy.

PROPOSITIONAL CONTENT

Truth-Conditional Semantics

The propositional content of an uttered expression is its specification, solely by virtue of its lexical content and syntactic structure, of existential features or properties constitutive of some state of affairs. Those features or properties, and thereby that state of affairs, can be asserted in declarative sentence forms, asked about in interrogatives, or specified as the object of the hearer's future act in imperative sentence forms. More precisely, propositional content specifies or models a state of affairs by the syntactic interrelationships among names of individuals and categories of object, action, quality, and quantity. These interrelated names and categories constitute the intension of the expression, and entail extensions in possible worlds relative to the physical and social environment of the expression's utterance (cf. Partee, 1976; Kempson, 1977).

It will hereafter be considered that informally, the propositional content of an uttered expression comprises a set of falsifiable assertions that are derivable from the surface lexicon of the uttered expression, ordered at a sufficiently deep syntactic level to make clausal, quantifier, and other dependency relations explicit.

Of course, there has been considerable controversy about the scope and autonomy of a semantic theory, enough to make tenuous the claim that propositional content is a distinct type of utterance meaning. On the one hand, there have been efforts to show that certain pragmatic features of sentence meaning could actually be accounted for within the framework of a semantic theory (e.g., Ross, 1970; Sadock, 1974; Gordon and Lakoff, 1975; Katz, 1977).

On the other hand, data and arguments have been produced that indicate that utterances often provide more information about an indicated state of affairs than is given by their truth conditions. This calls into doubt the adequacy of a truth-conditional semantic theory, and that in turn makes it unclear what distinguishes propositional content from other types of utterance meaning. However, on closer inspection these data involve inferences about indicated states of affairs beyond what is explicitly said about them. The occurrence of such inferences, and the basis for them, does not undermine the theoretical soundness of an autonomous, truth-conditional semantic theory.

Propositional Content versus Extralinguistic Understanding

Utterances provide more information about the states of affairs that their content specifies than is given by their truth conditions. This calls into question the adequacy of a truth-conditional semantic theory.

Katz and Fodor (1963) recognized this fact, and accordingly made a distinction between meanings that sentences have as a function of rules of semantic interpretation, and additional understandings based on the interpreter's knowledge of the world. Their contention was that, for example, [1a] and [1b] both involve the same ambiguity with respect to the rules of semantic interpretation, as to whether the indicated shoes are human footwear made from the animal's skin, or footwear for the animal to use:

[1] **a.** I just bought some alligator shoes.
b. I just bought some horseshoes.

Note that a truth-conditional analysis corresponds to Katz and Fodor's view that [1a] and [1b] are equivalently ambiguous. [1b] is true in a possible world where human footwear is made from horsehide as well as in the actual world where footwear is made for horses. [1a] is true in a possible world where footwear is made for alligators to wear as well as in the actual world where human footwear is made from alligator skin.

However, Katz and Fodor also note that [1a] and [1b] would normally not be understood as ambiguous, but as respectively about human footwear made from an alligator's skin and footwear made for horses to use. They attribute this disambiguation to special, additional understandings about the indicated states of affairs which result from the interpreter's extralinguistic knowledge about alligators, horses and human footwear.

However, distinguishing in that way between sentence meanings that follow from semantic rules, and further understandings which result from knowledge of the world, has been under attack almost from the outset as being ad hoc (e.g., Bolinger, 1965). It is still the focus of recent lines of argument by Searle (1980) against the notion that a self-contained semantic theory is possible.

Searle's view is that it is not possible to specify what a sentence is (truth-conditionally) about without reference to background knowledge people have about the world. For example, he contends that *cut* in [2a–d] below refers to substantially different operations on the indicated objects, but that the differences are not explicit in the meaning of the verb itself. If that is so, then it is not possible to specify the truth conditions of each of those expressions except on the basis of background knowledge about what is actually done in mowing lawns, slicing cake, severing wire, and making incisions in the skin:

[2] **a.** Bill cut the grass.
b. Bill cut the cake.

c. Bill cut some wire.
d. Bill cut his finger.

However, it is not the case that background knowledge is essential to derive the truth conditions for those sentences. If *cut* is read as an act in which a radical severance is inflicted on some object by a sharp implement, then [2a–d] specify that Bill inflicted such a severance (with an unspecified implement) on grass, cake, wire, and his finger. This unitary reading of *cut* (across its various realizations in practice) entails that [2a–d] can be collapsed into a single sentence without creating the problem that Searle predicts:

[3] Bill cut the grass, the cake, some wire and his finger.

The force of cases such as those Searle puts forward therefore does not preclude an independent truth-conditional semantics (that derives interpretations without reference to background knowledge). Rather, Searle's argument only supports the claim that propositional content—as defined by such a theory—does not capture further understandings that one undeniably has as a function of background knowledge. There is no reason to treat that as a failure of a truth-conditional semantic theory. In fact, precisely that aspect of a truth-conditional semantics makes it possible to explain how foreign interpreters knowledgeable of the rules and conventions of a language, but lacking certain background knowledge shared in the speech community, can be misled by an utterance without having misunderstood it.

Raskin (1985: 59–98) also views it as a defect of truth-conditional semantic theories that they derive propositional content narrowly, with insensitivity to further understandings that interpreters routinely have. However, in direct opposition to Searle, Raskin holds that this sort of defect in semantic theories can be rectified, that "background knowledge" can be incorporated into semantic theories by representing lexical items as covering terms for scripts.

Raskin's dissatisfaction with narrowly-drawn semantic theories is insensitive to the same concerns as Searle's. However, Raskin's data are richer than Searle's, and give rise to further, more complex issues. Consider for example [4a–c]:

[4] a. John was a dime short and had to do without milk.
b. Mary saw a black cat and immediately went back home.
c. Mary came into the room and all the men were charmed by her even before they sat down again.

It is natural (at least for native speakers of English) to read [4a] as asserting that John had no milk because he did not have enough money to buy some, to read [4b] as asserting that Mary went home as a result of encountering a black cat, and to read [4c] as asserting that Mary charmed the men almost immediately. But on truth-conditional grounds, none of those readings is justified. [4a] and [4b] only specify the conjunction of two events, not a causal relation between them; and [4c] only specifies that Mary charmed the men in the interval between her entrance and their sitting down, not that the interval was brief. The additional understandings of those three expressions derive, of course, from background knowledge about: (1) milk as a commodity, (2) the superstition that black cats bring ill fortune, and (3) the convention that men rise from their chairs and then (almost immediately) sit down again when women enter a room.

To get at the issue here, let us introduce the notion that an utterance has a *communicative point.* The communicative point of an utterance is the information or function it provides that is sufficiently newsworthy to warrant the inference that the reason for producing the utterance was to provide that information or function.

Now note that in the examples above, especially [4c], the truth conditions of each uttered expression miss the communicative point, miss precisely what each was evidently produced to communicate—that John did without milk *because* he lacked a dime; that Mary went back home *because* she saw a black cat; and in particular, that all the men were charmed by Mary *immediately* upon meeting her.

Raskin's concern, then, is really to expand the scope of a semantic theory so that it will specify meanings that capture the communicative point of utterances. But that disregards the fact that a distinction has to be made between the truth-conditional meaning of a proposition and the communicative point of its utterance. This is because the communicative point of an uttered expression often depends on whether it is true or false. For example, the communicative point of [5a–c] depends crucially on each being recognizably false:

[5] **a.** Jane's new car is two yards longer than the Queen Mary.
b. Jim ran his eyes around the room before resting them.
c. Now that I've fixed the TV, we need a repairman.

The force of Raskin's proposals is to collapse the distinction between the (truth-conditional) propositional content of utterances and their communicative point. This would have the undesirable consequence of obscuring the difference between expressions where the communicative point is implicated rather then being overt, as in [5a–c], and expressions where the communicative point precisely is made by the propositional content (e.g., *The St. Lawrence Seaway is the major commercial waterway in interior North America*).

Propositional Content vs. Conventions of Expression

There are various data that suggest that pragmatic aspects of speaking can affect the propositional content of an uttered expression, thus raising additional questions about the distinctness of propositional content as a type of meaning.

For example, the truth conditions of active and passive forms are identical (though this has to be qualified for sentence forms involving certain quantifiers), and so are alternate orderings of nouns around verbs marking bilateral relationships (e.g., *marry* and *resemble*). In that case, such variations in sentence form should not affect the deniability of the expression, yet they seem to make precisely that difference:

[6] **a.** S: John embarrassed Sally.
? H: No she wasn't.
b. S: Mary was embarrassed by John.
? H: No he didn't.
[7] **a.** S: John is married to Sally.
? H: No they're not.
b. S: John and Sally are married.
? H: No he's not.

These apparent shifts in what can be denied in response to different sentence forms make it seem that their propositional content is somehow different, even though their truth conditions are identical. However, these shifts do not involve changes in what can be denied, but changes in the way denials have to be expressed on pragmatic rather than semantic grounds.

What is involved stems partly from conventions about the surface order of 'old' and 'new' information that serve to mark the speaker's focus (Halliday, 1967; see also Chomsky, 1972: 89–102 for a related analysis of cleft-sentence forms). The contrasting sentence forms in [6] and [7] thus differ pragmatically, rather than semantically, in regard to the speaker's focus. Now consider that denials of some aspect of an utterance's content may involve the antecedent speaker's focus, or may not. If the focus is carried over into the denial, that continues the topic, but if the denial involves content not focused on, that functionally changes the topic. An important marker of topic continuity is the use of pro-forms with antecedents in prior utterances (Halliday & Hasan, 1976; Reichman, 1978). It follows that the oddity of the denials in [6] and [7] must involve their use of pro-forms even though the denials do not involve the antecdent's focus and thus have functionally changed the topic. This entails that all aspects of the content of an utterance can be denied, but that denials will seem odd if they misuse pro-forms with respect to continuing or breaking away from the antecedent's topical focus:

[8] **a.** S: Sally fired Pete.
H_a: No she didn't.
? H_b: No he wasn't.
H_c: No, Pete was reprimanded.
b. S: Pete was fired by Sally.
H_a: No he wasn't
? H_b: No she didn't.
Ha_c: No, Sally fired Mary.

A more complex case in which conventions of expression make it appear that the truth conditions of an expression are not the same as its propositional content is cited by Gazdar (1979, Chapter 7). In defending the position also taken here—that the semantics of an uttered expression are fully distinct from its pragmatic meanings—Gazdar professes an inability to explain away their apparent interrelation in [9] (from Wilson, 1975):

[9] Getting pregnant and getting married is worse than getting married and getting pregnant.

In truth-conditional terms, there is no difference between the content of the phrases *getting pregnant and getting married* versus *getting married and getting pregnant:* the semantics of *and* entail that the truth conditions of both phrases are satisfied by getting both married and pregnant no matter in what order. Yet those phrases are linked by a comparative, *worse than,* which presupposes that they are not truth-conditionally identical. In that case, either the sentence has no truth conditions and should be marked an anomaly, or it is false by definition, and should be marked an internal contradiction.

But this is intuitively unsatisfying. Those two phrases do indicate contrasting states of affairs, given the pragmatics of the connective *and* (Posner, 1980). *And* in this case marks the temporal ordering of the events referred to, so that [9] expresses a comparative evaluation of getting pregnant before marriage versus getting pregnant after marriage. This pragmatically based contrast can be verified or falisfied (has truth conditions). Gazdar thus considers these pragmatic meanings as part of the propositional content of [9].

However, consider that [10a–b] are directly analogous to [9], except that the contrasted subject and object phrases do not include constituents that pragmatically express their contrast:

[10] **a.** Making money is harder than making money.
b. Ending a lecture is better than ending a lecture.

It is nonetheless both possible and natural to read [10a] and [10b] as comprising dissimilar phrases, given the lexical ambiguity of *making money* (earning versus manufacturing it), and of *ending a lecture* (concluding versus disrupting one). The motivation for an interpreter to search out those contrasting readings, of course, is a pragmatic one—the presumption (under Grice's, 1975, Cooperative Principle) that the use of the comparative form is deliberate and sincere. This is also what is involved in [9]: there is a pragmatic motivation—and not a semantic one—for focusing on the (pragmatic) contrast between the two phrases.

Gazdar's principal concern of course remains: the fact that sentences like [9], [10a] and [10b] seem to take on truth values once they acquire a pragmatically motivated content. But it is not necessary to treat such acquired truth values as a function of the truth conditions of what was actually said. Such acquired truth values belong to a derived abstract entity, the *reinterpreted expression.*

That is, it is true of metaphors, just as it is true of [9], [10a] and [10b], that they can be judged true or false on the level of their metaphoric readings. But it would be theoretically incoherent to treat the truth or falsity of the metaphoric reading as entailing the truth or falsity of the uttered expression, rather than the truth or falsity of the derived entity, the reinterpreted expression. Metaphoric readings are distrinct from literal meanings, with any semantic defects in the literal reading being a motivation to derive the metaphoric reading (Sanders, 1973; Loewenberg, 1975). The same principle extends to instances such as [9] and [10]: it is the semantic oddity of the expression that on pragmatic grounds motivates a shift of interpretive focus.

The Status of Additional Understandings

The question, then, is not whether propositional content can be treated as the product of a truth-conditional semantic theory. The question is, given the propositional content (truth conditions) of an utterance, what is the status of additional understandings that are warranted by background knowledge and conventions of expression? This issue also applies to and can most easily be resolved in terms of similar understandings involving conventional implicatures and generalized conversational implicatures (Grice, 1975).

Conventional Implicature

There are certain connectives and modifiers that can be added or deleted without affecting the truth value of an utterance, but that mark certain additional understandings that the communicator has about the indicated state of affairs. For example, the modifiers *managed, even,* and *just* in [11a–c] make no difference to the propositional content of the respective expressions (given in brackets immediately below the original expression) but they conventionally implicate a further proposition (given in brackets as the second expression below the original):

[11] a. Peter managed to start the car.
[Peter started the car]
[Peter had trouble getting the car started]

b. Even John thought the movie was funny.
[John thought the movie was funny]
[Everybody thought the movie was funny, down to the hardest person to amuse, John]

c. That noise is just the wind rattling the windows.
[That noise is caused by the wind rattling the windows]
[That noise is commonplace and not a signal that something is wrong]

Consider that the communicator's liability for fostering implicatures that are false to the facts is much less severe than when the utterance's propositional content is false. If, for example, Peter in [11a] in fact had had no trouble, nor had been having trouble, starting his car, the communicator who authored [11a] would have spoken misleadingly, or at least have been sloppy in his phrasing. But if Peter did not get his car started in the current instance, then the communicator of [11a] would have been wrong, for reasons of deceit or ignorance.

Generalized Conversational Implicatures

Again from Grice's (1975) examples, there are certain sets of related terms, with the use of one rather than another fostering a further understanding regarding the indicated state of affairs. There is, for example, an array of terms involving number *(one, two, a few, several, many)* an array of terms involving authorization and permission *(order, authorize, permit, enable, prevent, not allow, preclude, forbid),* arrays of terms to distinguish kinship and types of interpersonal relationship, etc. These often form a 'scale' (Horn, 1972), such that use of a term located somewhere on such a scale implicates that conditions marked by terms higher or lower on the scale do not obtain:

[12] a. The General gave Private Smith permission to requisition a jeep.
b. Pete and Sally have been dating for almost two years.

Hence, it is implicated in [12a] that the General allowed—but did not order nor authorize—Private Smith to order a jeep. And it is implicated in [12b] that while Pete and Sally are romantically involved, they are not going steady or cohabiting. Note, however, that the communicator's liability for any incorrectness in these implicatures may even be lower than the liability for incorrect conventional implicatures.

This suggests that in these cases, and in general, there is a 'buyer beware' ethic associated with these additional understandings, where the communicator bears minimal responsibility for their correctness. This does not of course offset the temptation of relying on such additional understandings to improve the efficiency of information exchange. But this becomes increasingly risky the greater the extent to which communicators and interpreters cannot take for granted that they have largely the same background knowledge and follow the same conventions of phrasing and utterance (see Chapter 7 on communication under conditions of linguistic and cultural difference).

CONVERSATIONAL IMPLICATURE

The concern in this section is to show that (particularized) conversational implicatures are a non-exclusive, distinct type of utterance meaning. However, the reason this is in doubt is not because there are opposing conceptualizations and counterindications in the data (as in the case of propositional content). This is in doubt because the *assignment functions* and constituent features of conversational implicatures have never been made sufficiently explicit to support any conclusion, one way or the other, about their exclusivity and distinctness.

Grice's, (1967, 1975) analysis is vague on a number of key points, particularly on how and whether interpreters have any basis for a uniform understanding of what specific utterances implicate. Grice works from two core premises. The first is that the objective in speaking is to exchange information (though Grice, 1975: 47, acknowledges that that is an overly narrow characterization of the objectives of speaking). The second core premise is that interpreters presume that any entry in a discourse or dialogue is intended to be "cooperative"—to be a contribution that moves it forward.

When the goal is to exchange information, being cooperative entails that the propositional content of one's utterance satisfy certain requirements, which are codified by Grice in four "conversational maxims," i.e., an utterance must provide information that is: (1) topically relevant, (2) expressed perspicuously, (3) sufficient for the need at that juncture, and (4) believed to be true.

Grice's most basic postulate is that if (the form and content of) an utterance breaches one or more of those maxims, interpreters will make an effort to construe some rationale for the deviant utterance that upholds the presumption that the speaker intended to be cooperative. But Grice does not make clear that such construed rationales do not consist of propositions about some state of affairs, but rather they take the form of propositions about the communicator's subjective state regarding some state of affairs (belief, perception, feeling, desire). It is only with reference to some such subjective state that an offending utterance can have been intended to be as full a contribution as is either possible or necessary.

This characterization of conversational implicatures is borne out by Grice's (1975) chief exemplar, a letter of recommendation for a job applicant that praises the applicant's personal qualities but omits comment about the applicant's aptitudes and qualifications. Grice characterizes this as a breach of the maxim of quantity (insufficient information for the need) which he says implicates *the author's reluctance to publicly express that* the applicant's aptitudes and qualifications are inadequate.

The Apprehension of Conversational Implicatures

To take conversational implicature seriously as a type of utterance meaning, there must be a principled connection between the utterance's propositional content, the maxim(s) it breached, and what it implicates. But despite the importance of this issue, it has largely been disregarded. Even Grice (1975: 58) dealt with it only in a closing observation:

> Since, to calculate a conversational implicature is to calculate what has to be supposed in order to preserve the supposition that the Cooperative Principle is being observed, and since there may be various possible explanations, a list of which may be open, the

> conversational implicatum in such cases will be the disjunction of such specific explanations; and if the list of these is open, the implicatum will have just the kind of indeterminacy that many actual implicata do in fact seem to possess.

This conclusion is unsatisfying, particularly in view of its assumption that there is necessarily a lot of guesswork and haphazardness with regard to the apprehension of implicatures. That assumption is incorrect.

This is not to suggest that conversational implicatures are apprehended as a function of formal operations over some set of features of uttered expressions. However, the inferences that interpreters make to uphold the presumption that the Cooperative Principle is in force have a substantive foundation that constrains and structures them.

The Recognition of a Breach

The prerequisite for apprehending an implicated proposition is to recognize that one or another of the specific maxims has been breached. However, it is not an objective condition that some utterance breaches a maxim. It is a matter of judgment whether to regard an utterance as irrelevant, imprecise, insufficient, or insincere. To make such judgments, there must be some standard or expectation against which the utterance is measured.

For an utterance to be regarded as *topically irrelevant,* the interpreter must have some model of the state of affairs covered by the topic against which to assess whether the content of an utterance is (necessarily) about that same state of affairs. For an utterance to be regarded as providing too little or too much information, or to be regarded as being vague, ambiguous, or obscure, the interpreter must have some model or script regarding what the informational need is in order to achieve the (presumed) goal of the discourse or dialogue. And for an utterance to be regarded as sincere, the interpreter must have some model of the author's attitudes and beliefs about what he/she would want to make known and would believe to be true.

These models are presumably grounded in the interpreter's background knowledge and social experience. This makes it likely that there will be some individual differences in this regard, and thus some variation about when or whether a conversational maxim is breached. The ability of an author to make an implicature and of interpreters to apprehend it thus depends on there being substantial commonalities in the background knowledge and social experience of members of groups and communities.

Interpreters possess indefinitely large numbers of cognitive models that pertain to recognizing breaches of conversational maxims. It is thus a consideration whether there is some general basis for opting to utilize certain of one's cognitive models rather than others against which to test the relevance, perspicuity, sufficiency, and sincerity of an utterance. If there is a general basis for this, then at least it is not guesswork or haphazard to judge that a maxim has been breached.

There is obviously a shared basis for knowing what model to use in judging the relevance of an utterance—namely, the topic at hand. The model(s) used to judge the perspicuity and sufficiency of an utterance depend on what the present goals of the discourse or dialogue are understood as being. There are grounds for having common understandings of goals—namely, the explicit announcement of goals, or shared knowledge of the conventional goals related to the practice or institution into which the communicator has entered. There is least likely to be a shared basis for what model of the communicator to use in judging his/her sincerity. This predicts plausibly that there is the greatest likelihood of individual differences in apprehending that someone is kidding, or being ironic or being sarcastic. Given the communicator's identity, interpreters who know the communicator personally will have a richer model to utilize compared with interpreters who do not. Interpreters who do not know the communicator personally have to use models that apply to stereotypes based on the communicator's social-group memberships and/or role(s).

This can be illustrated in terms of the relationship between each of S's utterances and H's replies in [13]:

[13] **a.** S: You know, you still owe me for the $50 I loaned you.
H: My dentist just fitted me for three new crowns.
b. S: I need some advice about how to study for your midterm exam, Professor.
H: Read the book.

c. S: What a surprise running into you—it's been too long.
H: It really has. I'll call you for lunch real soon.

d. S: *Gandhi* is a brilliant film, a tribute to the best and finest qualities that people are capable of.
H: Oh yes, it's easily as profound and insightful as *Gone with the Wind.*

In [13a] the propositional content of S's utterance makes salient a model of borrowing, repayment, and indebtedness against which H's report of the need for dental work is irrelevant. In [13b] the propositional content (and apparent institutional context) of S's utterance introduces the goal of succeeding on an examination, making salient models of how that can be done against which H's reply is insufficiently informative. In [13c] the propositional content (and the conventional practices indicated thereby) of S's utterance introduces the goal of arranging social contact, making salient a model of how to go about that against which H's reply is vague. In [13d] the sincerity of H's reply depends on one's model of H. For illustrative purposes, let us say that as measured against S's model, H's reply is insincere.

The Content of the Resulting Implicature

Given that there is some systematic basis for recognizing that a maxim has been breached, the obvious next question is whether there is also a systematic basis for identifying what is thereby implicated. A conversational implicature is a proposition about the communicator's subjective state regarding some state of affairs, in light of which an evidently 'uncooperative' utterance can be regarded as cooperative after all.

The question then becomes whether there is any systematic way to apprehend what the communicator's subjective state is regarding what state of affairs, that explains away the apparent breach of a maxim and is thus implicated by it. The answer is yes, there is a way. The content of each maxim implies what the communicator would have to believe, perceive, feel or desire for a breach of that maxim to be only apparent.

The content of the conversational implicature that is predicated on the apparent breach of each particular maxim is as follows:

1. Breaches of the *maxim of relation,* which requires an utterance to be relevant: (the speaker believes or perceives that) there is a state of affairs that 'bridges the gap' and is relevant both to the propositional content of the utterance in question and of the antecedent topic.

2. Breaches of the *maxim of quantity,* which requires an utterance to provide just as much information as needed: there is a state of affairs that (the speaker considers sufficient to) prevent or dissuade him/her from supplying the missing information, or to motivate him/her to supply the excess.

3. Breaches of the *maxim of manner,* which requires an utterance to be clear and precise: there is a state of affairs that (the speaker considers sufficient to) prevent or dissuade him/her from being clearer.

4. Breaches of the *maxim of quality,* which requires the speaker to say what he/she believes to be true: (the speaker believes to be true) a topically relevant state of affairs that is the opposite or reciprocal of the one asserted or asked about.

Hence, an implicature must be a proposition, predicated on a subjective state of the speaker, about some state of affairs that conforms to one or another of the general requirements stated in 1–4 above, depending on which maxim was breached by the utterance in question. On the basis of applying 1–4 above to H's replies in [13a–d], the content of H's respective implicatures is given below.

In [13a] H's utterance about needing dental work is topically irrelevant, so that by 1 above the presumption of cooperation can only be upheld if there is some state of affairs relevant to both dental work and the antecedently mentioned loan. The common denominator between them of course is that both involve cash outflow, and if cash outflow for both purposes exceeds H's resources so that priorities have to be set, it is common practice to give health needs greater priority. On that basis, H's reply in [13a] implicates an intention to defer the obligation to repay the loan.

In [13b] H's reply is insufficiently informative, so that by 2 above the presumption of cooperation can only be upheld if there is some state of affairs that dissuades or prevents H from saying more. Considering that H is the (apparent) author of the examination in question, the insufficiency of information cannot be attributed to ignorance. Therefore, H must be dissuaded from saying more. Within the model of the indicated institution, professors can be dissuaded from advising students about how to study for particular examinations if, and H's reply thus implicates that: (1) they consider it incumbent on students to solve that problem independently, or (2) there is no advice that can be given which will avoid revealing the form and content of the examination, or (3) no method of studying for the examination improves upon fully reading the pertinent material. H's utterance is thus ambiguous as to its implicature. Disambiguating the utterance must be contingent on one's model of the speaker's beliefs and attitudes.

In [13c] H's reply is unclear about when arrangements to meet S will be made, so that by 3 above the presumption of cooperation can be retained only if there is some state of affairs that dissuades or prevents H from being clearer. One can only be prevented from knowing when to make arrangements for a meeting if making such arrangements is time-consuming and one's calendar is full; one can be dissuaded from being clear about when such arrangements will be made if one desires to avoid any firm obligation to make them. The former state of affairs is implausible, so that H's reply in [13c] implicates a reluctance to be committed to arranging for lunch (and having lunch) with S.

Finally, if H's assessment of *Gone with the Wind* is presumed to be insincere, then the principle of cooperation can be retained only if, by 4 above, there is a state of affairs H does believe to be true that is contrary to the one indicated and is topically relevant. The contrasting state of affairs to the one indicated is that *Gone with the Wind* is superficial and historically simplistic, which is topically relevant as a standard against which *Gandhi* is being measured. If one's model of H warrants considering that H would consider it true that *Gone with the Wind* is superficial and simplistic, not insightful and complex, then H's utterance implicates disagreement with S's evaluation of *Gandhi.*

The foregoing analysis can be summarized as follows. If the propositional content of an uttered expression, predicated on some cognitive model, breaches a conversational maxim, then a proposition is implicated that is a product of the intersection between objective conditions entailed by that cognitive model and the skeletal proposition presupposed by the breached maxim about the subjective state of the speaker towards such conditions. This can be expressed formally by a statement that ranges over the propositional content of the uttered expression (PC_{ue}), a cognitive model which has been salient antecedently (Mod_{η}), a conversational maxim (Max_{μ}), the skeletal proposition which that maxim presupposes ($[Max_{\mu}]Pr$), and the proposition which that utterance implicates ($ImPr_{ue}$):

[14] $([Mod_{\eta}]PC_{ue} \rightarrow \sim Max_{\mu}) \rightarrow ((Mod_{\eta} \cap [Max_{\mu}]Pr) = ImPr_{ue})$

This predicts that the chance of misfires and errors in deriving implicatures is smallest when the communicator and interpreter have an equivalent knowledge of the semantics of the language and equivalent cognitive models (e.g., are natives of the same speech community). The likelihood of misfires and errors should thus be very high not only when there are substantial differences in linguistic knowledge, but when there are substantial differences in the cognitive models utilized by the communicator and the interpreter (e.g., across disparate regions and cultures). By the same token, this predicts that there will be changes over time in what an interpreter takes to be implicated when a given utterance breaches a specific maxim, insofar as there are changes over time in that interpreter's pertinent cognitive models.

The Non-Exclusiveness of Conversational Implicatures

Grice (1975) implicates that if an uttered expression breaches one or more of the conversational maxims, and a proposition is thereby implicated, interpreters will focus on and respond to the implicature; the converse of this would be that if the utterance is cooperative in terms of its propositional content (at face value), then that is the type of meaning which interpreters will focus on and respond to. This is a natural point of view if the problem of focus is construed as a binary one, an either-or choice between the 'standard' and 'non-standard' meaning of an utterance.

It is obviously a central consideration here whether that view has merit—whether the mere fact of being able to derive an implicature warrants focusing on and responding to it, no matter how the utterance follows from its antecedents in the unfolding discourse or dialogue. Grice's tacit view that that is the case follows from his having construed the problem from the outset as a choice between two possible types or levels of meaning (Grice, 1957). But if one is not initially disposed to view the problem in this way, there is nothing else that motivates the assumption that the mere fact of breaching a maxim warrants focusing on the resulting implicature rather than on the utterance's propositional content.

Breaching a maxim implicates a state of affairs predicated on a subjective state of the communicator. However, in a given discourse or dialogue, the subjective states on which an implicature is predicated may be more tangential than the information provided by the utterance's propositional content (even though it is irrelevant, insufficient, imprecise, or insincere).

If this is correct, then it follows that when an utterance breaches a conversational maxim, in the absence of any more extended antecedent constraints on what specific interpretation to focus on, the interpreter can respond as coherently to the propositional content or illocutionary act as to the implicature. This is evident in [15] below. H's utterance breaches the maxim of relation, and is responded to by S_a in terms of what it implicates (that H believes that gas can be obtained most readily by telephoning for help)—but it is not anomalous for S_b to respond instead to its propositional content (about the location of a phone booth), or for S_c to respond to H's act of issuing a directive (by virtue of the implicature that they should telephone for help):

[15] S: I've run out of gas.
H: I saw a phone booth a block or two back.
S_a: It doesn't matter, there's a gas station down that way about a mile.
S_b: That's weird. Nobody lives around here anymore.
S_c: Who put you in charge? The one who's paying gets to work out the moves.

ILLOCUTIONARY ACTS

As in the preceding sections on propositional content and conversational implicature, the object here is to establish that illocutionary acts constitute a discrete and non-exclusive type of utterance meaning. This is in doubt for two reasons. First, while there is a 'standard' account of the interpretation of utterances as acts, it is vague in regard to particulars and evidently insensitive to numerous data. This being the case, there is little basis for concluding one way or the other whether illocutionary acts are a discrete and non-exclusive type of meaning. But second, Searle (e.g., 1969: 30) has nonetheless postulated that illocutionary acts are not discrete, that instead they mark the way in which (the speaker intended) propositional content should be utilized by the interpreter. Let us take these up in that order.

The Interpretation of Utterances as Acts

The Standard Account

Austin's (1962) foundational argument was that illocutionary acts are undertaken not only in the utterance of explicitly performative sentences—sentences with a prescribed utility in well-defined procedures and rituals—but that all utterances have, and are understood in terms of, a performative aspect (their social function) as well as their "constative" aspect (their propositional content). Although this is intuitively correct, it is problematic. If illocutionary acts were performed only in restricted contexts, then their production and understanding could be explained by anthropological and sociological studies that list ways of performing specific acts, and under which social circumstances. But Austin's (1962) thesis rules out such a direct approach. If all utterances are acts, then producing and understanding them must depend on knowledge of general relationships between social purposes and the form and content of utterances.

Searle's (1969) effort to make such relationships explicit rests on his supposition that there are a finite number of social purposes that utterances can serve, and that for each such purpose there are "constitutive rules" that specify what features of form and content an utterance must have, and what features the interpersonal situation must (be perceived to) have, for the utterance to serve the purpose.

However, utterances count as illocutionary acts (i.e., have social purposes) regardless of whether they include explicit verbal or nonverbal markers of their purpose (illocutionary force indicating devices). The problem thus resurfaces of how the act performed by making an unmarked utterance is understood.

The form and content of an utterance alone cannot uniquely identify the act it counts as. Numerous contrasting illocutionary acts have the same rules about the form and content of utterances used to perform them. A promise and a threat are both performed by uttering an expression that predicates a future act on the speaker. Advice and warnings are both performed by uttering an expression in which some eventuality is predicated on the hearer's present conduct.

Searle has not taken the problem here very seriously. Rather, he evidently takes for granted that the constitutive rules of any given illocutionary act are sufficiently unambiguous and explicit that knowing them is enough for interpreters to identify what act an utterance counts as, given its overt features and features of (what one knows about) the situation:

> Often, in actual speech situations, the context will make it clear what the illocutionary force of the utterance is, without its being necessary to invoke the appropriate explicit illocutionary force indicator. (1969: 30)

> In any speech situation there is a speaker, a hearer, and a speech act being performed by the speaker. The speaker and hearer share a mutual knowledge of those facts together with a mutual knowledge of the rules of performing the various kinds of speech acts. (1979: 167)

But this is unsatisfying. It is too vague to explain how interpreters go about doing this, or to support any conclusions one way or another about how reliable and systematic such understandings are.

The problem here is generally acknowledged (e.g., Stampe, 1975; Bach and Harnish, 1979; Edmondson, 1981; Green and Morgan, 1981), but it is not uniformly viewed as the result of a weakness in Searle's standard account. Green and Morgan (1981: 177) treat it as inherent in the nature of speech acts:

> Because the link between intentional acts—even speech acts—and their interpretation is so underdetermined by the objective data (that So-and-So has said "Thus-and-such"), and so dependent on the interpreter's beliefs about the actor's goals and motives, it should not

surprise us that it is a tenuous one, and that there will be many a slip twixt cup and lips.

Bach and Harnish also consider the basis for understanding the act an utterance counts as to be necessarily vague, and they tacitly give up on the feasibility of making explicit the basis for interpreting utterances as acts:

> How does [the hearer] *H* infer which meaning [which act] is operative? It would seem that he must reject all but one of the meanings of [the expression] *e* as contextually inappropriate and rely on certain mutual contextual beliefs to do this. . . . Usually, we seem just to hear (or read) and understand the expression *e* in the contextually most appropriate way—which is why we often miss subtle puns. Perhaps, then, the process of understanding an utterance involves operations that make certain readings more probable, given certain mutual contextual beliefs, and as hearers we often take these readings as first hypotheses concerning what [the speaker] *S* meant by *e* unless (or until) they are defeated by [mutual contextual beliefs], future remarks, and so on. (1979: 21)

But this type of utterance meaning cannot be taken seriously, any more than conversational implicatures could, if the explanation of how such meanings are connected to utterances with certain properties that occur in contexts with certain properties remains as vague as it is in the standard account.

Understanding Utterances as Acts on the Basis of Circumstantial Evidence

Let us stipulate that understanding an utterance as an act is never open-ended and unstructured, made in a vacuum. In a given context, there are at least two—and often three—independent variables that set parameters on what act(s) it is possible for a given utterance to count as. The intersection of these two or three sets of parameters isolates the few acts, often the single act, that the utterance could count as.

The act an utterance with a given form and content could count as, with reference to the constitutive rules of illocutionary acts, is narrowed by what acts are structurally called for or permissible at that juncture in the discourse or dialogue. The act an utterance could count as is also narrowed by what the communicator's character and traits dispose him/her to do.

The judgment of what act an utterance counts as is thus a product of the intersections of the set of acts that the uttered expression could count as given all applicable constitutive rules, {[Rules]Act}, the set of acts that are structurally called for in that segment of the discourse or dialogue, {[Need]Act}, and the set of acts the communicator is disposed towards, {[Disp]Act}.

However, the interpretation of an utterance as an act cannot be expressed formally as a simple product of the intersection of those three sets. Such an expression would entail the null set whenever there is no act the utterance could count as that is included in all three sets (i.e., when an act the utterance can count as according to the constitutive rules is not both structurally called for and consistent with the actor's dispositions as well). But it is incorrect to say that there is no act an utterance counts as in that circumstance. It is not uncommon, for example, for utterances to be understood as acts, but ones the communicator did not intend to perform. This would follow if the utterance could count as that act in terms of the constitutive rules or in terms of what is structurally called for, but not in terms of what the communicator's dispositions are (e.g., for person *A* to have said *X* is insulting, but it was probably not intended as an insult because *A* is my friend, and no display of hostility is called for in this interaction). Conversely, utterances are sometimes understood as acts which the communicator intended but misexecuted. This would follow if the act conforms to the speaker's dispositions and what is structurally called for, but the utterance does not have the form or content required by the constitutive rules of that act (e.g., because person *A* is hostile, and because an expression of hostility has a structural place in this interaction, *A* probably intended to insult me by saying *X*, but the content of *X* is actually not derogatory of anything to do with me).

Hence, in accordance with conventions of practical reasoning (cf. the forensic and scientific notions of circumstantial evidence) the principle here must be expressed so as to specify that any act the utterance can count as that is present in all three sets is more likely the intended one than one present in only two, and that any possible act present in two sets is more likely the intended one than an act present in only one. The appropriate expression of this comprises a series of different possible intersections of the sets {[Rules]Act}, {[Need]Act}, and {[Disp]Act}, ordered so that the act(s) which are products of the intersection of all three sets take precedence over acts which are products of the intersection of any two sets, and the act(s) which are products of the intersection of any two sets take precedence over act(s) which are included in any one set.

Of course, the merits of this analysis depend on there being a cognitive foundation for each of those sets of possible acts that is stable and does not have to be specified in an ad hoc way. Those cognitive foundations are as follows.

{[Rules]Act$_{ue}$}

As is evident from the criticisms above of the standard account, and as Stampe (1975) points out, given the various constitutive rules of possible illocutionary acts, an utterance in and of itself can count as any among a disjunctive array of possible acts. This is entirely compatible with the account here (whereas it is problematic in the standard account because understandings of utterances as acts are treated there as a function of constitutive rules alone, and such rules are obviously too weak to bear that load).

The rules of the various illocutionary acts can be regarded as a component of social knowledge, rooted in the speech community, relatively stable, and not ad hoc.

{[Need]Act}

Edmondson (1981) focuses on the existence of structural properties in conversation. Given those structural properties, only one from among a relatively small number of acts is called for (or at least permitted) at given junctures, and interpreters are accordingly disposed to regard any entry at such a juncture as one or another of those acts. Of course, the set of acts that are possible in terms of structural needs also has to include acts that reject or challenge what is called for structurally and acts that evade instead of rejecting what is called for structurally. For example, if there is a knock on the door, then with respect to what is needed in a 'summons-answer' sequence, the communicator can either answer, reject or challenge the legitimacy of the summons, or evade it. In that case, the utterance of *what do you want?* satisfies the requirements of both an answer and an evasion (by the constitutive rules of those acts) and could be interpreted as either.

The structural properties involved are either a product of the fixed relations among the components of standardized procedures and routines (e.g., Schegloff, 1972a, 1972b, 1982) or are the products of relations among categorical units of conversation that are emergent as the conversation unfolds (Edmondson, 1981: 82–136).

{**[Disp]Act**}

An interpreter has three principal ways of 'knowing' what a communicator's interpersonal attitudes and intentions are, or more precisely, what the valences of the communicator's dispositions are (e.g., liking, dislike, happiness, sadness, anger, caring, indifference). First, the valences of the communicator's present attitudes and intentions are often indicated nonverbally through vocal quality, facial expression, gaze behavior, posture, gesture, etc. Second, the communicator's declared role in a given instance generally carries with it an array of obligations and prohibitions (e.g., Goffman, 1959) that entail having (or more precisely, acting as if one had) certain interpersonal attitudes and intentions. Finally, insofar as the interpreter has had past dealings with the communicator, the interpreter will have been able to make inductions about the communicator's character and traits (by the methods described in Chapter 2) from which the communicator's dispositional valences in the present circumstance can be deduced.

The interpreter may of course have idiosyncratic and ad hoc knowledge regarding the acts a particular individual will perform in response to certain attitudes and intentions. But the attitudes and intentions attributed to an actor can be linked with acts that he/she is therefore disposed towards on a more general, less idiosyncratic basis. And there are conventions in the speech community about normal conduct in response to particular interior conditions (e.g., about what normal people who are jealous, sad, loving, antagonistic, etc. can be expected to do).

The Distinctness of Illocutionary Acts

I have postulated that interpreters have the option of focusing on and responding to what the communicator did (the illocutionary act) without focusing on and responding to what the utterance is about (its propositional content). The account of understanding utterances as acts given above supports this postulate by treating such understandings as functions of evidence pertaining solely to the utterance's social function. By the analysis above the interpreter's identification of the utterance's social function does not entail that the interpreter has used the utterance's content in the way the communicator intended.

It has of course been Searle's principal goal to show that propositional content in and of itself, without reference to the purposes for which it is been provided, is socially trivial, and that traditional semantic theories are correspondingly vacuous. Thus, Searle takes the view that illocutionary acts are directions to interpreters about how to use and respond to the content of the expression(s) uttered (whether to store it as valued information, apply it to the solution of a problem, make some change in the indicated state of affairs, provide information about the indicated state of affairs, etc.):

> From this semantical point of view we can distinguish two (not necessarily separate) elements in the syntactical structure of the sentence, which we might call the propositional indicator and the illocutionary force indicator. The illocutionary force indicator shows how the proposition is to be taken. (Searle, 1969: 30)

Consistent with this, Searle (1979: 117–136, 1980) explicitly rejects the presumptions of semantic and pragmatic theories that there are context-free sentence meanings—meanings that sentences have independent of what speakers (are perceived to) intend, and of the background knowledge and assumptions of interpreters.

The philosophical merits of this position are not at issue here, but its empirical merits are dubious. In saying that "[w]hen a proposition is expressed, it is always expressed in the performance of an illocutionary act," Searle (1969: 29) can have intended either a weak or a strong empirical claim. The weak version of this claim is merely a truism: that uttering an expression of language is always volitional and therefore purposeful. The strong version of that claim is arguably false.

The strong version of Searle's claim is that: (1) uttered expressions cannot be understood without reference to their illocutionary force, and (2) propositional content is not detachable from illocutionary force. The data do not support either of these.

There are instances contrary to the entailment that utterances are understandable only with respect to their illocutionary force, when an utterance is encountered and responded to without any basis for identifying its illocutionary force. I do not have in mind such artifices as a sentence in the so-called null context (e.g., a one-sentence anonymous letter) but such commonplaces as posted signs and notices, and any other instances where the communicator's social purpose is highly equivocal. [16] below could be posted in a storefront as an apology, an excuse, a warning, advice, a promise or an invitation to return:

[16] We will be closed for inventory Sunday and Monday, June 12–13, and will re-open at noon on Tuesday, June 14.

The equivocality of the act involved does not prevent an interpreter from understanding and utilizing the information provided in [16]. The propositional content of [16] follows from knowledge of the rules of English, and the interpreter has the option of utilizing that content as his/her needs dictate. This is precisely the way in which information is utilized which comes directly from the physical environment, and the way it can optionally be utilized even when the information has a source whose social purpose is unequivocal.

As for the claim that propositional content is not detachable from illocutionary force, one only has to consider such instances as in [17] below. The content of H's responses in [17] focuses on and responds to the content of S's utterances while disregarding their illocutionary force, but there is nothing anomalous about those responses.

[17] **a.** S: I demand a full refund on this defective toaster.
H: That? It looks like a microcomputer.
b. S: Anne is out to get you, so my advice is to double-check the facts in your report before you submit it.
H: I heard that she's being considered for a promotion.

SPECIFIC INTERPRETATIONS OF UTTERANCES

Propositional content, conversational implicatures and illocutionary force are discrete types of meaning that utterances have at the same time. This raises the question of what principled basis there is for focusing on and responding to a specific type of meaning at a given juncture in preference to the alternatives. This takes for granted that people do in fact assign specific interpretations to utterances and that they have a general, systematic basis for doing so. If this were not the case, then in light of the semantic chaining of entries in [18] below, it would be difficult to account for the intuition that nonetheless there is something wrong with B's responses to A, and that A's last entry does cohere with the antecedent sequence:

[18] A: Can you tell me where the public library is from here?
B: Oh sure, I've lived in this neighborhood all my life.
A: Great, because I have no idea where it is.
B: How come you haven't been there before? Not much of a reader?
A: No, no—I just moved into the area, so I don't know my way around yet. That's why I'll need very detailed directions.
B: Oh yeah? How come you moved? Where're you from?
A: Look, I really have to go—are you going to help me out, or not?

The next two chapters respectively: (1) make explicit the principles for focusing on specific types of utterance meaning, and (2) report laboratory data supporting them. Similar principles for assigning specific interpretations to nonverbals in their own right, and to nonverbals and utterances in combination, will be made explicit subsequently, in Chapter 6.

CHAPTER 4

The Relevance of Utterances: Warrants for Specific Interpretations

The objective in this chapter is to make explicit the principles that warrant focusing on specific utterance meanings or at least on meanings of a specific type at a given juncture. Informally, the question is, how do people judge which (type of) meaning is the 'correct' or intended one to focus on and respond to? Several factors can be posited a priori as having an effect on the interpreter's focus. However, on general theoretical grounds and for the purposes of this book, the most important one is that in order for an utterance to follow or contribute—i.e., be relevant— in the unfolding discourse or dialogue at that juncture, the interpreter has to focus on a specific (type of) meaning.

REASONS FOR INTERPRETIVE JUDGMENTS

There are at least three independent factors that can influence the specific interpretation of an utterance in a given instance:

1. Personal knowledge of the speaker and what he/she would characteristically have produced that utterance in that circumstance to express.
2. Conventional understandings of what that utterance would 'normally' be used to communicate in that circumstance.
3. What specific type of interpretation has to be focused on for the utterance to be relevant to its antecedents or consequents in the discourse or dialogue at hand.

These factors can either be complementary or in conflict. Let us postulate that in the normal case they are complementary, each warranting a focus on the same (type of) meaning.

On the other hand, when those factors support conflicting judgments it is an empirical question which of them will have the strongest effect, and why: their respective influences may be FIXED, the result of a hierarchical ordering among them; VARIABLE, e.g., a product of their relative salience in a given instance; or IDIOSYNCRATIC, ordered according to the interpreter's habits, dispositions, and biases.

However, that empirical question is secondary here. Regardless of the empirical strength of those factors, 3 above is the most important theoretically, both for accounting for specific interpretations of utterances, and especially for the concern in this book with the cognitive underpinnings of strategic communication.

First, 3 is the most generally applicable and available basis for making interpretive judgments. 1 and 2 do not consistently come into play. The (pertinent) knowledge people have about communicators is highly variable, and judgments of what (type of) meaning to focus on and respond to are often made despite substantial ignorance about the communicator. Similarly, the applicability of conventions about what certain utterances are used to communicate is highly variable. Utterances are often formulated in wholly nonconventional undertakings, such as collaborations on solving novel problems or completing novel tasks, coping with crises or catastrophes, and initiating, renegotiating, or terminating relationships.

In contrast, 3 is far less variable, and it almost always comes into play. The extent of the public record into which utterances are inserted is relatively a constant. In most instances there are at least constituents in the interpreter's personal or communal history from which even the first entries in discourses or dialogues follow, or consequences in the discourse or dialogue to which they contribute. Accordingly, 3 cannot fail to come into play except in the rare, often pathological, instances when utterances are produced in the absence of any (publicly evident) antecedent or consequent.

Second, 3 theoretically dominates 1 and 2. Consider that it is possible for an interpreter's personal knowledge about a communicator to be incorrect, or for the communicator to have changed, so that interpretive judgments based on such personal knowledge are incorrect. However, interpretive judgments based on one's knowledge of the communicator can be tested by reference to their consistency with interpretive judgments based on the relationship of the utterance to its antecedents and/or consequents. Similarly, errors in one's understandings of specific conventions about what utterances are used to communicate, or of when those conventions come into play, can be detected and corrected by reference to their consistency with judgments based on the relationship of the utterance to the public record.

Finally, 3 is the one basis for interpretive judgments that is reliably and unavoidably influenced by the way communicators formulate their entries in discourses and dialogues.[1] It is thus of central importance here as the one basis for specific interpretations that fosters, and thereby accounts for, strategic communication. By 3 the specific interpretation of one's utterances is influenced by formulating the current entry so that it will only be relevant to prior or subsequent ones with regard to the (type of) meaning it is desired be focused on. And conversely, the way one is understood can be influenced by making prior entries (in anticipation of the current one) or subsequent entries to which the current one will be relevant only in regard to the (type of) meaning it is desired be focused on.

Theoretical Antecedents and Present Advances

The central idea here—that an utterance's specific interpretation is decided so as to bear out the presumption of its relevance—has a clear precedent in Grice's (1975) thesis that when an utterance breaches the maxim of relation, it acquires the meaning of an implicature that sustains the presumption of its relevance. There is an even stronger precedent in Sperber and Wilson's (1982, 1986) idea that interpreters identify the intended meaning from among the possible contextual implications of an utterance as the one that makes the utterance maximally relevant in the given context.

However, the notion of relevance relied on by Grice and by Sperber and Wilson is simpler and more restricted than the one relied on here. This reflects core differences in what each account explains. Unlike the account of relevance and interpretation below, those precedents cannot (and were not intended to) explain (1) emergent constraints on what communicators say and do in discourses and dialogues, (2) the fluidity of the way entries are interpreted and cohered, nor (3) projections of the consequences of taking different options of content and style and formulating entries.

Grice and Sperber and Wilson seem to share the idea that relevance involves a connection between an utterance's propositional content and something like the topic of conversation, but only those aspects of the topic (it is here that their accounts are especially vague) about which the conversants have reason (in some sense) to be informative. In addition to this being vague, it is very narrow to conceive of an utterance's relevance just in terms of its propositional content (cf., Dascal, 1977; van Dijk, 1980). That narrowness makes the notion of relevance relied on by Grice and Sperber and Wilson insensitive to two facts about discourses and dialogues that are cited in Chapter 3 and below. First, utterances can be relevant in terms of their illocutionary force rather than their content. Second, because of that, even when an utterance's content is not topically relevant and an implicature results, the implicature will not necessarily be relevant at that juncture in the discourse or dialogue.

The principles developed below and empirically supported in Chapter 5 collectively specify the relevance of an utterance as being a product of its contribution to the coherence and progress of the unfolding discourse or dialogue. Such a notion is sensitive to the possibility of an utterance's relevance in terms of any of the different types of meaning it has, not just one. More importantly, it makes the relevance of an utterance contingent on its connection to properties of the discourse or dialogue that are emergent and fluid, the products of the adjustment of the interpretations of antecedent and consequent entries against each other to achieve coherence.

CONTRIBUTING TO THE COHERENCE AND PROGRESS OF SEQUENCES

The formulations of principles of relevance below differ importantly from what I originally proposed (Sanders, 1980, 1981). Along the lines taken by Grice (1975) and Sperber and Wilson (1982), I hypothesized that the different ways in which utterances are relevant involve links between the utterance's propositional content and features of the specific type of interpretation of a particular antecedent. However, in addition to the problems cited above with conceiving of an utterance's relevance just with respect to its propositional content, there are important weaknesses in conceiving of relevance as the product of a connection between the utterance and a particular antecedent. The most important one on meta-theoretical grounds is that that cannot distinguish antecedents that *warrant* a specific interpretation from antecedents that *entail* it. A further weakness on theoretical grounds is that defining relevance in that way resulted in formulations too weak to distinguish in many cases among the alternative types of interpretation. And finally, that approach failed empirically, laboratory tests having disconfirmed it (see Chapter 5). An analysis of these internal weaknesses, in combination with an analysis of the laboratory data, led to the revised formulations given below.

The revised formulations below premise that the relevance of an utterance in terms of one (type of) meaning or another has two semi-independent aspects. An utterance in terms of some (type of) meaning can be relevant to other entries in the unfolding discourse or dialogue if they share features that permit combining them into a larger whole. And an utterance on that type of interpretation can be relevant in the unfolding discourse or dialogue by making a functional contribution to it.

Coherence in Discourses and Dialogues

First, let us examine the relevance of an utterance to other entries on the basis of commonalities between the features of one of its (types of) meanings and features of its interpreted antecedents or consequents.

This involves a restatement of the core postulate here as the following: it is warranted to focus on that (type of) meaning of an utterance by which the utterance has commonalities with its interpreted antecedents or consequents.

Note that this does not entail taking the specific interpretations of an utterance's antecedents and consequents as givens, and adjusting the specific interpretation of the utterance so that it coheres with them. It follows just as much that the interpreter can take as given some specific interpretation of the utterance in question, and adjust the specific interpretations of antecedents or consequents so that they cohere with that. This does in fact happen, as in jokes, which trick one into focusing on the wrong meanings of components of the body of the joke, until the punch line reveals the trick. What this involves in the terms here is that none of the meanings of the joke's punch line coheres with the specific interpretations antecedently assigned to components of the body; however if some specific interpretation of the joke's punch line is taken as given, there is a way of changing the specific interpretations of components of the body so that they cohere with each other and with the punch line.

Hence, as a discourse or dialogue unfolds, specific (types of) meanings are focused on that have commonalities with interpreted antecedents, but those specific interpretations may subsequently be discarded and replaced by ones that have commonalities with the specific interpretation of utterances entered subsequently. For example, following S's utterance, it is warranted to focus on the content of H's reply, but S's subsequent entry warrants changing the focus from the content of H's utterance to the act it can count as:

[1] S: I can't figure out why my checkbook won't balance.
H: Let's see—Oh, you just have a dumb mistake in addition here.
S: You can't talk to me like that. Who do you think you are?

In that case, specific interpretations must be adjusted against each other as discourses and dialogues unfold, until each utterance has a specific interpretation that has commonalities with both its antecents and consequents. Let us say that a discourse or dialogue is *coherent* when that is achieved. And let us call the recurrent commonalities by which a given sequence of utterances is integrated into a whole the *grounds of coherence.*

This describes a checks-and-balances relationship between the specific interpretation of an utterance and the way a discourse or dialogue is cohered. Such a relationship can be illustrated at the level of the sentence, between the readings of individual words and the establishment of semantic commonalities that cohere them:

[2] Colorless green ideas sleep furiously.

Suppose that we take as given that the component terms of that expression must cohere in some way. Then the problem is to adjust the readings of each item against the other until they do cohere. First, given the pair *colorless green,* if *green* is read as 'a color', the reading of *colorless* as 'lacking color' has to be discarded in favor of reading *colorless* as 'lackluster'. However, given *[lackluster] green ideas,* if *ideas* is read as 'cognitions', then the reading of *green* as 'a color' has to be discarded in favor of reading it as 'unripened'. This adjustment requires no additional adjustment in the reading of *colorless.* Similarly, given *[lackluster unripened] ideas sleep,* against the reading of *ideas* as 'cognitions', the reading of *sleep* as 'temporary cessation of voluntary activity' has to be discarded in favor of reading *sleep* as 'lying dormant'. Finally, *[lackluster unripened ideas lie dormant] furiously* forces an adjustment of the reading of *furiously* away from 'violent' in favor of 'volatile'. Thus, [2] is interpreted roughly as [3]:

[3] Lackluster unripened ideas lying dormant are volatile.

Note that the readings of the items in [2] that are included in [3] are not ones that are immediately salient. They became salient in the effort to cohere the sentence. This corresponds to examples in Chapter 3 (examples [9] and [10]) where contrasting readings of lexically identical noun phrases became salient because they were linked by a contrastive verb phrase, and the sentence would not otherwise cohere. These cases suggest that once readings of enough lexical items in a sentence are found to create a ground of coherence, that sets parameters on what the readings of other items must be for them to be relevant. This not only warrants focusing on the readings of items that fit within those parameters, it makes those readings salient.

But it can sometimes happen that a lexical item (or an entry in a discourse or dialogue) has no readings that fit within parameters set by an assumed ground of coherence. It was noted above that this usually promotes reinterpreting other items and cohering them differently, as in metaphors and jokes (e.g., "Now take my wife--please!"). But if interpreters are unable or unwilling to reinterpret other items and cohere them differently, they can instead attribute a novel meaning to the item in question in order to make it relevant to the assumed ground of coherence. This is certainly done when interpreters have no previous understanding of an item, and attribute a reading to it that conforms to the parameters set by the assumed ground of coherence.

Correspondingly, at the level of discourses and dialogues, the specific interpretations that utterances can have narrow as the sequence unfolds and one or more grounds of coherence emerge. This generally makes salient, and warrants focusing on, one (type of) meaning that each next utterance has by virtue of rules of language and conventions of utterance. But as above, it is possible theoretically for the specific interpretation of an utterance to be some meaning that does not follow strictly from any applicable rules and conventions, but that is attributed to it anyway to make the utterance relevant to its antecedents or consequents.

This interdependence between specific interpretations and the coherence of the whole entails that specific interpretations will change over time as necessary to cohere entries with both their antecedents and consequents. But even though specific interpretations are inherently fluid, let us suppose that for reasons of expedience in most cases, specific interpretations become fixed once all the entries in the discourse or dialogue have been made and cohered.

Grounds of Coherence that Warrant Focusing on Propositional Content

It has been suggested that an utterance's propositional content is relevant if its presuppositions are borne out by prior entries or associated background knowledge (e.g., Kartunnen and Peters, 1979; Werth, 1981). The other principal idea put forward about this is that the propositional contents of utterances are relevant to each other if they are about components of some single institution, practice, or situation as defined in some knowledge structure (e.g., Schank and Abelson, 1977; van Dijk, 1980).

However, while both of these have merit as ways in which the content of utterances is related to the content of antecedents and consequents, such commonalities of content do not in themselves entail that the utterance is relevant on that basis to those antecedents and consequents. The additional consideration is whether the utterance adds to the coherence of the sequence by virtue of intersecting the established grounds of coherence in terms of its content.

The grounds of coherence in (some segment of) a discourse of dialogue are those features that all the constituents in that segment have in common. Thus, if the grounds of coherence warrant focusing on the propositional content of an utterance, by definition the content of the utterance must be about the same state of affairs that some *number* of other utterances in the sequence are also about. The strength of the warrant for focusing on propositional content (or any other type of meaning) is thus variable, and depends on how *many* consecutive utterances have those common features (α) and how *distant* from the utterance in question those consecutive utterances are (δ). The principle here can be expressed as follows:

> Given an uttered expression with some propositional content (PC_{ue}), it is warranted that PC_{ue} be the specific interpretation of the utterance when (1) over some segment of the discourse or dialogue contributions are relevant to each other by having certain features of their propositional content in common (P-REL), and (2) PC_{ue} is relevant to that segment by P-REL.

[4] $(PC_{ue} \cdot ((\alpha)(\delta)(\text{P-REL}_s)) \cdot (PC_{ue} \cap \text{P-REL}_s \neq \emptyset)) \Rightarrow (\alpha/\delta)(SI_{ue} = PC_{ue})$

where PC_{ue} = propositional content of the uttered expression.
α = a quantifier that indexes the number of antecedent occurrences of P-REL.
δ = a quantifier that indexes the distance between the current utterance and antecedent occurrences of P-REL.
P-REL_s = that ground of coherence in a segment of the antecedent or subsequent sequence which comprises features of a state of affairs specified by the propositional contents of the component utterances in that segment.
α/δ = a quantifier that indexes the strength of the warrant for focusing on propositional content, expressed as the ratio between the number of utterances in the segment cohered according to P-REL and the magnitude of the distance between the current utterances and that segment.
SI_{ue} = the specific interpretation of the utterance at that juncture.

It is entailed by [4] that when an utterance's propositional content is ambiguous by the rules of language and conventions of utterance, only those readings will be focused on that have features in common with the grounds of coherence. This accounts for the functional disambiguation of utterances in context. Such functional disambiguations result in the case of implicatures and illocutionary acts as well.

A preliminary test of [4] is that it correctly predicts when there is a warrant for focusing on the propositional content of utterances in a sequence, and when there is not. [5a] and [5b] below differ from one another because the ground of coherence that emerges in [5a] warrants focusing on propositional content, whereas the ground of coherence in [5b] warrants focusing on illocutionary acts. The propositional content of the utterances in [5a] is about a single state of affairs, and by [4] that provides a warrant for focusing on propositional content that becomes stronger as the dialogue proceeds. In [5b], on the other hand, the warrant for focusing on propositional content weakens as the dialogue progresses. Even though the content of each utterance in the sequence has features in common with the content of its immediate antecedent, no pair is about the same state of affairs as any other pair. Hence, no grounds of coherence develop that warrant with any strength a focus on propositional content:

[5] **a.** S: It's about time I cleaned up my desk; I don't know where anything is.
H: But it looks so organized; everything's neatly stacked and arranged.
S: Well, it's easy to just sweep papers and files into stacks as long as you do it haphazardly.
H: It's too bad it's so cramped in there. You really need a file cabinet.
S: I'm not sure filing the stuff haphazardly would improve things. I need a keeper.

b. S: It's about time I cleaned up my desk; I don't know where anything is.
H: Maybe then you can get those papers out of the dining room.
S: Where's the harm? It's not like we need it to entertain all our guests.
H: Look, if you want company, make some friends I can stand.
S: Come on, just because you don't like yourself doesn't mean you have to dislike everyone else too.

Grounds of Coherence that Warrant Focusing on Illocutionary Acts

It has been suggested that utterances in a discourse or dialogue are generally cohered on the basis of their connection to each other as acts, rather than on the basis of their content (Labov and Fanshel, 1977). Edmondson (1981) strengthened this idea considerably with his postulate that acts are interrelated as constituents of structured progressions from the introduction of an agenda to its outcome, and that utterances are understood both as conversational acts and as illocutionary acts in terms of what their structural place in such a progression is.

However, none of this speaks to the issue here. Labov and Fanshel's account offers no principle by which the relevance of acts to other acts can be gauged. Edmondson, on the other hand, presumes that utterances will be relevant as acts in one way or another in the progression from the introduction of an agenda to its outcome, and that they are interpreted accordingly. While this interpretive relativism is consistent with the general orientation here, Edmondson did not base it on a principled connection that 'utterances as acts' have to their antecedents or consequents that provides a warrant for focusing on that type of meaning.

Let us say that by definition what distinguishes 'utterances as acts' from utterances in terms of other types of meaning is that the former are predicated on a social purpose. Therefore, for an utterance to be relevant as an illocutionary act (as opposed to being relevant on the basis of its content) its social purpose must have some connection with its antecedents or consequents. Again, by definition, a social purpose has a connection with the antecedents or consequents of the utterance in question insofar as they provide a motivation (before the fact) or justification (after the fact) for that social purpose. The extent to which the grounds of coherence in some segment of a discourse or dialogue motivate or justify the social purpose of an utterance, determine the degree to which it is warranted to focus on the illocutionary act(s) that the utterance can count as.

The question is, what motivates or justifies performing a given illocutionary act? The most obvious answer is, the introduction in the discourse or dialogue of one or more of the *felicity conditions* of that act, (i.e., the social conditions that license or motivate that act). Therefore, insofar as features of one or more of the felicity conditions for the act are the grounds of coherence across some segment of the utterance's antecedents or consequents, there is a warrant for focusing on the utterance as act. For instance, if an utterance could count as a promise (on the grounds identified in

Chapter 3), and some segment of the antecedent or subsequent sequence is cohered by references to or expressions of the hearer's desire for what was promised, then to that extent it is warranted to focus on the utterance as act.

However, there are other ways in which an actor's social purpose can be motivated or justified. One is that he/she can be explicitly requested, charged or obligated to bring about some result, so that an utterance on this type of interpretation will be relevant insofar as it counts as having that purpose. A focus on the act is thus warranted insofar as features of such requests or imperatives are the grounds of coherence of some segment of the antecedent or subsequent sequence.

A third motivation or justification for an actor's social purpose is provided by antecedents or consequents that can themselves be interpreted as acts that the utterance in question conventionally reciprocates. This is typified by the relationship between first- and second-pair parts in adjacency pairs. Accordingly, an utterance on this type of interpretation will be relevant insofar as a segment of the antecedent or subsequent sequence is cohered by shared features of acts that initiate (and complete) pairs, triples, etc. of the same kind as the one in which the utterance in question is included (e.g., question-answer pairs, rebuke-apologize-forgive triples).

The warrant for focusing on one or more of the illocutionary act(s) that an utterance can count as can thus be expressed as follows:

> Given an uttered expression that counts as some illocutionary act (A_{ue}), it is warranted that A_{ue} be the specific interpretation of the utterance when entries over some segment of the discourse or dialogue are relevant to each other as requests for A_{ue}, reciprocals of A_{ue}, or conditions for felicitously performing A_{ue}.

[6] $(A_{ue} \cdot (\alpha)(\delta)(FC{:}A_s \vee R/I{:}A_s \vee (A^{-1}(+A))_s)) \Rightarrow (\alpha/\delta)(SI_{ue} = A_{ue})$

where A_{ue} = the illocutionary act that could be performed by the current utterance.

$FC{:}A_s$ = felicity conditions for the act in the antecedent or subsequent sequence.

$R/I{:}A_s$ = a request or imperative to perform the act in the antecedent or subsequent sequence.

$(A^{-1}(+A))_s$ = the reciprocal of the act in question (optionally, completed sequences of the same kind) in the antecedent or subsequent sequence.

A preliminary test of [6] is that it predicts when there is a warrant for focusing on utterances as acts and when there is not. In particular, [6] predicts that in [5b] above, it is warranted to focus on illocutionary acts rather than on content, and that in [5a] this is not the case.

To consider [5b] first, H's first rejoinder and the three entries following it can each be interpreted equivalently as acts of criticism and complaint, according to the principles given in Chapter 3. (By the constitutive rules of criticism and complaint, the content of each of those entries predicates a deficient state of affairs on the hearer; structurally, each is a 'counter-complaint' that challenges the immediate antecedent; and each actor is disposed towards criticism and complaint, as indicated by lexical choices expressive of a 'value conflict'.) Given that those entries each count as a criticism and complaint, then each is the reciprocal of the act that went before. The several repetitions of that connection, and the contiguity of the utterances involved, result in a ground of coherence that by [6] strongly warrants focusing on the illocutionary acts in [5b].

Conversely, if the utterances in [5a] are taken as acts, no pair of acts is connected on the same basis as any other pair, and therefore a ground of coherence involving 'utterance as acts' only weakly develops (especially compared with the strength of the warrant by [4] for focusing on propositional content). If S's first utterance counts as self-criticism, H reciprocates with a compliment; H's compliment on the other hand is reciprocated with a self-criticism; S's self-criticism is reciprocated by an absolution; and the absolution is reciprocated by a third self-criticism.

Grounds of Coherence that Warrant Focusing on Implicature

Dascal (1977) has proposed that utterances are fully relevant if their propositional content is relevant, and in addition if they have the illocutionary force called for at that juncture. If either the content or the force of an utterance is not relevant, then Dascal considers that the maxim of relation has been breached, and the utterance implicates some further proposition. This obviously lies in the direction being taken here, but for present purposes has two critical weaknesses. First, Dascal does not make explicit what is required for either the content or the force of an utterance to be relevant. Second, Dascal presumes that a focus on conversational implicatures is warranted just by a breach of the maxim of relation.

If a maxim is breached and some proposition is thus implicated, a focus on the implicature is not warranted unless the utterance is connected on that interpretation to some segment of the antecedent or subsequent sequence. The question is, in what way are utterances on their interpretation as implicatures distinctively connected to other utterances? The obvious answer in this case is incorrect. This would be to treat implicatures as indirectly expressed propositions about states of affairs, relevant to the content of antecedent or subsequent utterances on the same basis as overtly expressed propositions are, as given by [4].

Proceeding in that way returns to essentially the position taken by Grice (1975), that a focus on either propositional content or implicature is contingent on which has more commonalities with the content of the utterance's antecedents or consequents. But this fails because in many cases, the utterance's content and the implicature are about the same state of affairs, and thus will be warranted to the same degree by their connection to the content of other entries in the sequence. This is the case in the following:

[7] S: I need some advice about how to study for your midterm exam, Professor.
H: Read the book.

The propositional content of H's utterance (that reading the book is a sufficient means of studying for the examination) and H's implicature (the student will get no help with special tactics for studying) are equally relevant to the content of S's request. Hence, it is an inadequate warrant for focusing on an implicature that the content of the implicature have features in common with the content of antecedents or consequents.

Intuitively, whether to focus on the content of H's utterance in [7] or on the implicature depends on what one assumes H's beliefs and attitudes are about S, about students in general, and about education. This intuition is justified. In judging whether an implicature is relevant, the issue is not whether the content of the implicated proposition is relevant, but whether the fact of the implicature is relevant. Implicatures are predicated on (inferences about) the communicator's subjective state (salient beliefs, perceptions, feelings, desires). Hence, an implicature is only relevant insofar as the subjective state on which it is predicated is relevant—is antecedently caused or symptomized, or subsequently symptomized, by other entries in the discourse or dialogue. The absence of antecedents or consequents in [7] that foster or symptomize the subjective state on which H's implicated refusal to help is predicated accounts for the absence of a warrant for focusing on the implicature.

It should be the case if the foregoing is correct that [7] can be expanded to provide warrants for focusing on the implicature, and expanded alternatively to not provide warrants for focusing on the implicature. In [8a] below, there is no expression subsequent to the utterance in question of a subjective state on which the implicated rebuff is predicated, and thus no warrant for (retrospectively) focusing on that type of interpretation. In [8b], on the other hand, subsequent entries by H do express the beliefs and attitudes on which the implicature is predicated, and to that degree a retrospective focus on H's utterance as a rebuff is warranted:

[8] **a.** S: I need some advice about how to study for your midterm exam, Professor.
H: Read the book.
S: Well, yes, of course I will, but I'm not sure what to focus on.
H: The book provides support for a single thesis, so I think you'd be making a mistake if you didn't read it comprehensively.
S: But there are so many facts and figures, it'll be an enormous job to memorize them in time for the exam.
H: I understand that, but those data have to be mastered if you're going to be prepared for advanced work in this area.

b. S: I need some advice about how to study for your midterm exam, Professor.
H: Read the book.
S: Well, yes, of course I will, but I'm not sure what to focus on.

H: If you've paid any attention to my lectures, you should be able to figure that out.
S: But there are so many facts and figures, it'll be an enormous job to memorize them in time for the exam.
H: Sounds like you want me to do the work for you, but that's not how the game is played, at least not in this class.

The warrant for focusing on what an utterance implicates can thus be represented formally as follows:

> Given an uttered expression that implicates some proposition (Imp_{ue}), it is warranted that Imp_{ue} be the specific interpretation of the utterance when (1) over some segment of the discourse or dialogue entries cohere as expressions of some subjective state, and (2) the subjective state on which the implicated proposition is predicated is approximately the same as the one expressed elsewhere.

[9] $(Imp_{ue} \cdot ((\alpha)(\delta)(SS_s)) \cdot (SS{:}Imp_{ue} \approx SS_s)) \Rightarrow (\alpha/\delta)(SI_{ue} = Imp_{ue})$

where Imp_{ue} = a proposition implicated by the utterance in question by virtue of breaching some maxim.
SS_s = a subjective state of the communicator that one or more entries in the antecedent or subsequent sequence conventionally disclose, 'cause' or result from, or on which an implicature is predicated.
$SS{:}Imp_{ue}$ = the subjective state on which the implicature in question is predicated.

Progress in Discourses and Dialogues

An utterance is also relevant in a discourse or dialogue insofar as it makes a contribution to the sequence's progression towards an outcome. As Schank (1977) argued, utterances that are *wholly redundant* are not responsive (relevant), and as Tracy (1982) argued, neither are utterances that are *beside the point.*

[10] **a.** S: My car's in the shop and I need a lift.
?H: Cars have to be serviced every so often.[2]
b. S: John needs cheering up; he flunked his exam.
?H: Fred saw John at dinner last week.

Suppose that we say an utterance is relevant on a type of interpretation if it contributes to the progress of the discourse or dialogue towards a resolution (is neither wholly redundant nor beside the point). Edmondson (1981) has defined the notion of "progressing towards a resolution" in structural terms. With particular attention to exchanges in which a tangible outcome is at issue, Edmondson considers that they are minimally required to have a component that sets the agenda for the exchange (a "proffer") and a component that resolves that agenda (a "satisfy"). Intermediate entries (if any) contribute if for example they challenge the premises of a proffer or of some other intermediate component, correct their content or reject the entire undertaking. Such intermediate entries may themselves initiate an agenda that has to be resolved before the main business can be resumed and concluded. Certain proffers and their satisfaction may in turn be preliminaries to some further agenda, or may be entered into in consequence of the way prior ones were satisfied.

While there are important shortcomings in Edmondson's analysis (in particular that his structural categories seem ad hoc and ill-defined, and that the generality of the analysis is unclear), the basic idea survives and is useful here. One can at least accept that discourses and dialogues are punctuated by the introductions of agenda and their resolution, and that it is with reference to such agenda whether a given juncture of a discourse or dialogue lies between transition boundaries, or is a transition boundary.

Let us then stipulate that an agenda for (some segment of) a discourse or dialogue is established by an utterance on whichever interpretation: (1) states a purpose or objective, (2) is called for by conventions in the institution at hand about what the business to be transacted is and how it is to be done, or (3) poses questions, makes requests, issues imperatives, airs grievances or in some other way makes a demand on the audience.

On that basis an utterance is wholly redundant on an interpretation if it neither expresses nor constitutes new information, and its entry does not effect a change in what remains to be done to bring about a resolution of the current agenda. Similarly, an utterance is beside the point on an interpretation if it does express or constitute new information, but it does not effect a change in what is required to bring about a resolution.

The principle by which utterances contribute to the progress of discourses and dialogues can thus be expressed as follows:

> It is warranted to focus on that meaning of an uttered expression ($MG\gamma_{ue}$) by which (1) it is a proffer (i.e., introduces a new agenda), or (2) it reduces or enlarges the minimal number of entries that are projected to be necessary subsequently to satisfy an outstanding proffer.

[11] $((MG\gamma_{ue} = PR) \Rightarrow (SI_{ue} = MG\gamma_{ue})) \vee$
$(([PR](\alpha+\beta = S) \cdot [PR]((\alpha+MG\gamma_{ue}) + (\beta \pm i) = S)) \Rightarrow (SI_{ue} = MG\gamma_{ue}))$

where $MG\gamma_{ue}$ = one of the alternate meanings of the uttered expression.
PR = a proffer.
SI_{ue} = the specific interpretation of the uttered expression.
α = the number of entries subsequent to PR up to the present juncture that affected progress towards a resolution.
β = the minimal number of entries needed subsequent to the present juncture to satisfy PR.
i = one or more entries in the discourse or dialogue.
S = satisfaction of PR.

An initial test of the adequacy of [11] is whether it predicts what is necessary to foster an interpretive focus on one or another of the possibilities in a given case. Let us therefore test [11] first against a negative case, [12], where a specific interpretation is not warranted on intuitive grounds. The question is whether [11] can account for S's being able to focus equally well on the different meanings of H's utterance:

[12] S: I've run out of gas.
H: I saw a phone booth a block or two back.
S_a: That's weird. Nobody lives around here anymore
S_b: It doesn't matter, there's a gas station down that way about a mile.
S_c: Who put you in charge? The one who's paying gets to work out the moves.

It follows from [11] that no specific interpretation is warranted insofar as there is no agenda against which to measure the contribution of the utterance in question. That predicts that any of the meanings of H's utterance in [12] can be focused on and responded to because S's initial utterance is equivocal as to the intended agenda. If S's utterance is read as an observation about the present situation, then H's utterance contributes by also being read as an observation about the situation, and S_a's response is predicated on that reading. If S's utterance is read as implicating a call for action, then H's utterance contributes by being read as a proposal for action, and S_b's response is predicated on that reading. Finally, if S's utterance is read as an act of declaring that there is an 'emergency' situation, then H's utterance contributes by being read as an imperative, and S_c's response is predicated on that reading.

The more substantial test of [11] is whether it predicts what revisions of [12] are necessary to establish a warrant for a specific interpretation of H's utterance. It is clear from the above that the needed revision is to make more explicit the agenda S sets in the first utterance. This is done in [13a–c]:

[13] a. S: I've run out of gas, but at least nothing's standing in this urban wasteland for muggers to hide behind.
H: I saw a phone booth a block or two back.
S_a: That's weird. Nobody lives around here anymore.
(?) S_b: It doesn't matter, there's a gas station down that way about a mile.
? S_c: Who put you in charge? The one who's paying gets to work out the moves.

b. S: I've run out of gas, but it won't take long to get going again.
H: I saw a phone booth a block or two back.
? S_a: That's weird. Nobody lives around here anymore.
S_b: It doesn't matter, there's a gas station down that way about a mile.
? S_c: Who put you in charge? The one who's paying gets to work out the moves.

c. S: I've run out of gas, so I want you to flag someone down and go for help while I watch the car.
H: I saw a phone booth a block or two back.
? S_a: That's weird. Nobody lives around here anymore.
(?) S_b: It doesn't matter, there's a gas station down that way about a mile.
S_c: Who put you in charge? The one who's paying gets to work out the moves.

COHERENCE, PROGRESS, SPECIFIC INTERPRETATIONS AND MEANINGS

Coherence and Progress

There are two ways in which an utterance can be relevant: (1) by contributing to the coherence of an antecedent or subsequent part of the discourse or dialogue, or (2) by contributing to progress towards a resolution of some agenda. The obvious question is, is there an interrelation between them?

Even though utterances are normally relevant in both ways, this is not necessary in principle. It is possible that an utterance on a specific interpretation contributes to the coherence of a segment of a discourse or dialogue without affecting progress on an agenda (e.g., when an utterance provides information regarding an agenda which has already been satisfied). Likewise, utterances can affect progress on the agenda at hand without contributing to the coherence of an antecedent or subsequent segment (as when an impasse on an agenda is attributed to a tacit disagreement, so that the specific interpretation of an utterance that is produced to overcome the tacit disagreement will not have features in common with the specific interpretations of antecedents that preceded it).

However, in practice those two ways in which utterances are relevant exert an influence on each other. First, given that an utterance is relevant insofar as it contributes to the ground of coherence in some segment of the antecedent or subsequent sequence, the boundaries of such segments are often defined in terms of the various agenda that are introduced in the discourse of dialogue. Second, conversely, agenda and their resolution are defined less often by being explicity announced, than implicitly, by the introduction or termination of a chain of entries that cohere in some consistent way.

Specific Interpretations and Meanings

In the formulations above, a specific interpretation is one (type of) meaning from among the alternative meanings of an utterance. The meanings of utterances are generally givens prior to and independent of their contribution to the discourse or dialogue, products of rules of language and conventions of utterance. This has the merit of distinguishing between the meanings an utterance has by virtue of its form and content and the social conditions of its utterance, and those of its meanings that are salient in the present discourse or dialogue because it is those that affect the interests of communicator and interpreter.

It follows from that unidirectional relationship between an utterance's meanings and its specific interpretation that the strategic control of understandings is contingent on applying the rules of language and conventions of utterance so that the meanings of each utterance include the intended one. This would necessarily result in whatever coherence, constraints on what can be said next, and progress towards some outcome is (or is not) created in the discourse or dialogue.

However, the relationship between an utterance's meanings and its contribution to the unfolding discourse or dialogue is not invariably unidirectional. Consider that utterances can be ill-formed or misarticulated, so that the interpreter cannot know what their meanings are, and yet the interpreter may consider that he/she knows what specific interpretation was intended. Further, interpreters at times stop listening, though they continue (inattentively) giving signals of acknowledgment, and yet may contribute relevantly when they are given the floor despite not knowing what in particular was said or done antecedently. Along the same lines, interactants sometimes anticipate what the other's utterance is intended to express, chiming in with the speaker to complete the utterance or interrupting the speaker to reply.

These commonplaces of everyday interaction entail that interpreters have some basis for forecasting what the communicator intends to communicate at a given juncture. The principles of relevance here provide such a basis. As a ground of coherence emerges prior to some juncture, increasingly narrow parameters emerge on the specific interpretations that subsequent utterances can relevantly have. As progress towards satisfying an agenda is made, then on that basis also, increasingly narrow parameters emerge on the specific interpretations of subsequent utterances. This is analogous to the increasing grammatical and semantic limits on the lexical items that can be entered in an unfolding utterance. On that basis, just as a meaning can often be attributed to lexical items that are unfamiliar or not well articulated, so intended meanings can be attributed to utterances that are not understood or attended to. This is the foundation for communication between people from different speech communities, different cultures and even different language communities (see Chapter 7).

NOTES: CHAPTER 4

1. This does not deny that entries in the present dialogue or discourse can also be formulated to affect inferences about the communicator, pertinent to 1, and understandings about what conventions and norms are in force, pertinent to 2. However, such entries will not reliably influence interpretive focus. In the case of 1, when the communicator is already known to the interpreter, then to the extent of the number and variety of the previous encounters in which that knowledge was formed, the influence of present entries on 'new' inferences will be inhibited. It is only when the communicator is wholly unknown with regard to reputation as well as previous acquaintance (which in general is a rare circumstance) that inferences about him/her based on current entries will influence the specific interpretation of subsequent entries. In the case of 2, though the conventions and norms in force can be influenced to some degree by the way the communicator formulates his/her entries, they are also defined to some extent by extrinsic factors that are beyond the communicator's control. The influence of entries in discourses or dialogues in this regard is thus unreliable.

2. Marking such utterances as odd indicates that the utterance does not follow or contribute in the sequence, so that its specific interpretation is equivocal, and it warrants explicit puzzlement or dismissal, e.g., *Why did you say that?* or *Yeah? Well, anyway . . . .*

CHAPTER 5

Laboratory Studies of the Specific Interpretation of Utterances

This chapter reports six experimental studies that were designed to test first the general premise, and then particular hypotheses, that the specific interpretation of utterances is a product of the way they are relevant to other constituents of the discourse or dialogue.

These studies contribute to a meager pool of data. Little is known in fact about how consistent or varied people are in understanding utterances, what types of meanings they focus on and what factors above and beyond the rules of language and conventions of utterance—within the discourse or dialogue and extrinsic to it—affect their understandings and specific interpretations of utterances.

Much of the experimental work about understanding has actually involved studies of information processing (e.g., Lachman, Lachman and Butterfield, 1976). Some studies have used the way respondents paraphrase text stored in memory as evidence of the way in which discourse is processed, stored, and retrieved (e.g., Keenan and Kintsch, 1974; Harris and Monaco, 1978). These paraphrases are also indicative of understandings.

The only empirical work that bears directly on the issues of interest here has been done with regard to the way in which words are cohered in the interpretation of sentences. Carpenter and Daneman (1981) found that homographs (e.g., *tear* from the eyes, and *tear* in fabric) are interpreted so that they cohere with the antecedent sequence until and if subsequent entries force a reinterpretation (e.g., *Cinderella was sad because she couldn't go to the dance that night. There were big* ***tears*** *in her dress.* Similarly, Townsend and Bever (1982) found that the interpretation of ambiguous noun phrases of the general form *verb-ing + noun-pl* (e.g., *diving submarines, racing* *cars*) depends on which reading coheres with the antecedent sequence. On a more general level, Begg and Harris (1982) found that interpreters who had prior knowledge of syllogistic forms and conventions tended, more than interpreters who did not have such background, to over-interpret syllogistically organized statements so as to make them cohere in the expected way.

SYNOPSIS OF RESEARCH ON PRINCIPLES OF SPECIFIC INTERPRETATION

The six studies reported below represent a progression of theory and data that begins with the premise that utterances' specific interpretations depend on the basis of their relevance to single constituents of the antecedent sequence (Studies I–IV). The data did not support that premise. This fostered the development of different principles of relevance, the ones detailed in Chapter 4. These more complex formulations were then tested (Studies V and VI). The data upheld them.

The methods and findings of each study are summarized below. The experimental materials used and the data are presented thereafter.

Synopsis of Part I (Studies I–IV)

The first set of four studies showed generally that manipulating dialogues so as to vary the constituent immediately antecedent to an utterance had relatively little effect on its specific interpretation.

Study I

Three pairs of dialogues were constructed, with the test utterance being the last entry in each dialogue. On the assumption that utterances are normally relevant to the constituent of the dialogue immediately antecedent to them, each pair of dialogues comprised the same entries, whose sequence differed in each member of the pair, so as to vary which constituent was entered immediately before the test utterance (e.g., Dialogue 1a comprised utterances 1-2-3-4, and Dialogue 1b comprised utterances 3-2-1-4).

To measure shifts in the specific interpretation of the test utterance, respondents were asked to select the 'best' among alternative ways in which to reply to the test utterance in a continuation of the dialogue. Dialogues were presented and responded to in writing. Each respondent was shown three dialogues, one from each of the three pairs.

The test was administered at a large Pacific university, with respondents grouped for purposes of analysis as 'Eastern' (if they gave their ethnic identity as Korean, Japanese, or Chinese) or 'Western.' Despite considerable variation in response among individuals, there were no substantial effects related to manipulations of the dialogues or to the ethnic identities of the respondents.

Study II (Potoker, 1982)

The second study was designed to investigate whether the results of the first study stemmed from methodological failures or theoretical ones. The methodological concern was that the measure used in Study I was flawed: changes in the specific interpretation of an utterance might not correspond systematically with changes in preferences among ways of responding to it. The theoretical issue focused on was whether interpretations of an utterance are contingent on its relevance to the overall situation or to a particular antecedent.

Two triples of dialogues were constructed. Two dialogues of each triple were constructed as in Study I, with each comprising the same utterances but ordering them differently. The third dialogue of each triple ended with the same test utterance as the other two, but its antecedents differed entirely from its antecedents in the other dialogues. As a result, the immediate antecedent of the test utterance was varied across all three dialogues of a triple, but the overall situation was the same in the first two dialogues and varied in the third. It was reasoned that if preferences among alternative meanings are based on the relevance of utterances to particular antecedent constituents, those preferences would vary between each dialogue of the triple. But if such preferences among alternative meanings are based on the relevance of utterances to the overall situation, those preferences would differ between the third dialogue and the first two dialogues, but not between those first two dialogues.

Respondents were asked to both select the best paraphrase of the test utterance from a written set of alternatives, and to select the best way of continuing the dialogue. Each respondent was shown two dialogues, one from each of two triples.

Preferences among alternative meanings of the test utterance differed with respect to both measures for both triples of dialogues. The results involving the first triple conformed to what was predicted if specific interpretations are based on the relevance of utterances to the overall situation. However, the results involving the second triple conformed to neither hypothesis on one measure, and on the other measure conformed to what was predicted if specific interpretations are based on the relevance of utterances to particular antecedents.

Post hoc accounts of these findings suggested that the utterance's relevance to the overall situation had an effect on preferences among alternative meanings only when some overall issue emerged in the dialogue (as in a conflict). Such preferences were otherwise contingent on the utterance's relevance to particular antecedents. The data did not indicate any substantial difference between the two ways in which changes in specific interpretation were measured.

Study III (with Sharon N. Potoker)

The third study was designed to test specific hypotheses about the relationships between utterances and particular antecedents that condition their specific interpretation, depending on the type of dialogue in which the utterance occurs. Four triples of dialogues were constructed. Each triple of dialogues involved a different type of situation: a conflict; coordination and cooperation; talk about a conflict; and chitchat. The dialogues within each triple comprised the same utterances, except for the immediate antecedent of the test utterance. The immediate antecedent of the test utterance was varied within a triple so that the test utterance was relevant on a different basis to the immediate antecedent in each dialogue.

The same three immediate antecedents were used to establish a given basis of relevance in each of the four triples. The test utterance was the same across all twelve dialogues. Each respondent was given one practice dialogue, and one of the twelve "test" dialogues.

It was predicted on the basis of the results in Study II that preferences among alternative meanings of the test utterance would vary within a triple, given different immediate antecedents, when only chitchat was involved, but would not vary despite different immediate antecedents when a conflict was involved. It was taken as a research question whether the overall situation would in any other case override the influence of immediate antecedents on the preferences among alternative meanings of the test utterance. Respondents were asked to select the best paraphrase of the test utterance from a list of alternatives.

The data showed that manipulations of the antecedents of the test utterance had no substantial effect on preferences among alternative meanings of the test utterance within any of the triples of dialogues. It should be emphasized that this was the case even when the test utterance breached the maxim of relation, which by Grice's (1975) analysis should have fostered a shift in focus from propositional content to an implicature.

A debriefing of respondents elicited two criticisms of the test materials that might account for the results in this study. The respondents were largely undergraduates, and objected that the dialogues involved situations and attitudes alien to their interests and experience. The second criticism was that none of the alternative meanings given was quite right (usually because they considered the 'tone' with which those meanings were expressed to be wrong—either too hostile, too indifferent, too stilted, etc.).

Study IVa

To follow up on the criticisms of Study III elicited from respondents, two triples of dialogues were constructed involving 'undergraduate' situations. One triple involved a conflict, the other chitchat. As in Study III the constituents of dialogues within each triple were the same, except for the immediate antecedent of the test utterance.

All three dialogues of one triple or the other were given to respondents, who were asked to supply paraphrases of the test utterance in each case. The paraphrases generated by respondents varied from one dialogue version to the next, precisely in the way expected from the basis of the test utterance's relevance to the immediate antecedent. The substance of the various paraphrases of the test utterance in each dialogue exhibited such consistent, recurrent features that it was straightforward to cluster them and formulate single composites of each cluster.

Study IVb

Each of the dialogues utilized in Study IVa was distributed separately to respondents, who were asked to select the best paraphrase of the test utterance from a set of the composite paraphrases drawn from those provided by respondents in Study IVa.

However, in contrast with Study IVa, no substantial difference in preferences among alternative meanings of the test utterance was exhibited within each triple of dialogues.

Synopsis of Part II (Studies V and VI)

The findings of those initial studies were taken to provide some weak evidence that the specific interpretation of utterances is contingent on their connection to their antecedents (Studies II and IVa), but to disconfirm the general hypothesis that specific interpretations are contingent on the relevance of utterances to particular constituents of the antecedent sequence.

The findings of Study II, together with the recurrent findings that interpretations do not vary as long as the overall sequence is constant and only the immediate antecedent varies, were taken as evidence that specific interpretations depend on the utterance's relevance to the common thread that runs through and links together groups of constituents of the antecedent sequence.

At the same time, the findings of Study IVa indicate that the type of meaning focused on does vary in conformity with the type of relevance the utterance has to its antecedents. It was concluded from this that the basis of relevance involved has to be exhibited recurrently among the antecedents of the test utterance before there is a sufficiently strong warrant to focus on one rather than another type of meaning.

Study Va

This study was designed as a preliminary test of the revised theory. Three dialogues were constructed that each began with the same stated agenda (a young man is puzzled about what to buy his friend's fifteen-year-old sister for her birthday) and ended with the same test utterance (the brother asking *Would you consider something like perfume or jewelry for her? Something feminine?*). The entries between the first utterance and the test utterance differed in each dialogue, however, so as to manipulate the ground of coherence. In Dialogue 1, entries were cohered in terms of their propositional content, and it was predicted that respondents would take the brother's final question literally. In Dialogue 2 entries were cohered in terms of the brother's subjective state (anxiety about the sister being attracted to the friend), and it was predicted that respondents would take the brother's final question as implicating a query about the friend's motives. In Dialogue 3 entries were cohered in terms of felicity conditions for the act of insult (the brother's hostile and disapproving view of his sister), and it was predicted that respondents would take the brother's final question as an attack on his sister's femininity.

Respondents were given one of the three dialogues and asked to identify the best paraphrase of the test utterance among a list of five: two of the five paraphrases were 'dummies' not warranted theoretically; the other three paraphrases involved the test utterance's propositional content, the implicated query, and the act of insulting the sister's feminity.

Respondents focused on propositional content significantly more than on the alternatives when focusing on propositional content was warranted theoretically. Respondents also focused on the illocutionary act significantly more than on the alternatives when focusing on the illocutionary act was warranted theoretically. However, when it was warranted to focus on the implicature, respondents focused on propositional content as much as on the implicature.

Study Vb

This follow-up study was designed to test whether respondents' preferences for the implicature and the illocutionary act would be dminished if Dialogues 2 and 3 were revised so that all of the entries were substantially the same, but with more explicit commonalities of content.

In the case of Dialogue 3′, these revisions did have the effect of diminishing respondents' focus on the illocutionary act (though respondents' focus did not shift to propositional content, but became random instead). However, in the case of Dialogue 2′, these revisions had the reverse effect, making the focus on the implicature more pronounced.

The post hoc account of these findings was that a focus on an implicature is warranted primarily by indicators of the subjective state involved antecedently, regardless of whether overt breaches of conversational maxims are evident. The revised dialogue made the brother's subjective state more explicit, but did not include any breaches of the maxim of relation that had been evident in the original version. At the same time, the revision of Dialogue 3 appears to have made it more difficult to interpret the illocutionary act itself, by obscuring the brother's dispositions and making the structural 'need' for an insult less obvious. This would explain why respondents' preferences for a way of paraphrasing the test utterance in Dialogue 3′ because more random: none of the alternative paraphrases to choose from would have been satisfactory.

Study VI

The final study in this series replicated Study V, but strengthened the rigor of the study by involving a larger number of respondents, and subjecting the data to a more powerful statistical analysis (MAN-OVA) than the Chi-Square statistic utilized in the other studies.

However, the study was expanded to determine whether variations in the (type of) meaning focused on were a product of inductions about the communicator, based on the content of his entries, rather than a product of the ground of coherence emergent in each dialogue. This was tested by providing respondents with prologues in which the conversants were characterized. The three prologues constructed gave the same information, except for the attitudes they attributed to the brother about his sister (proud of her accomplishments, distrustful of her judgment and maturity, and detached, respectively).

The respondents focused on the meaning that was theoretically warranted in each dialogue. The prologues characterizing the brother's attitudes towards his sister had no significant effect on the specific interpretation of his question.

Taken collectively, these studies strongly support both the general theoretical premise here—that specific interpretations are a function of the relationship of utterances to their antecedents (or consequents)—and beyond that, these studies support the particular formulations given in Chapter 4. The test dialogues were constructed to create warrants in the ground of coherence for focusing on one type of meaning or another, and the meaning of the test utterance that respondents focused on differed in each dialogue as predicted.

TEST MATERIALS AND RESULTS FOR STUDIES I–VI

Study I

Dialogue 1a

Lee: Here—let me give you a hundred dollars towards what I owe you.
Kim: I'm really upset that I haven't been able to find you the last two weeks.
Lee: I wish you weren't feeling so hostile about the money I borrowed.
Kim: I badly needed cash this week.

Dialogue 1b

Lee: I wish you weren't feeling so hostile about the money I borrowed.
Kim: I'm really upset that I haven't been able to find you the last two weeks.
Lee: Here—let me give you a hundred dollars towards what I owe you.
Kim: I badly needed cash this week.

Results

LEE'S NEXT RESPONSE	RELEVANT TO	DIALOGUE	1A	1B
2. I thought you had overdraft privileges. 4. Why? Something wrong with your car?	} content {	'Western' Ss	11	10
		'Eastern' Ss	9	12
1. I've been out of town. 3. I'm sorry, but you gave no deadline.	} implicature {	'Western' Ss	16	17
		'Eastern' Ss	39	40

A. Preferences for replies did not vary significantly between Dialogues 1a and 1b.
B. 'Western' respondents exhibited no statistically greater preference for replies to content (utterances 2 and 4) over replies to the implicature (utterances 1 and 3) in either dialogue.
C. 'Eastern' respondents preferred replies to the implicature over replies to content in both dialogues (for Dialogue 1a, $\chi^2 = 15.1$, df = 1, $p<.01$; for Dialogue 1b, $\chi^2 = 18.7$, df = 1, $p<.01$).

Dialogue 2a

Kim: Call a meeting of the committee for next Thursday and make the election of a chair the first item on the agenda.
Lee: I think we should see how much desire there is for that kind of structure.
Kim: This group badly needs a strong leader.
Lee: We've been functioning very smoothly without any formal leadership.

Dialogue 2b

Kim: This group badly needs a strong leader.
Lee: I think we should see how much desire there is for that kind of structure.
Kim: Call a meeting of the committee for next Thursday and make the election of a chair the first item on the agenda.
Lee: We've been functioning very smoothly without any formal leadership.

Results

LEE'S NEXT RESPONSE	RELEVANT TO	DIALOGUE	2A	2B
2. We're working too slowly for the deadline. 4. Groups that are too smooth do sloppy work.	} content {	'Western' Ss	22	26
		'Eastern' Ss	33	37
1. Whatever your opinion, set up that meeting. 3. It's frustrating when you try to block me.	} act {	'Western' Ss	5	2
		'Eastern' Ss	16	16

A. Preferences for replies did not vary significantly between Dialogues 2a and 2b.

B. 'Western respondents preferred replies to content (utterances 2 and 4) over replies to the illocutionary act in both dialogues (for Dialogue 2a, $\chi^2 = 10.7$, df = 1, $p<.01$; for Dialogue 2b, $\chi^2 = 20.6$, df = 1, $p<.01$).
C. 'Eastern' respondents also preferred replies to content over replies to the illocutionary act in both dialogues (for Dialogue 2a, $\chi^2 = 5.9$, df = 1, $p<.025$; for Dialogue 2b, $\chi^2 = 8.3$, df = 1, $p<.01$).

Dialogue 3a

Kim: You seem edgy around your fiancée these days.
Lee: I'm afraid to do anything. I've seen her rant about some petty issues.
Kim: That must be hard to take—could someone in her family help?
Lee: Her uncle is nagging her to delay the marriage.
Kim: Well, seeing her aunt is the last thing you should do.

Dialogue 3b

Kim: You seem edgy around your fiancée these days.
Lee: Her uncle is nagging her to delay the marriage.
Kim: That must be hard to take—could someone in her family help?
Lee: I'm afraid to do anything. I've seen her rant about some petty issues.
Kim: Well, seeing her aunt is the last thing you should do.

Results

LEE'S NEXT RESPONSE	RELEVANT TO	DIALOGUE	3A	3B
2. Yes, her uncle's stubborn about his opinions. 4. Maybe we should delay the marriage then.	content	'Western' Ss 'Eastern' Ss	20 39	15 35
1. I hate it when you joke about my problems. 3. Listen—I said I've seen her *rant*.	wordplay	'Western' Ss 'Eastern' Ss	7 11	12 15

A. Preferences for replies did not vary significantly between Dialogues 3a and 3b.
B. 'Western' respondents exhibited a greater preference for replies to content (utterances 2 and 4) over replies to wordplay in Dialogue 3a ($\chi^2 = 6.26$, df = 1, $p<.01$), but did not significantly favor replies to one type of interpretation over the other in Dialogue 3b.

C. 'Eastern' respondents exhibited a greater preference for replies to content in both dialogues (for Dialogue 3a, $\chi^2 = 15.68$, df = 1, $p<.01$; for Dialogue 3b, $\chi^2 = 5.45$, df = 1, $p<.025$).

Study II (Potoker, 1982)

Dialogue 1a

A: That's really a shame about your job. Job hunting is tough—why don't you let me help?
B: Well, I've been reading this really good book about interviewing techniques and it's got a lot of really good stuff in it. Really made me think.
A: I love to read, but I never seem to find the time—especially when it's school work! I promised my roommate we'd study for our philosophy test together, but I haven't even started reading the text yet.
B: I don't think people should say things they can't live up to.

Dialogue 1b

A: I love to read, but I never seem to find the time—especially when it's school work! I promised my roommate we'd study for our philosophy test together, but I haven't even started reading the text yet.
B: Well, I've been reading this really good book about interviewing techniques and it's got a lot of really good stuff in it. Really made me think.
A: That's really a shame about your job. Job hunting is tough—why don't you let me help?
B: I don't think people should say things they can't live up to.

Dialogue 1c

A: I just can't believe my uncle turned you down for that job. It really gets to me how he went back on his word after he has assured me you would be offered the position.
B: Well, I'm really pissed. I mean, I moved all the way here because I trusted that his word was good.
A: I'm really sorry. It wasn't my fault though. Anyway, you can count on me to help you find a job.
B: I don't think people should say things they can't live up to.

Results

INTERPRETATIONS OF UTTERANCE 4	DIALOGUE		
	1A	1B	1C
1. B is implying A breaks promises.	13	23	11
2. B thinks people should promise sincerely.	7	3	2
3. B is implying A won't help B with job hunting.	3	3	15
4. B considers A's uncle wrong for breaking his promise.	15	12	12

A. Preferences for interpretations were not significantly different between Dialogues 1a and 1b.

B. Preferences for interpretations differed between Dialogues 1a and 1c ($\chi^2 = 9.82$, df = 3, $p<.05$);

C. Preferences for interpretations differed between Dialogues 1b and 1c ($\chi^2 = 12.33$, df = 3, $p<.01$).

RESPONSES TO UTTERANCE 4	DIALOGUE		
	1A	1B	1C
1. Don't take your anger out on me.	5	7	9
2. It's a problem when people are undependable.	15	12	8
3. I am going to read that book and study.	12	19	1
4. I agree—my uncle's act was surprising.	2	0	16

A. Preferences for responses were not significantly different between Dialogues 1a and 1b.

B. Preferences for responses differed between Dialogues 1a and 1c ($\chi^2 = 19.07$, df = 3, $p<.01$).

C. Preferences for responses differed between Dialogues 1b and 1c ($\chi^2 = 23.60$, df = 3, $p<.01$).

Dialogue 2a

A: You know, my doctor was telling me about how the sun causes cancer. That shouldn't bother us though—we'll never get a chance to use the beach this summer.

F: Oh, but I love the summer. I've been dreaming about relaxing on a nice sandy beach. I can feel the warmth already as I soak up some of those rays.

A: Well, we really need to get great jobs this summer if we have any plans to buy that car. You know it costs $3000, and the salesman said it was a steal at the price.
B: Sometimes people will say anything to get their way.

Dialogue 2b

A; Well, we really need to get great jobs this summer if we have any plans to buy that car. You know it costs $3000, and the salesman said it was a steal at the price.
B: Oh, but I love the summer. I've been dreaming about relaxing on a nice sandy beach. I can feel the warmth already as I soak up some of those rays.
A: You know, my doctor was telling me about how the sun causes cancer. That shouldn't bother us though—we'll never get a chance to use the beach this summer.
B: Sometimes people will say anything to get their way.

Dialogue 2c

A: You know, if you don't help me with my statistics homework I really think I will fail the exam.
B: I have a lot of work to do for class tomorrow, but I think I can squeeze some time in for you.
A: My statistics professor said that a lot of students have approached her about delaying the exam. They told her that she didn't give us enough time to prepare.
B: Sometimes people will say anything to get their way.

Results

INTERPRETATIONS OF UTTERANCE 4	DIALOGUE		
	2A	2B	2C
1. B thinks people are deceitful in pursuing goals.	8	9	13
2. B is accusing A of manipulating B.	9	26	10
3. B resents having to comply with A's request.	7	3	2
4. The people A referred to are manipulative.	14	3	15

A. Preferences for interpretations differed between Dialogues 2a and 2b ($\chi^2 = 16.09$, df = 3, $p<.01$).
B. Preferences for interpretations were not significantly different between Dialogues 2a and 2c.

C. Preferences for interpretations differed between Dialogues 2b and 2c (χ^2 = 16.03, df = 3, p<.01).

RESPONSES TO UTTERANCE 4	2A	2B	2C
1. I didn't tell you that just to get my way.	8	21	1
2. Yes, people do say whatever will get their way.	21	6	8
3. No, it's true—I wouldn't need help with more time.	4	0	8
4. They're right, she didn't give us enough time.	1	1	22

A. Preferences for responses differed between Dialogues 2a and 2b (χ^2 = 17.73, df = 3, p<.01).
B. Preferences for responses differed between Dialogues 2a and 2c (χ^2 = 39.50, df = 3, p<.01).
C. Preferences for responses differed between Dialogues 2b and 2c (χ^2 = 46.12, df = 3, p<.01).

Study III (with Sharon Potoker)

Dialogues 1a–1c: Conflict

K: I'm looking forward to spending this holiday weekend at home with the kids.
P: Oh, you are? Well, if you insist on that, remember that the fence needs repair and the garden hasn't been weeded.
K: I've been planning on chores—work like that relaxes me after being cooped up in the office all the time.
P: I wouldn't expect the kids to let you relax much. All their friends are going somewhere for the holidays.
K: Well, if it gets that bad I'll take them to the movies or maybe shopping for your birthday present. They'll enjoy that.
  P_a: You seem to be juggling your priorities around.
  P_b: Are you aware of all the special deals there are, like weekend package rates at the big resorts?
  P_c: Watch out when you're worrying about the kids that you don't totally forget about the fact that adults have needs too.
K: My only priority is not to be hassled.

Results

POSSIBLE INTERPRETATIONS OF K'S LAST UTTERANCE	DIALOGUE		
	1A	1B	1C
I only care about being left alone.	6	8	7
I don't need to be concerned with that.	1	3	1
Don't muddy the waters with side-issues.	3	2	1
We've talked enough; my wants are clear.	8	7	11

There were no significant differences in preferences of interpretation across the three dialogues.

Dialogues 2a–2c: Mutual Support

K: I wonder if we'll be able to afford a weekend outing before winter hits.
P: That would be great. Were you thinking of something in particular?
K: I'd like to try putting up at a resort where there are all sorts of things to do right on the grounds.
P: Sounds like it would be fun—especially if there were entertaining things for the kids too.
K: The Smiths told me they had a nice time at the Delmont Hotel because there's so much in the area for kids—even an amusement park and a riding stable in the next town.

P_a: You seem to be juggling your priorities around.
P_b: Are you aware of all the special deals there are, like weekend package rates at the big resorts?
P_c: Watch out when you're worrying about the kids that you don't totally forget about the fact that adults have needs too.

K: My only priority is not to be hassled.

Results

POSSIBLE INTERPRETATIONS OF K'S LAST UTTERANCE	DIALOGUE		
	2A	2B	2C
I only care about being left alone.	15	10	12
I don't need to be concerned with that.	1	6	1
Don't muddy the waters with side-issues.	0	1	2
We've talked enough; my wants are clear.	3	1	3

Preferences for interpretations differed between Dialogues 2a and 2b (χ^2 = 6.49, df = 2, $p<.05$).

Dialogues 3a–3c: Talk about Conflict

K: Nan's been snapping at me a lot recently—I can't figure out what I'm supposed to be doing wrong half the time.
P: She's been pretty irritable in general, I think, but my guess is that she's feeling pressured about money, and you haven't exactly been saving.
K: She's got to learn to trust me more and stop looking over my shoulder. I never spend money just for the fun of it.
P: Maybe it'd be smart if you two just sat down and talked over what the needs are—you know, try to set reasonable limits.
K: Sounds good, but I've tried that before, and we always end up fighting because I like to pick up little extras for the kids, and she wants to put that kind of money away for vacations.
P_a: You seem to be juggling your priorities around.
P_b: Are you aware of all the special deals there are, like weekend package rates at the big resorts?
P_c: Watch out when you're worrying about the kids that you don't totally forget about the fact that adults have needs too.
K: My only priority is not to be hassled.

Results

POSSIBLE INTERPRETATIONS OF K'S LAST UTTERANCE	DIALOGUE		
	3A	3B	3C
I only care about being left alone.	11	5	13
I don't need to be concerned with that.	1	1	2
Don't muddy the waters with side-issues.	1	2	0
We've talked enough; my wants are clear.	5	5	6

There were no significant differences in preferences of interpretation across the three dialogues.

Dialogues 4a–4c: Chitchat

K: I saw Jim and Sally downtown yesterday in their new car.
P: The downtown is sure getting run down—inflation is driving all the stores out to the malls.
K: I hate the malls. It's so impersonal out there. It's shopping by the numbers, and like it or lump it. I want to be catered to.
P: The thing that frustrates me when I go shopping is how little choice there is—hardly any variety and the prices all the same.

K: It's good enough for the kids and they're the ones with all the money. You just can't get away from it—it's plain good business to give them what they want. Pleasing adults doesn't matter.

P_a: You seem to be juggling your priorities around.

P_b: Are you aware of all the special deals there are, like weekend package rates at the big resorts?

P_c: Watch out when you're worrying about the kids that you don't totally forget about the fact that adults have needs too.

K: My only priority is not to be hassled.

Results

POSSIBLE INTERPRETATIONS OF K'S LAST UTTERANCE	DIALOGUE		
	4A	4B	4C
I only care about being left alone.	9	14	9
I don't need to be concerned with that.	1	2	3
Don't muddy the waters with side-issues.	1	1	1
We've talked enough; my wants are clear.	7	4	2

There were no significant differences in preferences of interpretation across the three dialogues.

Studies IVa and IVb

Dialogues 1a–1c: Conflict

C: Hey—how ya doin'?

M: Good—you?

C: OK *(pause)*. Listen, we're just on the way to that fancy French place downtown for dinner. It's my birthday. Wanna come?

M: Sure; yeah, thanks.

C: OK, we'll wait here while you go change.

M: No need—I'm neat and clean. Let's just go.

C: Come on—I've seen you wear some really fine looking things.

M_a: Yeah, but you're not usually worried about this kind of thing. I don't see what difference it'll make if I change clothes.

M_b: Yeah, but you're just pushing this because you think I'll end up embarrassing myself. Let people point. I can handle it.

M_c: Yeah, but you're just pushing this because it's your birthday and you're using that to throw your weight around.

C: You can't go in there dressed in shorts.

Results of Study IVa: Composites of Respondent-Generated Interpretations

INTERPRETATION OF C'S LAST UTTERANCE	DIALOGUES		
	1A	1B	1C
Informational: the restaurant bans shorts.	13	4	7
Implicature: it would be inappropriate to wear shorts. } Implicature: I'm [C] afraid that you'll [M] embarrass me.	2	11	2
Illocutionary Act: I [C] request/order you [M] to change.	1	1	8

A. Types of interpretations generated differed between Dialogues 1a and 1b ($\chi^2 = 10.99$, df = 2, $p<.01$).
B. Types of interpretations generated differed between Dialogues 1a and 1c ($\chi^2 = 12.49$, df = 2, $p<.01$).
C. Types of interpretations generated differed between Dialogues 1b and 1C ($\chi^2 = 7.74$, df = 2, $p<.05$).

Dialogues 2a–2c: Chitchat

M: Hi—it's a long drive down here, but I made it. *(C gets in M's car).*
C: Great you're here—this'll be worth the drive.
M: Yeah, a Stones concert, maybe the last one ever. How'd you get the tickets?
C: I have an in at campus security; somebody lost 'em.
M: Freebies! All the better! Now all I have to do is find someplace to park.
C: Look—there's a lot over there. Oh, oh; it's staff parking.
M_a: But it's late in the day; I don't see what difference it makes.
M_b: Well, the gate's open, nobody's looking—I'll just sneak in.
M_c: But with your in at campus security, you can get it fixed.
C: You can't leave your car in there without a permit.

Results of Study IVa: Composites of Respondent-Generated Interpretations

INTERPRETATION OF C'S LAST UTTERANCE	DIALOGUES		
	2A	2B	2C
Informational: a permit is needed to park there.	8	2	1
Implicature: I [C] disapprove of your parking there. } Implicature: it's risky to leave your car parked there.	7	6	0
Illocutionary Act: I [C] warn you not to park there. } Illocutionary Act: I [C] decline to help you park there.	0	7	14

A. Types of interpretations generated differed between Dialogues 2a and 2b (χ^2 = 10.68, df = 2, p<.05).
B. Types of interpretations generated differed between Dialogues 2a and 2c (χ^2 = 26.44, df = 2, p<.01).
C. Types of interpretations generated differed between Dialogues 2b and 2c (χ^2 = 24.27, df = 2, p<.01).

Results of Study IVb

INTERPRETATION OF C'S LAST UTTERANCE	DIALOGUES		
	1A	1B	1C
Informational: the restaurant bans shorts.	7	5	7
Implicature: I'm [C] afraid that you'll [M] embarrass me.	11	14	8
Illocutionary Act: I [C] request/order you [M] to change.	8	7	10
Meta-talk: I [C] reiterate that I want you [M] to change.	5	6	13

Preferred types of interpretation were not significantly different between the three dialogues.

INTERPRETATION OF C'S LAST UTTERANCE	DIALOGUES		
	2A	2B	2C
Informational: a permit is needed to park there.	9	11	9
Implicature: I [C] disapprove of your parking there.	9	8	7
Illocutionary Act: I [C] warn you it's risky to park there.	13	17	11
Illocutionary Act: I [C] decline to help you park there.	1	2	4

Preferred types of interpretation were not significantly different between the three dialogues.

Study Va

Dialogue A (Ground of coherence based on propositional content about Sally's character and traits)

D: I've been trying to figure out what Sally [K's sister] would like for her birthday.
K: Yeah, that's coming right up, isn't it? 15 already.
D: Uh, huh. Say, she's pretty young for a high school junior, now that I think about it. She skip a grade?
K: Two—2nd and 5th. She's smart but she hardly works at it. She'll take dancing over reading every time.

D: Well, there goes my idea of giving her some kind of book.
K: Would you consider something like perfume or jewelry for her? Something feminine?

Dialogue B (Ground of coherence based on K's subjective state regarding D's involvement with Sally)

D: I've been trying to figure out what Sally [K's sister] would like for her birthday.
K: What for? Just because you're my buddy? Come on, forget it.
D: No, no; her feelings'd be hurt if I let it go. Besides, I'd like to give her a little something.
K: Swell, and then she ends up with a crush on you. You want to turn into some kind of cradle-robber?
D: She'll be 15. Anyway, we're pals, her and me. We talk sometimes when I'm waiting on you, walk to the park once in a while; you know.
K: Would you consider something like perfume or jewelry for her? Something feminine?

Dialogue C (Ground of Coherence based on felicity conditions for K's insulting Sally)

D: I've been trying to figure out what Sally [K's sister] would like for her birthday.
K: That's strictly up to you—it's no good coming to me for advice. I want to stay out of it.
D: You must really resent her. I've never understood it.
K: Don't waste your time probing for hidden feelings. I just think I should stay out of her life now that she's growing up, almost 15.
D: That's some number you're trying to do, but I'm betting you can't handle her being a better athlete than you. As if that changes the fact that she's your sister.
K: Would you consider something like perfume or jewelry for her? Something feminine?

Results

INTERPRETATIONS OF K'S FINAL UTTERANCE	DIALOGUE		
	A	B	C
1. K is recommending D not give a childish gift.	2	0	0
2. K is asking D to indicate any interest in that gift idea.	12*	10	6
3. K is probing whether D has romantic interest in Sally.	2	11*	0
4. K is putting Sally down.	0	0	15*
5. K is probing whether D would chip in with K on a gift.	0	0	0

*Predicted to be the preferred interpretation in that condition.

A. Preferences for interpretations differed between Dialogues A and B ($\chi^2 = 7.87$, df = 3, $p<.05$).
B. Preferences for interpretations differed between Dialogues A and C ($\chi^2 = 20.77$, df = 3, $p<.01$).
C. Preferences for interpretations differed between Dialogues B and C ($\chi^2 = 27.0$, df = 3, $p<.01$).
D. Interpretation #2 was most preferred in Dialogue A as predicted ($\chi^2 = 44.1$, df = 3, $p<.01$).
E. Interpretation #4 was most preferred in Dialogue C as predicted ($\chi^2 = 12.58$, df = 3, $p<.01$).

Study Vb

Dialogue B′

D: I'm trying to figure out what Sally [K's sister] would like for her birthday.
K: If you're concerned about giving her something just because we're friends, you don't have to go to the trouble.
D: That's not my reason. I'd like to give her something, and I'm afraid she'd be hurt if I didn't. So you don't have to worry about it.
K: I'm just concerned that she might form a crush on you if you make the gesture. I can't believe you'd want to get romantically involved with her—she's just a baby.
D: She'll be 15, but that's beside the point. We've gotten to be pals, talking sometimes when I've been waiting on you, walking to the park once or twice, that sort of thing. None of which is much help in coming up with ideas for a gift.
K: Would you consider something like perfume or jewelry for her? Something feminine?

Dialogue C′

D: I'm trying to figure out what Sally [K's sister] would like for her birthday.
K: I hope you won't mind if I don't offer any suggestions. It'll be a better gift if you pick out something on your own, and anyway I'd rather not get involved.
D: I'm not surprised you feel that way; I've noticed you putting Sally off a lot, as if you resent her. I just don't understand it.

K: It's not resentment at all, you're wrong about that. Now that Sally is growing up—about to be 15 and all—I think she'd prefer it if I didn't get involved in her affairs.

D: I'm sure she doesn't feel that way. And that's not really how you're acting. My bet is that you have a hard time accepting that she's a better athlete than you. None of which is much help in coming up with ideas for a gift.

K: Would you consider something like perfume or jewelry for her? Something feminine?

Results

INTERPRETATIONS OF K'S FINAL UTTERANCE	DIALOGUE B′	DIALOGUE C′
1. K is recommending D not give a childish gift.	1	2
2. K is asking D to indicate any interest in that gift idea.	5	8
3. K is probing whether D has romantic interest in Sally.	12	3
4. K is putting Sally down.	0	7
5. K is probing whether D would chip in with K on a gift.	0	0

A. Preferences for interpretations differed between Dialogues B′ and C′ (χ^2 = 13.32, df = 3, p<.01).

B. Interpretation #3 was most preferred in Dialogue B′ (χ^2 = 10.33, df = 3, p<.025).

Study VI

Introductory Prologues

1. The two speakers, D and K, are male undergrduates here at [Ss university]. They have been close friends since high school.
2. a. Follow-up interviews revealed that D is aware of feelings K tries to hide—this includes K's pride about how 'together' and mature his younger sister, Sally, is.
   b. Follow-up interviews revealed that D is aware of feelings K tries to hide—this includes K's fears that Sally is too foolish to look out for herself.
   c. Follow-up interviews revealed that D is aware of feelings K tries to hide—this includes K's view that Sally is nice enough, but a little insensitive.

Dialogue A (as in Study Va)

D: I've been trying to figure out what Sally [K's sister] would like for her birthday.

K: Yeah, that's coming right up, isn't it? 15 already.

D: Uh, huh. Say, she's pretty young for a high school junior, now that I think about it. She skip a grade?

K: Two—2nd and 5th. She's smart but she hardly works at it. She'll take dancing over reading every time.

D: Well, there goes my idea of giving her some kind of book.

K: Would you consider something like perfume or jewelry for her? Something feminine?

Dialogue B (as in Study Va)

D: I've been trying to figure out what Sally [K's sister] would like for her birthday.

K: What for? Just because you're my buddy? Come on, forget it.

D: No, no; her feelings'd be hurt if I let it go. Besides, I'd like to give her a little something.

K: Swell, and then she ends up with a crush on you. You want to turn into some kind of cradle-robber?

D: She'll be 15. Anyway, we're pals, her and me. We talk sometimes when I'm waiting on you, walk to the park once in awhile; you know.

K: Would you consider something like perfume or jewelry for her? Something feminine?

Dialogue C (as in Study Va)

D: I've been trying to figure out what Sally [K's sister] would like for her birthday.

K: That's strictly up to you—it's no good coming to me for advice. I want to stay out of it.

D: You must really resent her. I've never understood it.

K: Don't waste your time probing for hidden feelings. I just think I should stay out of her life now that she's growing up, almost 15.

D: That's some number you're trying to do, but I'm betting you can't handle her being a better athlete than you. As if that changes the fact that she's your sister.

K: Would you consider something like perfume or jewelry for her? Something feminine?

Results

INTERPRETATIONS OF K'S FINAL UTTERANCE	DIALOGUE		
	A	B	C
1. K is recommending D not give a childish gift.	5.92	6.27	6.16
2. K is asking D to indicate any interest in that gift idea.	[1.96]*	3.18	2.61
3. K is probing whether D has romantic interest in Sally.	4.06	[1.83]*	4.55
4. K is putting Sally down.	4.92	4.29	[2.74]*
5. K is probing whether D thinks Sally too young for such gifts.	3.29**	3.85	4.49

A. Respondents rated the alternative interpretations on a Likert-type 7-place scale, with 1.0 being the highest possible rating and 7.0 being the lowest possible rating.

B. The ratings of the interpretation warranted theoretically in each dialogue are bracketed.

*This interpretation was rated significantly more favorably in this dialogue than in the other two, $p<.05$.

**This interpretation was rated significantly higher in Dialogue A than in Dialogue C, $p<.05$.

Statistics from the MANOVA Test

A. Multivariate analysis of variance revealed main effects on ratings of the alternative interpretations by the different dialogues (Hotelling's T = .70: F = 15.58, df = 10,444, $p<.01$).

B. Multivariate analysis of variance revealed no main effects on ratings of the alternate interpretations by background information regarding K's attitudes towards Sally (Hotelling's T = .074: F = 1.63, df = 10,444).

C. Univariate F-tests revealed significant effects on the ratings of interpretations 2–5 by the different dialogues, as follows:

INTERPRETATION	HYPOTHESIZED MS	ERROR MS	F
1.	2.67	2.13	1.25
2.	30.14	2.68	11.24*
3.	161.61	3.31	48.87*
4.	96.98	3.99	24.33*
5.	28.23	3.26	8.66*

* $p<.01$

Part III

Controlling Understandings in Different Media and in Different Cultures

This section of the book generalizes the idea that specific interpretations are contingent on which possible meanings are relevant, and that options of content, style, and delivery are constrained by projected interpretive consequences.

The first part of Chapter 6 makes explicit principles of relevance that apply to nonverbal displays, and serve as warrants for judgments of what meaning(s) of nonverbals to focus on and respond to. For example, it is possible to understand a smile as a spontaneous expression of felt pleasure or as a formal, insincere gesture. The judgment of which such meaning to focus on depends on which is relevant to antecedents in the discourse or dialogue.

Given that the specific interpretations of nonverbal displays and of utterances are contingent on their relevance to antecedents, each can function as antecedents of the other and influence the other's specific interpretation. The middle part of Chapter 6 details the influence that utterances on each type of specific interpretation exert on the specific interpretations of subsequent or concurrent nonverbals, and conversely, the influence that nonverbals with specific interpretations exert on the specific interpretation of subsequent or concurrent utterances.

In the last part of Chapter 6 the interpretive connections between nonverbal displays and utterances are applied to contrasting communications media. Print media at one extreme, which include little or no basis for displaying nonverbals, provide a more restrictive set of resources for controlling understandings than do audio-visual media at the other extreme.

In Chapter 7, principles of relevance and their role in controlling understandings are given the status of universals of communication competence. Because of the interpretive connections between utterances and nonverbal displays, interpreters who are culturally and linguistically different from communicators can nonetheless detect misunderstandings, and thus be guided in a trial-and-error procedure to achieve correct understandings. This enables the formulation of ad hoc ways of communicating certain information, even between foreigners and natives who are maximally different. The principles of relevance formulated in Chapters 4 and 6 thus entail what has to be done in such circumstances to make oneself understood, and what kinds of understanding are possible in those circumstances.

CHAPTER 6

The Specific Interpretation of Nonverbal Displays in Different Media, Alone and in Combination with Utterances

The preceding account of the specific interpretation of utterances does not address the effect of the communicator's nonverbal displays on the interpreter's judgments. But that failing is widespread. Despite a general recognition that (some) utterance meanings and, in the terms used here, their specific interpretations are critically influenced by the nonverbal displays that accompany them, little has been done to make explicit the interdependence between the meanings or specific interpretations of utterances, and the meanings of the nonverbal displays that accompany them. Hence, the variety of evidence cited by Friedman (1982) only shows indirectly that nonverbal displays exert an important and complex influence on the meanings and specific interpretations of utterances.

The dearth of efforts to formulate the way utterance meanings and nonverbal meanings influence each other results at least in part from the persistence of views that these involve two discrete channels of communication that parallel each other rather than interact (e.g., Watzlawick, Bateson, & Jackson, 1967; Mehrabian, 1972; Norton, 1983). Utterances are taken to generally function as channels for information about the objective environment (though the connotation of words and phrases are informative about the actor's subjective state). Conversely, nonverbal displays are taken to generally function as channels for information about the actor's subjective state (though certain deictic and mimetic gestures are informative about the objective environment). Although this view would no longer receive much explicit endorsement, studies of nonverbal displays sustain it tacitly by focusing on the psycho-social causes and the social functions of *isolated* gaze behaviors, facial expressions, vocal inflections, gesture, posture, and bodily movement (Harper, Wiens, and Matarazzo, 1978; Malandro & Barker, 1983).

Before an account can be given of the influence exerted by nonverbal displays on the meanings and specific interpretations of utterances (and vice-versa), it has to be made explicit what the characteristics are of nonverbal meanings, and what gives a nonverbal display the meaning it has.

A few nonverbal displays conventionally express a proposition (the circling of thumb and index finger to express approval or appreciation about something, the hitchhiker's upraised hand/thumb to request a ride). But nonverbal displays generally are characterized as having signal-like meanings. Their meanings are specified in terms of states and conditions which cause them or with which they co-occur, and whose occurrence they consequently signal. In some cases, these are states or conditions interior to the actor, in other cases they are states or conditions in the social or physical environment. Some nonverbal displays are understood as symptoms of physical or emotional states (e.g., facial expressions, gaze behavior, muscular tension, vocal inflections, posture). Other displays are conventional deictic or mimetic signals of the location or characteristics of objects, events, and situations (e.g., facial expressions, gestures, vocal inflections). Still other displays are conventional signals of intention, role definition, or social relationship during the actor's participation in the practices and rituals of an institution (e.g., a handshake, genuflection, a student's raised arm, a salute, a hug). Even Birdwhistell's (1970) structural analysis of nonverbal displays, which borrows formally from the approach to word strings by structural linguists, characterizes the meanings both of primitive units of nonverbal display and complexes of those units in signal-like terms.

While nonverbal displays have cognitively simpler meanings than utterances do, understanding a display in any instance is just as complicated. Most nonverbal displays do not have just one signal-value (signal just one state or condition) or one social function. Their signal-values and functions vary across contexts. This ambiguity requires interpreters to judge which of a nonverbal display's possible signal-values or functions should be focused on in a given instance, depending on their context.

This motivates an extension of the distinction between possible meanings and specific interpretations to an account of the way nonverbal displays are understood, and the way in which those understandings are influenced by what actors say and do antecedently and subsequently. This not only provides a more powerful and explicit account of nonverbal communication, but prepares the way for detailing the influence that nonverbal displays in discourses and dialogues exert on the meanings and specific interpretations of utterances, and vice-versa.

It is hypothesized in this chapter that a specific interpretation of a nonverbal is warranted insofar as the nonverbal, with regard to one of its possible meanings, follows from antecedents or fosters consequents (i.e., is relevant) in an unfolding dialogue or (orally presented) discourse (Sanders, 1985). My intention is to specify the principles that warrant specific interpretations of bodily and vocal displays in dialogues and discourses. On that basis, it will be possible to make explicit the mutual influence of nonverbals and utterances on their respective and conjoint specific interpretations. Finally, this account of the interrelationship between utterances and nonverbals will be applied to distinguishing between print, audio-only and audio-visual media, particularly in terms of their strategic utilities and limitations.

THE INTERPRETATION OF BODILY AND VOCAL DISPLAYS

There has been increasing sensitivity to indications in the empirical data that nonverbal behaviors in human communication are often not involuntary signals with fixed meanings (analogous to behavioral signals in other animal species)—that instead they are displayed strategically in many instances. This further indicates that judgments have to be made about what their specific interpretation should be (was intended to be) at a given juncture in a dialogue or discourse.

The trend towards this point of view has been fostered in part by data that indicate that there is considerable variability in the meanings (signal-values) of nonverbals. Munn (1940), Frijda (1958) and Kuleshov (1974) found variability in interpreters' judgments of the emotive value of facial expressions out of context, and a considerable influence on those judgments by context (although Ekman, Friesen and Ellsworth, 1972, have shown that signals of certain core emotions are reliably identifiable and that interpreters can be further trained towards high reliability).

More recently, Volkmar and Siegal (1982) found that consistent versus inconsistent combinations of verbalized message and accompanying nonverbal behaviors in making requests of children had contrasting effects on their responses. While the experimenters viewed these patterns in their data as indicating that each different combination had a particular meaning, their data can just as well be read as showing that in the face of the ambiguity of those combinations, respondents had different strategies of interpretation and social coping. Some children responded to the mere fact of being addressed no matter what the actual message combinations were. Others responded just to the verbal component regardless of whether accompanying nonverbal behaviors were consistent with it. Others responded just to consistent pairings of verbal and nonverbal, etc. Zivin (1982) has provided data that indicate a developmental progression from childhood to adulthood away from displaying and responding to nonverbals as involuntary displays and toward treating them as conventional or contrived expressions of belief, attitude, or feeling. In the terms being employed here, Zivin's distinction is between nonverbals that are (interpreted as being) non-strategic, or expressive, and nonverbals that are (interpreted as being) strategic, displayed for effect.

Ekman and Friesen (1969, 1975) have identified numerous strategic aspects in the display of nonverbal behaviors, such that the degree to which they are actually 'spontaneous,' involuntary signals is conceivably small. Ekman and Friesen (1969) noted that while certain nonverbal behaviors are universal signals of particular interior conditions, there are culture-specific restrictions on displaying them. This suggests that the meaning of any such nonverbal behavior is not fixed, but varies with its conformity to or breach of those restrictions on its display. Buck (1982: 37) has characterized nonverbal displays that conform to such restrictions as 'false' expressions of interior states which accordingly take on a strategic rather than expressive character. Ekman and Friesen (1975) have also distinguished among facial expressions that: (1) exaggerage, (2) understate, (3) belie or (4) fully conceal felt emotions—an explicit identification of strategems in the display of nonverbal behaviors.

There are at least three possible grounds for judging the likeliest 'correct' meaning of a nonverbal at a given juncture of an unfolding social transaction. These correspond to the three factors posited in Chapter 4 as influencing the specific interpretation of utterances:

1. Personal knowledge about the actor and what he/she would characteristically display the nonverbal in such circumstances to express.
2. Conventional understandings of what displaying that nonverbal would 'normally' express in that circumstance.
3. Which of the nonverbal's meanings would have to be focused on for the nonverbal to be relevant to its antededents or consequents in the dialogue or discourse at hand.

For the same reasons given in Chapter 4, 3 above is the most theoretically important of the three factors, and the only one that makes a nonverbal's specific interpretation reliably and unavoidably contingent on how the communicator formulates entries in the dialogue or discourse.

The question, then, is what makes a nonverbal relevant or not in a dialogue or discourse? The answer again parallels the case of utterances, but the parallel is not exact. First, nonverbals are relevant only insofar as they contribute to the coherence of the discourse or dialogue. Nonverbals in their own right do not contribute substantively to the progress of a discourse or dialogue towards a resolution, except insofar as they contribute to its coherence.

Second, the warrants for focusing on one meaning among possible alternatives do not involve the different ways that types of meaning are connected to antecedents and consequents. The several meanings of most nonverbals are of the same type (signals of interior conditions, illustrative or indicative signals, or conventional signals within institutions). Rather, nonverbal displays are signals (whether spontaneous or contrived), and the problem for interpreters is to judge which—among the various things some nonverbal could signal—it would be relevant to signal at that juncture.

Insofar as the condition or state of affairs that it is possible for a nonverbal to signal has been introduced antecedently in the public record or becomes evident subsequently, the nonverbal is relevant to that condition or state of affairs, and it is warranted to focus on that signal-value.

This is clearest in the case of nonverbals with signal-values that are indicative or illustrative. For example, jerking the forearm up towards the shoulder, with the fingers closed into a fist and the thumb upraised towards oneself, mimes or illustrates either: (1) that one is going in the indicated direction and wants (free) transportation, (2) that something is located in the indicated direction (behind one) or (3) that the person being addressed should go away. The signal-value it is warranted to focus on in any instance is of course the one that mimes or illustrates something that has been entered into the antecedent discourse or dialogue. Similarly, a nonverbal that among other possible signal-values has a particular conventional value within some institution (e.g., a student raising his hand in class) has that value relevantly—and focusing on it is warranted—insofar as utterances, conduct, and physical 'props' distinctive of the institution have been entered antecedently (or are entered subsequently) in the dialogue or discourse.

Even nonverbals that (nominally) signal interior sensations, feelings and cognitions are relevant to exterior antecedents or consequents. For most interior conditions that can be signalled nonverbally, there are exterior causes that are conventionally held as being sufficient to produce that condition, or exterior consequents of the interior condition (aside from the nonverbal itself) that it is conventionally held as being sufficient to produce. Hence, such a nonverbal is relevant to any antecedents or consequents in the dialogue or discourse (or in the communicator's immediate physical environment) that are sufficient to cause or result from an interior state it can signal. It is warranted to focus on that signal-value insofar as there are such antecedents or consequents. Some empirical support for this is provided by Kuleshov's (1974) experiments with montage. Viewers were shown a series of juxtapositions of the same image of an actor's face with shots of each of several objects (e.g., a bowl of soup, a dead woman in her coffin), giving the impression (by film conventions) that the actor was looking in each scene at one of those objects. Viewers interpreted the facial expression as signaling the interior condition that would conventionally result from contemplation of each object (e.g., hunger, sadness).

The warrant for focusing on a specific signal-value of a nonverbal display can therefore be expressed as follows.

> Given a nonverbal display that can have as its signal value that certain conditions exist ([NV]S:C_j), and given that those conditions are entailed by certain objects, events or situations (OES), then a focus on that signal value of the nonverbal display is warranted when entries in a segment of the discourse or dialogue cohere as references to or instances of OES.

[1] $(([NV]S{:}C_j) \cdot (OES \rightarrow C_j) \cdot (\alpha)(\delta)(OES_s)) \Rightarrow (\alpha/\delta)(SI_{NV} = S{:}C_j)$

where α = a quantifier that indexes the frequency with which OES occurs in the segment.
δ = a quantifier that indexes the distance between NV and OES.
α/δ = a quantifier that indexes the strength of the warrant for focusing on S:C_j as the ratio of α to δ.
SI_{NV} = the specific interpretation of the nonverbal display.

It follows from [1] that the probability that a nonverbal display will receive some specific interpretation depends on where the display occurs in an unfolding discourse or dialogue. The display of nonverbals must therefore be as constrained (though perhaps not as controllable) as the production of utterances. There is a constant potential entailed by [1] for a conflict between the nonverbals actors are disposed by their thoughts or feelings to display, and what the interpretive consequences would be of that display at that juncture. This predicts that even when actors cannot control the nonverbals they display, they will try to at least manage their timing so that they occur at a juncture where it would be warranted to focus on the intended meaning, or at least not warranted to focus on an undesired meaning. Zivin's (1982) findings bear this out, that as actors grow to adulthood they become increasingly calculated and less spontaneous about displaying nonverbals, and their displays correspondingly tend to be understood as more calculated and less spontaneous.

For example, a smile of pleasure at seeing someone may be displayed when no pleasure is felt, but to express such pleasure, at the juncture where the actor is observed to be looking at the person—

whether observed by the person or by a third party. By the same token, even when pleasure is felt at seeing the person, a signal of the emotion may nonetheless be suppressed until that juncture where one is observed to be looking at the person, because the antecedent of the display is then observable and a focus on the intended meaning thus warranted. Similarly, there is a greater likelihood that smiles or laughter will be displayed when watching television in the company of others, at junctures where the antecedents of the display are evident, and less likelihood that they will be displayed when one is alone or when their antecedents cannot be identified by others.

But note that even though [1] has considerable explanatory power, it is too powerful. It predicts that any nonverbal display that occurs in the absence of conditions it standardly signals will not cohere in the discourse or dialogue, and thus cannot be reliably understood. In some cases this is correct (e.g., when someone blushes in the absence of any antecedent condition conventionally sufficient to cause an interior condition signaled by blushing). But there are instances to the contrary and [1] is insensitive to them.

Nonverbals that are standardly displayed within some institution (such as a military salute, a student's raised hand, an actor's bow) are sometimes displayed in non-institutional settings. These displays are not necessarily incoherent. For example, an actor with no military rank in a civilian setting who nonetheless displays a military salute could be understood to thereby be attributing military qualities to the situation if the actor had been asked or told to do something. An actor in a social context in the company of peers might nonetheless raise his/her hand to get the floor to speak, and be understood thereby to be attributing to the situation a school-like inequality of access to the floor if he/she had not been getting opportunities to take the floor. An actor in a social context in the company of peers might nonetheless take an actor's bow, and be understood to be attributing entertainment-value to something he/she just done if others had stood by just observing him/her.

The common denominator in each case is that even though the nonverbal was displayed in the absence of any state or condition it standardly signals, its antecedents had some of the features definitive of those states or conditions. The military salute was displayed following the issuance of a directive, which has authoritative elements in common with military institutions. The raised hand was displayed after rights to the floor were usurped by some and denied to the actor, which has features of the inequality definitive of regulated forums, including classrooms. The theatrical bow was displayed after the actor performed while others watched, a social relationship that has features in common with those definitive of staged entertainments.

Of course, not every nonverbal that is displayed in the absence of a condition it standardly signals can be reinterpreted so that it coheres with its antecedents or consequents. Such reinterpretations, and a focus on them, are warranted when [1] fails if and only if there are components of the discourse or dialogue that have features in common with objects, events, or situations, that the nonverbal standardly signals. The principle here can be expressed as follows:

> Given a nonverbal display that standardly signals that some condition exists ($[NV]S{:}C_j$), and given that those conditions are entailed by certain objects, events or situations (OES), then when NV is displayed and OES is not present in a given segment of a discourse or dialogue, it is warranted to focus on NV as an attribution of the distinguishing features of OES to entries in that segment with which OES has certain other features in common.

[2] $([NV]\Sigma \cdot (\Delta)(\sim OES_s \cdot ((\alpha)(\delta)(Ent_s) \cap OES \neq \emptyset))) \Rightarrow (\alpha/\delta)(SI_{NV} = CL{:}(Ent \rightarrow C_j))$

where $[NV]\Sigma$ = the normal condition in (1), $([NV]S{:}C_j) \cdot (OES \rightarrow C_j)$.
Δ = a quantifier that indexes the extent of the segment in which OES does not occur.
Ent_s = entries in a segment of the discourse or dialogue.
$CL{:}(Ent \rightarrow C_j)$ = a claim that Ent are sufficient causes of the signaled condition C_j.

THE RELATIONSHIP BETWEEN NONVERBAL DISPLAYS AND UTTERANCES

If the specific interpretation of nonverbal displays depends on their relevance to antecedents and consequents in the discourse or dialogue, then their specific interpretations could be influenced by utterances that are treated as antecedents or consequents. Conversely, the specific interpretations of utterances could be influenced by nonverbal displays that are treated as antecedents or consequents. In that case, the specific interpretations of utterances and nonverbal displays must theoretically be interdependent. For example, if a speaker asserts that the hearer has bad taste, the hearer would be less likely to focus on the illocutionary force of that utterance (an insult) if the speaker subsequently smiled than if the speaker frowned. This in turn would influence the specific interpretations of subsequent entries, and possibly antecedent ones as well. Conversely, if one person slapped another person on the buttocks, the specific interpretation of that behavior would be different if the actor said nothing than if the actor said (either beforehand or afterwards) that a mosquito had landed there. Again, this in turn would influence the specific interpretation of subsequent and possibly antecedent entries.

The influence nonverbal displays have on the specific interpretation of utterances in discourses and dialogues, and the reverse, are detailed below. But this has to be justified first, considering that it is widely held to the contrary that utterances and nonverbal displays are products of independent channels of communication. Laboratory studies have seemed to confirm that utterances and nonverbal displays do involve independent channels of communication to which interpreters respond differentially. When respondents were presented with inconsistencies between the information provided in each channel, they attended to the information provided nonverbally (e.g., Mehrabian & Ferris, 1967; Mehrabian & Wiener, 1967; Bugental, Kaswan, & Love, 1970).

However, these findings are misleading. The studies involved did not define pairings of utterances and nonverbal displays as being consistent or inconsistent in terms of their meanings. Rather, if the affect states or attitudes they projected had the same valence (were both positive or both negative) they were defined as being consistent, and if they had opposite valences they were defined as being inconsistent. The laboratory findings thus were actually that when the valences of an utterance and an accompanying nonverbal display were different, the valence of the nonverbal display predicted effects on respondents.

However, this finding has to be greatly qualified in light of the post hoc examination by Bugental, Kaswan, and Love (1970) of the meanings of inconsistent pairs. They found that positively valued utterances paired with a negatively valued facial expression and vocal qualities were judged by respondents to be sarcastic; negatively valued utterances paired with positively valued nonverbals were judged to involve joking. While the valence of the nonverbal display does predict the valence of these meanings, it is critically important here that these meanings are single, unitary interpretations of the pair. It indicates that respondents did not focus on the meaning of the nonverbal display instead of the utterance. Rather, respondents must have adjusted the separate meanings of the utterance and the nonverbal against each other. This is to be expected on the strength of the Gricean presumption that actors intend to be Cooperative and make contributions, so that when they accompany an utterance with a nonverbal display, they intend that the two will cohere.

The theoretical conclusion here that the specific interpretations of utterances and nonverbal displays are interdependent thus does not contradict any laboratory findings, but if anything is borne out by them. Before detailing this interdependence, it only remains to consider whether the observed dominance of the valence of nonverbal displays is inherent or contingent.

In general, when a nonverbal display is inconsistent with an utterance, it is easier (it takes less cognitive work) to hold constant the warranted interpretation of the nonverbal display, and adjust the interpretation of the utterance to it so that they cohere. This is not because nonverbal displays are more spontaneous or harder to control, and thus more believable. Rather, most nonverbal displays have narrower ranges of meaning than utterances, and this makes it harder to adjust their specific interpretations to cohere with the specific interpretation of an utterance than vice-versa. The valences of many nonverbal displays are often the same across their possible signal-values (a downward-turning facial expression has a negative valence no matter which of its possible signal-values is focused on). In contrast, the valences of the attitudes and feelings projected across the possible (types of) meanings of an utterance can easily differ. If a speaker says "Here comes my bus," that could implicate relief at being able to go home (positive valence) or disappointment at having to take leave of the hearer (negative valence). In that case, all else being equal, there is much more latitude to adjust the specific interpretation of an utterance so that it coheres with an interpreted nonverbal than the reverse.

The foregoing indicates that it is contingent rather than inherent that the interpretations of utterances tend to be adjusted to cohere with the interpretations of nonverbals. In that case, it should happen at least occasionally that the specific interpretations of nonverbal displays are adjusted so that they cohere with accompanying utterances. Moreover, it is a theoretical imperative that this be the case whenever the warrant for the specific interpretation of the utterance is stronger than the warrant for the specific interpretation of the nonverbal display. Such reverse influences do occasionally occur, as in stock movie scenes when something the heroine has wanted for some time comes to pass (e.g., the hero agrees to hang up his guns), and the heroine says, "I'm so happy" and then proceeds to weep. The warrants for focusing on the content of such an utterance are so strong that the specific interpretation of the accompanying nonverbal display is adjusted to cohere with it.

Of course, it is conceivable that a strong warrant for focusing on some type of utterance meaning could develop, without it being possible to adjust the specific interpretation of the given nonverbal so that it coheres (e.g., if someone was ordering from the menu in a restaurant, and at the same time repeatedly describing a square by movements of one or both hands with outstretched index fingers, or moving the arm rhythmically in the manner of an orchestra's conductor). Let us suppose that such an interpretive impasse is an initial condition for treating the nonverbal display in what are actually fairly common ways—disregarding it as gratuitous, or explicitly asking the actor for its meaning.

The Effect of Utterance Meanings on Interpretations of Nonverbals

Nonverbals that Signal Interior Conditions

For nonverbals that can signal an interior condition, specific interpretations are contingent on which of their possible signal-values is relevant, and in what way, to antecedent causes or subsequent symptoms of the interior condition. Such antecedents and consequents may be physical conditions in the environment of the dialogue or discourse, or may be interpreted utterances. It is the latter that are of interest here.

Utterances can be sufficient causes of feelings and cognitions with regard to each possible type of meaning. The propositional content of an utterance may provide information about a state of affairs that is sufficient to precipitate certain interior conditions (e.g., an announcement of the winner of a lottery). An implicated proposition—and particularly the communicator's subjective state on which it is predicated—can similarly be a sufficient cause of an interior condition (e.g., implicated disrespect for one's professional judgment), and so can the performance of an illocutionary act (e.g., a threat). Thus, a distancing posture, muscular tension, and a direct gaze following an insult merit a different interpretation from when that display follows a request to perform an unpleasant duty (a power display in the first instance, a defensive recoil in the second).

Conversely, interior conditions can be sufficient causes of subsequent utterances that warrant retrospectively a specific interpretation of some nonverbal display. When the effects of interior conditions surface in uncalculated ways, they are unlikely to be relevant to the propositional content of the communicator's subsequent utterances. However, nonverbal signals of the communicator's interior condition would most probably be relevant to and retrospectively interpreted in terms of subsequent utterances with types of meaning that symptomize the communicator's interior condition: implicatures predicated on the interior condition in question, or illocutionary acts that presuppose certain interpersonal attitudes.

Nonverbal Deixis and Mimesis

When nonverbal behaviors can be interpreted as informative or illustrative regarding objects, situations, or events, their referents do not necessarily have to be in the physical environment. Utterances, particularly with respect to their propositional content, may identify objects, situations, or events that can be nonverbally indicated, mimed or illustrated. Speech where the ground of coherence involves propositional content is of course commonly accompanied by indicative and illustrative gestures, which have specific interpretations on the basis of their relevance to (features of) the propositional content of antecedent, concurrent or subsequent utterances. Conversely, because utterances with specific interpretations as implicatures or illocutionary acts do not identify objects, situations, or events that can be nonverbally indicated or mimed, such utterances cannot be antecedents or consequents that influence the specific interpretation of deictic or mimetic nonverbals.

Nonverbal Signals in Institutions

A variety of nonverbal displays have a standard signal-value when they occur within a particular institution (e.g., a handshake, a salute, genuflection). Nonverbals with regard to that standard signal-value are relevant to antecedents or consequents that situate the display within that institution. While these antecedents and consequents often involve components of the physical setting, they can include or consist entirely of utterances. Given that such nonverbals tend to be displayed during certain rituals and routines, utterances to which they are relevant will typically also be components of those rituals and routines, particularly on their interpretation as illocutionary acts (e.g., approaching someone with one's hand and lower arm extended towards them will be interpreted as the initial phase of a handshake if accompanied by the utterance of a greeting, but not if the utterance is "You forgot to return my book").

It is of course possible to introduce or cite certain rituals, routines, and institutions by utterances with a certain propositional content (e.g., "We are gathered here today for the purpose of . . ."). It is also possible to do this by utterances with implicatures that are predicated on certain subjective states that concern the norms of a ritual, routine or institution (e.g., the example in Chapters 3 and 4 of the professor who gave insufficient advice about how to study for an exam, and thereby could have implicated that the norms of the institution dissuaded him/her from saying more). Finally, certain illocutionary acts are only performed in the course of—and therefore functionally introduce or cite—particular rituals, routines or institutions.

When displays of this type of nonverbal do not satisfy [1], but do satisfy [2], this is often the result of producing accompanying utterances that are conventional within some institution, but without being in the conventional physical setting. For example, suppose that one person is questioning another intensively, evincing skepticism about some antecedent claim(s). If the person being interrogated or a third party picks up some object and bangs it on a table several times, it would be warranted to judge the specific interpretation of that nonverbal as being the attribution of qualities of a forensic cross-examination to the questioning, rather than as gratuitous and disruptive, if the actor also produces an utterance that is conventional in courts of law, such as "Out of order—your questions are irrelevant, immaterial, and incompetent."

The Effect of Nonverbal Meanings on the Meanings and Specific Interpretations of Utterances

Propositional Content

Nonverbal behaviors have a relatively small influence on the assignment of propositional content to utterances, given that (truth conditional) propositional content is a function of the structure and lexicon of the expression uttered, regardless of any interior or exterior conditions signaled by accompanying nonverbals.

However, gaze and gesturing behavior can substitute for or referentially disambiguate lexical constituents of an utterance. In addition, vocal stress contributes to distinguishing certain homonymous parts of speech (e.g., pérmit versus permít, cóntent versus contént). Finally, though this is as much a pragmatic consideration as a semantic one, vocal stress and intonation contours distinguish what is being presupposed by the communicator from what is being asserted (Lakoff, 1971; Chomsky, 1972; Grice, 1978; Coulthard and Brazil, 1982):

[3] **a.** I asked Mary to *dance*
b. I asked *Mary* to dance
c. I *asked* Mary to dance.
d. *I* asked Mary to dance.

Nonverbals also have little bearing on whether it is warranted to focus on propositional content. The warrant for such a focus is that the ground of coherence of some segment of the discourse or dialogue consists of features of propositional content that are shared by the content of the utterance in question, independent of the interior or exterior conditions signaled by accompanying nonverbals. Of course, insofar as the nonverbals displayed have specific interpretations as propositions, as a function of [2] above, those nonverbals may contribute to the ground of coherence that warrants focusing on the propositional content of antecedent or subsequent utterances.

For example, suppose that someone at a symphony concert is asked how they enjoyed the performance of some avante-garde composition, and that the person 'replies' with a nonverbal display that standardly signals gastric distress (a certain facial grimace, and arms gripped across the abdomen). In the absence of a conventionally sufficient cause of gastric distress, the nonverbal is a claim, by [2], that the music was nauseating. This coheres with the propositional content of the antecedent question, and adds to a ground of coherence that may warrant focusing on the propositional content of subsequent utterances.

Conversational Implicatures

Nonverbals play a critical role in deriving implicatures, largely by marking breaches of a conversational maxim. First, it is problematic with reference to utterance content and conversational demand alone to distinguish utterances that breach the maxim of relation from utterances that introduce new topics (Grice, 1975: 46). It is thus significant that there are intonational patterns that have been identified as characteristic of topic shifts (Brown, Currie and Kenworthy, 1980: 34–36). When such a pattern occurs in uttering an expression that breaches the maxim of relation, it presumably constrains against the derivation of an implicature.

Second, a breach of the maxim of quality (be sincere, say what you believe to be true) can be recognized not just on the basis of the interpreter's models of the communicator's beliefs and values (as in Chapter 3), but also on the basis of nonverbal behaviors that have been identified as naturally or conventionally signaling insincerity, primarily lower body movements and vocal qualities (Bugental, Henker and Whalen, 1976).

Third, the reason that both the maxim of quantity and the maxim of manner are breached is either an inability to be more complete or more precise on one hand, or an unwillingness to be so on the other; what such breaches implicate depends in part on which of those is perceived as the cause. Those two general states have somewhat different nonverbal correlates. States of uncertainty or ignorance at a juncture are often exhibited in gaze behavior (Galin and Ornstein, 1974), vocal hesitation phenomena (Hart and Brown, 1974), and gesture and posture (Sousa-Poza and Rohrberg, 1977). In contrast, states of anxiety or hostility that would generally precipitate a reluctance to be complete or precise tend to be exhibited in various bodily movements (Ekman and Friesen, 1972).

Nonverbals also contribute importantly to the warrant for focusing on a conversational implicature. That focus is warranted if there is a ground of coherence consisting of features of the subjective state on which the implicature is predicated. In particular, nonverbals that signal the communicator's interior condition add to, and in some cases wholly construct, that ground of coherence.

Illocutionary Acts

Nonverbal behaviors also contribute critically to the interpretation of utterances as illocutionary acts. Searle (1969: 30) has noted that illocutionary force indicators include such nonverbal components of utterance as stress and intonation contours—but this is vague and incomplete. Consider that the constitutive rules of illocutionary acts cite (the interpreter's beliefs about) the interpersonal attitudes and intentions of the communicator. Whether a communicator is understood to be making a promise or a threat, giving advice or a warning, issuing an imperative or making a request, and so forth depends on whether the communicator is perceived to be supportive or hostile, selfish or other-directed, etc. For example, saying "I want you to come back" can count as a plea or an imperative; saying "the movie already started" can count as a justification for not going in, advice to proceed more rapidly to the theatre, or a reprimand for being late. The different valences of interpersonal attitude and intention that distinguish among such alternative readings of an utterance are often marked by nonverbal signals of interior conditions, especially vocal quality, facial expression, gaze, posture, and movement (e.g., Birdwhistell, 1970; Scheflen, 1972; Malandro and Barker, 1983).

Similarly, nonverbals contribute to the warrant for focusing on the act an utterance can count as. In particular, insofar as the felicity conditions for an act are introduced antecedently or subsequently, it is warranted to focus on the utterance as that act. And the felicity conditions of a considerable number of acts include the desires, needs, intentions or interpersonal attitudes of the communicator and/or interpreter. These may be entered into the discourse or dialogue nonverbally.

The Interrelation of Interpreted Nonverbals and Utterances

It was noted in Chapter 4 that the specific interpretations of utterances in a discourse or dialogue are interdependent, and have to be adjusted against each other to foster (as much as possible) consistent grounds of coherence among them. This interdependence extends to the relationship between utterances and nonverbals as well. The specific interpretation of nonverbals is contingent on the specific interpretations of antecedent or subsequent utterances. Conversely, utterance meanings of each type, and the specific interpretation of utterances, is contingent (to varying degrees) on the specific interpretations of the nonverbals that precede, accompany, or follow them. In that case, as a dialogue or discourse unfolds, the interpretations of nonverbals may have to be adjusted so that they cohere with interpreted utterances, and vice versa.

In consequence of this process, nonverbals and utterances are assigned specific, complementary interpretations in conjunction with one another which may differ from what their specific interpretations would be individually. These adjusted, complementary interpretations can be identified with the holistic messages that Friedman (1982) and Poyatos (1983) consider to emerge from conjunctions of utterances and nonverbals.

NONVERBALS AND UTTERANCES IN MASS MEDIA

The principal aim below is to utilize the account here of the interrelation of nonverbals and utterances to compare different communication media. The object is to account for the communicative value both of visuals and of visuals combined with copy in television and film, and on that basis to make explicit the strategic capabilities of those media compared with audio and print media.

The Communicative Value of Visuals

The public interest first in movies and then in television presumably results from their capacity to display not simply visuals but kinetic visuals, rather than linguistic reconstructions of the depicted objects, situations and events. However, beyond their greater density of information per unit of time and space, it has not been explained why (kinetic) visuals have any particular communicative utility or attractiveness—what if anything they function to communicate that cannot just as well be communicated linguistically (in audio-only and print media). Their communicative utility has generally been addressed from two perspectives, both of which are essential but insufficient because they do not make clear the communicative utility of visuals versus linguistic messages, nor explain why kinetic visuals are different in kind from static ones.

To take those concerns in reverse order, visuals have a particular communicative utility compared with linguistic messages insofar as they depict nonverbal behaviors, particularly nonverbals that can be interpreted as signaling interior states or sensations. Although it is possible to assert, implicate or presuppose linguistically that one has general dispositions and intentions, or to describe narratively transient feelings and sensations after the fact, it is only through nonverbal behaviors that it is possible to express (and conversely, be informed about) such transient internal states at specific junctures of an unfolding transaction. Hence, media that can display nonverbal behaviors with high fidelty enable the communication not only of more information, but of different, more complex messages, than media that do not have that capability.

But visuals have communicative utility even when they could be replaced (albeit with less economy) by linguistic messages. First, studies of the visual arts (e.g., Veltrusky, 1976) treat visuals as expressive of perceptions and feelings through the use of color (especially warm versus cool colors), light and dark, uses of space (under/over, bottom/top, 'edge'/center), texture, shape, and representations or visual analogs of nonverbal behaviors (slumped versus erect, open versus closed, downward-turning versus upward-turning).

Note that the 'meanings' of visuals that result from such qualities are unlike the meanings of nonverbal behaviors, in that they are not contingent. There are no principles such as [1] above that have to be applied by the (acculturated) interpreter in order for a work of art to express or stimulate perceptions and feelings by virtue of its uses of color, light and space, shape, etc.

On a second level, however, there is considerable need for judgment about the specific interpretation of a visual. Novitz (1977) has argued that an adequate account of visuals has to include a distinction corresponding to the one between propositional content and illocutionary acts. His thesis is that what is *pictured* in a visual is a necessary but not sufficient factor in our understanding of what the visual *depicts.* What a visual depicts is contingent on what the point of displaying the picture is, on what is accomplished by means of that display:

> Take, for example, a picture of a dog at his master's grave which is entitled *Devotion.* It is sometimes supposed in virtue of its title this picture must be a picture of devotion; but this supposition involves an important oversight. It involves ignoring the distinction between pictures on the one hand, and the use made of pictures on the other. In the present case we have what is admittedly a picture *of* a dog at a graveside. However, the picture sports a title which, to some extent at least, functions as a use-indicator, giving an audience a clue about how the picture is being used. It is being used, perhaps, to illustrate a tale of devotion. But to illustrate a tale of devotion with this picture, is not to picture devotion: no more than the use of the sentence "The ice is thin" to warn someone about the danger of falling into a pond presupposes that the sentence means that there is a danger of falling into a pond. (p. 13)
>
> . . . the intended or planned use of an envisaged picture frequently influences the way it is created. It has an important bearing on what shapes and colours are brought to the canvas and the relation in which they stand to one another: in short it affects and moulds the structure of the picture. Conversely, the way in which lines and colours are arranged in depicting will often, although by no means invariably, determine the possible uses of the picture. (p. 67)

Accordingly, in addition to the affective qualities resulting from their intrinsic properties, visuals are also informative, illustrative, sermonic, and the like, depending on what we believe we should (i.e., are intended to) use them for.

Following Novitz, interpretations of what a visual depicts are contingent on such use-indicators as titles or other linguistic accompaniments, and the manner and location of their display. These follow if the principle given in Chapter 3 for judging the meaning of an utterance as an act is applied to visuals as well. That principle linked the interpretation of an utterance as an act to: (1) the constitutive rules of acts that the utterance could count as, (2) the actor's disposition toward one or another of those acts, and (3) the structural need for one or another of those acts. Analogous to the constitutive rules of illocutionary acts, there are often conventions about what the possible uses are of a visual with certain features. The interpreter is as likely to have beliefs about the dispositions of the person who displays a visual as the person who performs an illocutionary act. And like utterances, visuals are generally displayed in the course of a progression from the start of some agenda to its resolution, such that there is a structural need for the display.

Kinetic Visuals and Accompanying Utterances

The specific interpretation of nonverbal behaviors and of utterances is hypothetically a function of their relationship to elements and/or patterns of development in the antecedent sequence of utterances, behaviors and events. This presumes that the constituents of the antecedent sequence are ordered: hence, even if an interpreter is knowledgable of what the constituents of a given sequence are, but is ignorant of where in the sequence a nonverbal or an utterance occurred, then the interpreter cannot judge what specific interpretation the nonverbal or utterance should receive.

The communicative difference between static and kinetic visuals, then, is that kinetic visuals are informative about where in a sequence of utterances, behaviors and events the pictured entities (especially nonverbal behaviors) occurred. This provides a basis for assigning specific interpretations to the nonverbal behaviors pictured in kinetic visuals—to gaze, facial expression, gesture, posture, and the like. Conversely, static visuals, especially representational paintings and photographs, provide interpreters with an otherwise unattainable opportunity to break away from normal perceptual and interpretive processes, and visually decompose persons, objects and scenes into their constituent parts (cf. Sontag, 1977).

Film (at least since 1927) and television not only have the capability of displaying kinetic visuals, but of doing so in conjunction with utterances. Hence, the interrelation of nonverbal behaviors and utterances detailed above can be exploited in these media to influence the specific interpretations of each, and to construct composite whole messages.

But the strategic utility of both film and television derives not just from this capability to display sequences, but from the capability through the framing and selection of camera shots, and through editing, to manipulate the sequencing of visuals with respect to each other, and with respect to utterances. This is particularly significant in the case of televised news: it entails not only that the interpretation of displayed visual material (as Novitz suggests) and depicted nonverbal behaviors is manipulable by what the reporter says prior to and concurrent with it; more interestingly, it entails that the interpretation of what is said by reporters is manipulable by the visuals displayed prior to and concurrent with their utterances.

For example, a televised report in 1980 on President-elect Reagan's tardiness in making major cabinet appointments utilized visuals in conjunction with utterances to imply that the cause of the delay was a chronic tendency by the Reagan staff to be interested in ethically dubious candidates. The report began with film of Mr. Reagan at an airport in California telling reporters that delays were the result of slow-downs caused by cumbersome disclosure requirements under new ethics legislation. The story was continued by a reporter in Washington who was (visually recognizable as) one of the network's featured commentators and sometime anchorperson. The reporter was visually located at the Lincoln memorial, standing with his back to the statue of the sitting Lincoln—an icon of honesty and integrity—which was looming above him, glowering over the reporter's shoulder into the camera. Meanwhile, the reporter added linguistically to the report by saying that the Reagan staff was embarrassed by the number of candidates they had approached who had declined to be considered because of those disclosure requirements, and concluded by reciting a lengthy list of their names. The presentation of those facts, in conjunction with the visual of Lincoln gratuitously in the background, implicated that contrary to Reagan's statement, the problem was that ethical deficiencies were chronic among high-ranking Republicans.

From this perspective, the difference between television and film on one hand, and radio, telephone and print media on the other, is a function of: (1) what can be communicated, and (2) what devices are available to influence specific interpretations of utterances and nonverbals. In contrast with film and television, audio-only media obviously have no capability to display any but vocalic nonverbals, but they do enable the sequencing of utterances. While print media also enable the sequencing of utterances, and in addition the display of visuals, they do not enable the sequencing of visuals relative to each other, or the sequencing of visuals with respect to utterances, except in a crude and highly attenuated way.

NONVERBALS AND STRATEGIC COMMUNICATION

Given their interpretive interrelationship with utterances, nonverbals are constrained with respect to their projected effect on the interpretation of contemplated utterances; but by the same token, nonverbals expand the options of expression in utterances, and more generally, the options of expression of information, intentions, and attitudes. It is this latter aspect that deserves special emphasis here.

Nonverbals in conjunction with certain utterances expand the options of expression by enabling the utterance of the same expressions with differing attitudinal valences. For example, when people engage in teasing, their utterances make salient and comment on weaknesses or perceived deficiencies in the other person, but this can be accompanied by nonverbals such that the teasing is either an affectionate or hostile act. More generally, nonverbals in conjunction with utterances enable the communication of certain information, perceptions, attitudes, and the like in such a way that the communicator is not accountable for the actual message, given what is materially in the public record. Thus, for example, claims for the virtues of some practice or commodity can be implicated by the utterance of purely descriptive expressions, with no evaluations on the public record, if the descriptions are accompanied by nonverbal expressions of enthusiasm and gratification.

The foregoing is something of a departure from the view that nonverbals are a means of expression and a source of information independent of spoken and written language. It suggests that nonverbals are more a resource in strategic communication than a mode of producing discrete entries in dialogues and discourses, except with respect to [2] above. This is consistent with the distinctions made above between media in terms of their capacity to display nonverbals.

CHAPTER 7

Universals of Communication Competence: On Understanding and Being Understood by Foreigners

The objective in this chapter is to support the claim that the principles of specific interpretation given in Chapters 4 and 6 are universals.

Aside from formal universals of language and some nonverbals whose meanings appear to be universal, the resources for linguistic and nonverbal communication that have been identified in work to date are culture- and community-specific. The syntactic rules and lexicon one has to know in producing and understanding sentences differ substantively from one language to the next. Conventions of phrasing, and of what utterances to produce under which circumstances, vary across communities and cultures. The conventional meanings of nonverbals (excepting universals) also vary across communities and cultures, as do conventions of nonverbal display (e.g., Wittgenstein, 1953; Hymes, 1964; Garfinkel, 1967; Labov, 1967; Kochman, 1973; Ekman and Friesen, 1975; Grice, 1975; Philipsen, 1967; Schank and Abelson, 1977; Harper, Weins and Matarazzo, 1978; Ladd, 1980; Searle, 1980; Coulmas, 1981; Tannen, 1981; Gumperz, 1982; Poyatos, 1983; Levinson, 1983).

However, there are facts that indicate that resources must exist for communication across the boundaries of communities, cultures, and languages. If utterances and behaviors were produced and understood just with respect to community-specific rules and conventions, then it would not be possible for people to communicate who have different languages, know different conventions of utterance and behavior, and have different background knowledge.

But to the contrary, people are able to communicate despite having in common few if any such resources. It is true that as the degree of difference increases, the effortfulness of communication goes up, and so do limits on what can be communicated, and how it can be communicated. But people are never wholly prevented from communicating, even under conditions of maximum difference.

It is not sufficient to account for the facts of communication under conditions of maximum difference just with reference to nonverbals with universal meanings, though of course such nonverbals contribute. First, while the meaning of some nonverbals is universal, conventions of their display are generally not. Therefore, when there are cultural and communal differences such that those conventions are not shared, the probability of error in the specific interpretation of such nonverbals will be high. Second, such nonverbals can only enable the expression of certain feelings and interpersonal orientations (e.g., pleasure/happiness, sadness, anger, incomprehension, confusion), whereas communication between people who share only those means of expression must be and is more substantive than that.

If individuals who lack shared resources for expressing themselves can nonetheless communicate, that must be a function of a capacity to improvise ways to make themselves understood, at least sufficiently to meet minimal needs under the circumstances. Given that this is done, then in the course of repeated interactions, regularities in what aliens say and do as grounds of coherence emerge will enable interpreters to detect and remedy misunderstandings of utterances and behaviors. The detection and remedy of misunderstandings in turn supports inferences of at least some rules and conventions of expression in the alien community. This correctly predicts that foreigners—conceivably including children in the process of first-language acquisition—have a systematic basis for learning (some portion of) unknown languages and dialects without the benefit of third-party mediators, insofar as circumstances necessitate having to communicate repeatedly with natives.

If people who do not have shared resources for communication are nonetheless able to improvise ways of making themselves understood, that must be predicated on a universal inferential procedure that enables (provisional) attributions of the intended meaning to alien utterances and behaviors. An adequate representation of that inferential procedure should not only explain the capacity of alien communicators to make themselves understood, but should also account for (1) the limits on what can be communicated, and how, as the degree of difference increases, (2) the increasing effortfulness of communication as the degree of difference increases, (3) learning alien rules and conventions over time, and (4) detecting and remedying misunderstandings.

The thesis here is that the principles of specific interpretation above provide the foundation for an inferential procedure which is adequate to account for both the feasibility, and details of the practice, of communication under varying conditions of difference. In particular, the application of those principles enables the (provisional) attribution of intended meanings (specific interpretations) to alien utterances and behaviors, and more importantly, the detection and remedy of misunderstandings over time. The detection and remedy of misunderstandings in turn enables inductions about alien rules and conventions of expression, and background knowledge.

The principles of specific interpretation formulated in Chapters 4 and 6 thus have the utility and power of universals of communicative competence, at least according to the criteria proposed by Gumperz (1982b).

Background Research

Studies of communication between natives and foreigners (or non-natives) are a relatively new development, and have originated largely in the context of work on teaching English as a second language. The focus of this work has been on what kinds of errors are made in communication between natives and foreigners (Chun, et al., 1982; Varonis & Gass, 1985), what compensatory strategies natives and foreigners adopt to minimize or correct such errors (Long, 1983; Gass & Varonis, 1985), and what linguistic and cultural knowledge foreigners need to avoid these errors (Gumperz, 1977; Thomas, 1983).

It is natural and reasonable for that research to have focused on discovering what can be done to help non-native speakers overcome their communicative handicaps. But as a result the fact has been under-appreciated that natives and foreigners with varying degrees of difference nonetheless improvise ways of communicating.

The ways that natives and foreigners have been observed to compensate for their differences are (1) foreigners' requests for help with vocabulary, and natives' correction of foreigner's errors, particularly vocabulary errors and discourse errors regarding topic and turn-taking (Chun, et al., 1982), and (2) natives' simplifications of their utterances, particularly through adoption of simpler syntax and greater referential explicitness by the abandonment of pro-forms (Long, 1983; Gass & Varonis, 1985).

However, the communication problems of natives and foreigners are often more complex than those compensatory responses suggest. Varonis and Gass (1985) examine a revealing instance of this. It indicates that a key problem for natives and foreigners in dialogues is to establish and verify a shared goal. But while Varonis and Gass provided a model that enabled them to characterize the problem and identify the particular ways in which it surfaced and was responded to in the conversation, it was too weak to help them explain how the conversants were able to detect the problem and the measures they took to correct it.

The case provided by Varonis and Gass (1985: 332-333) makes salient the checks and balances relationship specified in Chapters 4 and 6 between the way in which entries in a discourse or dialogue are understood, and the way they are cohered.

The conversants were a native (NS) who operated a television repair service, and a non-native student (NNS) who thought he had called a television retail outlet, and was trying to find out the price of a new television. It is likely that the confusion this produced lasted throughout the conversation because the student was foreign. This is not because of the student's speech (which does not seem to have gotten in the way except in turns 39-40 in the second excerpt below). It is because the student and service person alike seem to have attributed their confusion to the mere fact of his being a foreigner.

But more important than the source of their confusion is the fact that the student and service person were able to detect misunderstandings and attempt to remedy them. This is what is of particular interest here, and can be explained in terms of the checks and balances relationship between the way entries are understood and the way they are cohered.

1. NS: Hello.
2. NNS: Hello. Could you tell me about the price and size of Sylvania color TV?

3. NS: Pardon?
4. NNS: Could you tell me about the price and size of Sylvania TV . . . color?
5. NS: What do you want? A service call?
6. NNS: —seventeen inch—
7. NNS: Hunh?
8. NS: What did you want? A service call, or how much to repair a TV?
9. NNS: Yeah. Eh TV color.
10. NS: Seventeen inch?
11. NNS: O.K.
12. NS: (pause) Well is it a portable?

The service person evidently interpreted and cohered the student's entries in turns 2, 4, 6, and 9 as requests to know the price of repairing a Sylvania color TV which he already owned. The service person's question in turn 10 about the size of the TV which she presumed the student owned thus coheres with those antecedents. But the student's reply at turn 11, "O.K.," is not relevant on any of its conventional usages to those antecedents cohered in that way. The student's reply thus reveals for the first time that there might have been antecedent misunderstandings. It is consistent with this that the service person pauses for the first time, perhaps trying to read "O.K." as affirming that the television is seventeen inches, before going on in turn 12 to try finding out more about the student's TV.

As the conversation progresses, the service person gives up trying to get information and in turn 24 starts asking the student to bring his TV in for an estimate, a request which could not have been relevant in terms of any of its possible meanings with the way the student would have been trying to cohere its antecedents. This warrants the student's effort in turn 37 to break off the conversation and restart it. The result is a near miss:

36. NS: The only thing you can do is bring it in, you know, and let him (the repairman) look at it 'n go from there.
37. NNS: (long pause) New television please. (clears throat)
38. NS: Oh, you wanna know (long pause) how much a new television is?

39. NNS: Yeah, I wan' buy one please.
40. NS: (pause) Do we wanna buy one?
41. NNS: uh hunh.
42. NS: Is it Sylvania?

It is not evident from the content of the student's utterance in turn 37 that there was any particular warrant for the service person to have understood it (correctly) as a statement that his goal was to purchase rather than repair a television. The utterance could just as well have been understood as a statement that the television was new that he wanted repaired. It is thus likely that the service person's specific interpretation was based first on indications that something was wrong with her construction of the antecedent ground of coherence, given both prior coherence problems, and the long pause before the student spoke in turn 37. In addition she would have had to realize that if the student's utterance in turn 37 were understood as re-presenting his agenda, it would be possible to reinterpret and differently cohere antecedent entries in accordance with that. This speculation is consistent with three subsequent facts. The service person hesitated before stating what she newly understood his goal to be. She asked for verification that her new understanding was correct instead of just taking it for granted. And she promptly abandoned this new understanding upon mishearing the student's response.

In the end, the steps taken by the student and service person to overcome their misunderstandings did not fully succeed. But they did detect and respond to their misunderstandings. And they had nothing to work from in doing this except the interconnection between the way the sequence cohered and the way entries were interpreted.

A CASE STUDY OF COMMUNICATION UNDER CONDITIONS OF MAXIMUM DIFFERENCE

Beyond the data being produced in studies of second-language learners, and anecdotes in the journals of explorers and tourists, there is an additional, non-obvious source of data about communication between natives and foreigners—the work of clinicians with brain-damaged and communicatively dysfunctional children. The work of F. Lowenthal (1982, 1984) is of particular interest in this regard.

Lowenthal (1984) reports work with an aphasic Moroccan child, Saïd, in Belgium for a period of two years that began when the child was 5.5 years old. Saïd is further described as being able to differentiate only highly dissimilar sounds (a man laughing from a cow mooing, but not a bell from a flute). Saïd exhibited only two gestures that were utilized in a consistent way: a thumbs-up gesture to mean 'good,' and the right thumb pointing towards his chest to mean 'me.' He responded consistently only to a few individual words—*Saïd, good, bad, yes, no* and *more*—and Lowenthal gives his opinion that Saïd's ability to discriminate among those words depended heavily on intonation.

Saïd is therefore an individual whose resources for communication differed in extreme ways from those of Lowenthal and the others who worked with him. Yet on at least one occasion Saïd improvised a way of expressing an abstract social perception in the absence of a shared vocabulary or nonverbal means of doing so.

Lowenthal's work with Saïd consisted of instructing him in solving certain kinds of problems using nonverbal communication devices (NVCDs), comprising objects of different colors and shapes that could be categorized and sequenced in various ways. The clinical objective was to expand Saïd's communication resources by providing him with alternative means of learning and performing basic logico-linguistic operations. This method met with some moderate success, but that is not the point here.

Teaching Saïd the use of NVCDs was of course predicated on being able to give him feedback using the primitive vocabulary he already had (particularly the evaluative terms *good, bad, right,* and *wrong*). Because he had this vocabulary in common with the clinicians from the outset, neither this teaching nor even Saïd's increased proficiency in solving problems with NVCDs represents the improvisation of ways of making oneself understood under conditions of maximum difference. However, Lowenthal (1984: 7) reports Saïd's "making jokes *about* the device and . . . expressing his jokes *through* a (purposely) inadequate use of the material."

> On June 27 (approximately 7 months after sessions began) he made a . . . mistake and immediately looked at the experimenter's face, (sic) he obviously expected the usual "No". The experimenter did

> not react and the child immediately put his hands in front of his face in a gesture apparently meaning "Oh! What did I do?", (sic) he then corrected his . . . mistake and looked, laughing, at the experimenter . . .

Saïd's laughter, a critical resource in this incident, is a nonverbal with a universal meaning—but the laughter does not in itself express Saïd's social perception nor warrant those attributions of what meaning Saïd intended to communicate. Rather, Saïd managed to express himself by sequencing his behaviors in such a way that they had antecedents and consequents that warranted attributing the intended meanings to them, along the lines of the principles for inductions about others' intentions in Chapter 2, and for interpreting nonverbals in Chapter 6. It is in particular the self-correction following eye contact with the experimenter, and laughter following the self-correction, that by the principles here (see below, in particular) suffices as an improvised way for Saïd to joke about (and perhaps to assert his transcedence of) the learning situation.

A PROCEDURE FOR INTERPRETING ALIEN UTTERANCES AND BEHAVIORS

As described in Chapter 4, there is a circular, checks-and-balances, relationship between the specific interpretations by which antecedent entries are cohered in a discourse or dialogue and the specific interpretation of the current entry. Either the specific interpretations of antecedents are taken as given, and the meaning of the current entry is focused on that coheres it with those antecedents—or some meaning of the current entry is focused on, and the meanings and/or specific interpretations of antecedents are revised to cohere them with the current entry. This checks-and-balances method of interpreting utterances and behaviors, and cohering them, enables interpreters to attribute intended meanings to alien utterances and behaviors, and enables communicators to improvise ways of making themselves understood.

The question is, how does this method for adjusting specific interpretations against each other generalize to the problem of communicating under conditions of linguistic and cultural difference? As given in Chapters 4 and 6, that method is predicated on there being a set of possible meanings of each utterance and nonverbal—assigned on prior, independent grounds—such that the interpreter focuses on the one(s) that cohere the sequence. Yet in communication with aliens the problem is precisely that interpreters have impoverished grounds, and sometimes virtually none, for knowing the possible meanings of utterances and behaviors.

Recall, however, that it was also noted in Chapter 4 that an interpreter can project from the emergent ground of coherence some features of the specific interpretation of subsequent entries. This compares with the problem interpreters have in identifying the specific interpretations intended by alien communicators. If the ground of coherence has been sufficiently well established, the applicable principles of specific interpretation warrant projections of at least some features of the meaning that the communicator (on the presumption that he/she intended to make a contribution) must have intended be focused on at that juncture.

Hence, insofar as the interpreter who is faced with alien utterances and behaviors has some basis for construing the grounds of coherence in the sequence, then the applicable principles of specific interpretation warrant projections of (features of) at least the intended specific interpretation. The basis for construing grounds of coherence in discourses and dialogues is described in the two sections below, under conditions of moderate linguistic and cultural difference and under conditions of maximum difference.

Communication under Conditions of Moderate Difference

The problem of an interpreter faced with a single entry that he/she does not understand generalizes straightforwardly to interactions where (1) participants speak the same language, but one or more speaks it as a second language or speaks a different dialect, and (2) participants are from dissimilar communities and cultures. In such cases, the interpreter who applies his/her native rules and conventions to assigning possible interpretations to alien utterances and behaviors will (probably) misunderstand some entries and/or overlook intended meanings. Focusing on incorrect meanings will result in persistent difficulties in identifying a ground of coherence that applies uniformly to entries in the discourse or dialogue. Such difficulties will foster the detection of at least the existence of misunderstandings.

The alien interpreter in that circumstance can (provisionally) favor a ground of coherence that applies to at least some entries. That ground of coherence might be favored on some such practical criterion as that it applies to the largest possible number of entries given their presumed meanings, or it applies to entries about whose meaning the alien interpreter is certain. On the basis of that (provisional) ground of coherence, entries that do not then cohere can be identified as having been misunderstood. Given entries that have been identified as having been misunderstood, it is possible to project what features their intended meaning would have to have in order for them to be relevant to the presumed meanings of other entries, to contribute to the ground of coherence.

The contrast between the (apparent) misunderstanding and projected correct meaning enables the inference of the revisions that would be necessary in the rules and conventions that one applied that were presumably incorrect, to arrive at the correct (intended) meaning. Such inferences of alien rules and conventions can be subsequently tested against the coherence of the meanings they specify for subsequent entries. Hence, the principles of specific interpretation above apply in conditions of moderate difference both to the detection and (progressive) correction of errors over time, and to the concomitant inference of alien rules and conventions.

Errors and Their Detection Regarding Nonverbals

Given gaps in one's knowledge of a community's practices and conventions, the interpreter is most likely to misunderstand or not understand (at least some) conventional nonverbal displays. This also applies to nonverbals that are displayed in the absence of conditions they standardly signal, to make an attribution of certain features of those conditions to non-standard antecedents.

With regard to conventional nonverbals, errors in understanding or specific interpretation will be evident insofar as (1) the display does not have a known signal-value, or (2) the nonverbal is displayed in the absence of antecedents or consequents to which the alien interpreter considers it relevant. These errors can be corrected over time either by explicitly asking for and obtaining an explanation of their meaning, or by observing regularities in the features of antecedents or consequents in the interactions, practices or institutions within which those nonverbals are displayed.

The calculated display of nonverbals in the absence of antecedents or consequents they standardly signal, so as to attribute certain qualities to other antecedents or consequents, will be more problematic for alien interpreters. While errors in one's understanding of such nonverbals will be detected in the same way as described above, remedying such errors is more difficult. Observing regularities over time in the context in which such nonverbals are displayed will reveal meanings different from what the intended meaning was in displaying them deviantly. Further, given that the strategic value of displaying nonverbals deviantly is to make implicit claims about utterances, behaviors, situations or events, the actor may not be willing to provide an explanation of the intended meaning. The only recourse in that case is for the alien interpreter to consult third-party informants.

Errors and their Detection Regarding Propositional Content

Although an alien interpreter who knows the rules of language will generally be equipped to derive the propositional content of utterances, there will be obstacles presented by unfamiliar lexical items or familiar items with novel definitions. An additional source of error is that background knowledge enables native interpreters to obtain more information than aliens about an indicated state of affairs, given the phrasing and syntax of the uttered expression (Searle, 1980; also see the section on propositional content in Chapter 3).

Errors in the definitions of words or in further understandings of the state of affairs indicated by an utterance's propositional content can be detected in particular cases by their inconsistency with the signal-values of any accompanying deictic or mimetic nonverbals. Such errors can of course be detected more generally if the utterance in question does not cohere with the overall sequence by the applicable principle of specific interpretation.

The definitions of alien lexical items can either be asked for directly, or, corresponding to the central idea here, be projected on the basis of the grammatical and semantic requirements created by the rest of the sentence for items in the slot(s) they fill.

Further understandings about indicated states of affairs can also be asked about directly, or the background knowledge one lacks can be obtained from participation in the indicated behavior, situation, event or activity. But the more general and reliable remedy is to infer those further understandings over time, as features that the state of affairs in question would have to have for utterances about that state of affairs to contribute to the grounds of coherence in the sequence, and/or to progress towards the resolution of an agenda.

Errors and their Detection Regarding Illocutionary Acts

Given differences between the interpreter and alien communicators in background knowledge regarding social practices, roles, rights and obligations, there is a considerable potential for misunderstanding the illocutionary force of utterances under conditions of moderate difference. There are, however, three grounds for detecting such errors, the second and third of which also play a critical role in communication under conditions of maximum difference. First, of course, the utterance may not be relevant to antecedents or consequents in terms of that misunderstood illocutionary force. Second, accompanying nonverbal signals of interior conditions may be contrary to, or not relevant to, the felicity conditions of the presumed act.

Third, insofar as the utterance in question occurs as part of a standardized practice, task or institution, and the alien interpreter has a cognitive schema (e.g., a script) that calls for certain acts at certain junctures, then by that schema the misunderstood illocutionary force of the utterance will give it the status of a deviant entry. But particulars of the cognitive schema one applies may also be in error about alien practices and institutions. Hence, utilizing such schemata to detect and remedy errors in understanding the illocutionary force of utterances requires that there be some basis for also detecting and remedying errors in the schema. This is feasible to a degree by a checks-and-balances procedure, where one's understandings of the illocutionary force of utterances is adjusted against what one's cognitive schema calls for, and one's cognitive schema is adjusted against the illocutionary force that is attributed to utterances in terms of principles of specific interpretation. Of course, this makes it cumbersome to utilize cognitive schemata to detect and remedy misunderstandings. Their utility is more substantial under conditions of maximum difference, where alternative methods of detecting and remedying misunderstandings are more sparse.

Hence, principles of specific interpretation play a substantial role in remedying misunderstandings of illocutionary force under conditions of moderate difference, whether or not the alien interpreter also utilizes cognitive schema for that purpose. Those principles provide a basis for projecting what the illocutionary force of the utterance would have to be on the three grounds below:

1. What the illocutionary force of a given utterance would have to be for it to cohere with accompanying nonverbal signals of interior conditions.
2. What the illocutionary force would have to be for it to add to the ground of coherence created by antecedently asking that some act be done, entering reciprocals of it, and in particular, by what is done subsequently in response.
3. What the force of the utterance would have to be to contribute to resolution of the present agenda at that juncture.

Errors and their Detection Regarding Conversational Implicatures

The greatest potential for interpretive errors under conditions of moderate difference involves conversational implicatures. The models that interpreters have to bring to bear in recognizing that a conversational maxim has been breached (that the alien communicator's utterance was topically irrelevant, insufficient, vague or insincere), and in deriving the implicature, are heavily dependent in their details precisely on the background knowledge that members of different communities and cultures do not share.

Errors in recognizing the breach of a conversational maxim can be detected largely on the grounds that the utterance in question does not cohere with and contribute to the progress of the sequence at that juncture in terms of its other (types of) meanings. However, even if one has reason to believe that it is an error to focus on the propositional content or illocutionary force of an utterance, and that some proposition must have been implicated, it is difficult to remedy this by identifying what maxim, if any, was breached. Certain nonverbals that might accompany the utterance do signal interior conditions that foster the breach of particular maxims (see also Chapter 6): insincerity, which fosters breaches of the maxim of quality (e.g., Bugental, Henker and Whalen, 1976), and uncertainty or ignorance, which foster breaches of the maxims of quantity and manner (e.g., Galin and Ornstein, 1974; Hart and Brown, 1974; Sousa-Poza and

Rohrberg, 1977). But this is unreliable, given that there may not be antecedents or consequents to which such nonverbals are relevant that warrant focusing on those signal-values, except for the utterance whose meaning is precisely what is in question.

But even if breaches of conversational maxims are correctly identified, differences in background knowledge are likely to foster misunderstandings of what is thereby implicated. This is a critical point. The specific proposition implicated (upon breaching a specific maxim by an utterance with a specific content) is a function of certain models about the communicator, social practices and obligations, and of various relationships, situations and events in the world. To the degree that communicator and interpreter do not share that background knowledge, misunderstanding the implicature is likely. Further, the key basis for detecting and remedying such misunderstandings—the ground of coherence at the given juncture—applies to the subjective state on which implicatures are predicated, but not the substance of the implicature itself.

Philipsen (1984) has shown this in his analysis of a speech by the late Mayor Daley of Chicago. The speech coheres with respect to implicatures that are made on the basis of background knowledge specific to the Mayor's ethnic traditions, but the speech was regarded as rambling and incoherent by reporters (alien interpreters) who had no basis for detecting their interpretive errors.

To the degree that alien communicators and interpreters are sensitive to this problem, they are likely to avoid producing or focusing on implicatures. There is some weak empirical support for believing that interpreters are conservative in that way. When respondents in experimental studies of specific interpretation (reported in Chapter 5) were provided with conversations in which there were few cues about the situation and about the speaker's intentions, they tended to focus on prospositional content even when the utterance in question breached the maxim of relation (see especially data for Dialogues 2a and 2b in Study I; for Dialogues 1b, 2b, 3b and 4b in Study III; and for Dialogue B in Study Va).

In sum, despite a greater likelihood of short-term errors in interactions under conditions of moderate linguistic and cultural difference compared with interactions between natives, there will be little diminution of the ability of aliens to exchange information and to recognize and perform such acts as promising, advising, threatening, apologizing, congratulating, etc. But communication in such circumstances will be handicapped by the relative unreliability of methods of implicitly expressing oneself nonverbally—and especially verbally—that make exchanges more efficient, and that afford communicators the strategic resources to avoid having to be publicly accountable for what they communicate. This riskiness (and thus the practical loss) of ways of expressing oneself implicitly entails that alien communicators will find it more effortful to formulate utterances and behaviors that cohere with the unfolding sequence and contribute to its progress in the desired way. This also entails that alien interpreters will experience both more effort and heightened insecurity about whether they are 'missing something.'

Communication under Conditions of Maximum Difference

When an interpreter is maximally ignorant of the alien communicator's rules of language, conventions of utterance, conventions of nonverbal meaning and display, and background knowledge, then in contrast to the situations above, the interpreter does not have rules and conventions for assigning meanings sufficient to (provisionally) identify grounds of coherence. Therefore, there must be an extra-discursive basis for attributing intended meanings and construing the ground of coherence in sequences where the meaning of alien entries is consistently unknown.

The Utility of Nonverbal Displays

The principles for assigning specific interpretations to nonverbals are therefore of particular importance in this circumstance (and in fact are relied on heavily under conditions of maximum difference). Insofar as nonverbals are displayed so as to have a marked connection with particular antecedents and consequents, intended meanings can be attributed to them (Saïd's strategy in the case study above). Over the course of repeated interactions, displays (and also evident suppressions) of nonverbals will exhibit regularities that support the inference of at least some rules and conventions of expression in the alien community.

But in addition, certain of the intended meanings of utterances and behaviors can be attributed at particular junctures with reference to the cognitive schema of the task, practice or institution in which they were entered. Such cognitive schema represent goals and sufficient means of achieving them, such that they project a ground of coherence in the interaction, and attribute intended contributions (meanings) to alien utterances. This entails what intuitively seems to be true; that under conditions of maximum difference what can be communicated is limited to just what is required to transact business in particular settings and institutions (e.g., markets, places for obtaining food, shelter or transportation, offices of the civil authorities).

Acts and Reactions in Public Settings

The components of such cognitive schemata are generally acts, so that the ground of coherence in interactions under conditions of maximum difference will involve the illocutionary force of alien utterances and behaviors, and/or the felicity conditions created by them. The content of alien utterances in such circumstances could only be identified (at least initially) to the degree that the constitutive rules of the (schematized) acts require the utterance(s) involved to have content with certain features.

Of course, the particulars of an alien interpreter's cognitive schemata about tasks, practices and institutions in a foreign place will be incorrect, often to a considerable degree, and therefore many of the possible interpretations assigned will be incorrect. The critical issue, then, is whether the checks-and-balances method for adjusting meanings and specific interpretations against each other applies in this case to detect errors, and on that basis, produces learning and improved understandings over time.

Given the principles in Chapters 4 and 6, errors in a cognitive schema—and resulting errors in the understanding and specific interpretation of utterances and behaviors—can be detected in two ways. First, any given schema will specify that certain acts have to be performed at certain junctures. At least some of the utterances produced that are thus schematized as particular acts will be accompanied by nonverbals that have universal meanings, or whose meanings have been learned, as signals of the communicator's subjective state. Insofar as those nonverbals do not signal subjective states called for in the performance of the presumed act—do not cohere with the utterance(s) they accompany as those have (provisionally) been understood—it is warranted to consider the schema in use and the illocutionary force attributed to the utterance incorrect in at least that particular. Second, given that one knows the intended meaning of one's own entries, then insofar as they do not receive the schematized uptake (to the extent that that can be detected from accompanying nonverbals, as above), there are errors in one's own schema relative to the schemata of alien respondents.

Of course, there is also likely to be some degree of confirmation of projected illocutionary acts, and thus of (parts of) one's schema. The contrast between utterances and behaviors with meanings the interpreter considers are known and ones that were misunderstood is likely to reveal some alien conventions of utterance and of nonverbal display.

Information Exchange

Information exchange in the absence of a shared language depends on identifying referents by means of mimetic and deictic nonverbals, and on the creation of an ad hoc vocabulary. However, the pertinent gestures and utterances are unlikely to be interpreted as informational unless (illocutionary acts of) seeking and providing information are called for in one's schema, or having or providing certain information is a prerequisite to performing some schematized act. Given that felicity conditions for acts of information exchange are thus introduced, the content one then attributes to specific utterances and behaviors can be tested, as above, in terms of whether the contribution of subsequent nonverbals and vocabulary items contributes to the (presumed) ground of coherence that emerged from that attributed content.

On these foundations, at least some lexical items and rules of an alien language can be inferred from first acquiring ad hoc vocabulary items and other features of utterances presumed to have a certain propositional content. The propositional content of an alien communicator's utterances can in turn be inferred, first, from the evident performance of some illocutionary act where the utterance's propositional content must have certain features, and second, in terms of what content is relevant given the ground of coherence that has emerged antecedently.

Implicatures

Obviously, the impediments to the detection and remedy of errors that arise under conditions of moderate difference in understanding implicatures arise here as well, but to a greater degree. First, the detection of breaches of conversational maxims depends on shared background knowledge by which an utterance is markedly insufficient, vague or imprecise, insincere, or topically irrelevant, and such shared knowledge is obviously a sparse commodity under conditions of maximum difference. But even if an alien interpreter did have such background knowledge, utilizing it to detect breaches requires understanding the propositional content of utterances.

Of course, these barriers to detecting breaches of conversational maxims would erode over time, to the degree that the interpreter had learned some rules and conventions of expression of the alien community, and on that basis, some of the community's background knowledge. But even if breaches of maxims could be detected to some degree, and on the basis of that same background knowledge, implicatures could be derived, it would still be difficult to detect and remedy errors, for the same reasons that it is difficult under conditions of moderate difference. Implicatures cohere with respect to the subjective states on which they are predicated, not the substance of what is implicated. Consequently, errors in understanding an implicature cannot be detected by difficulties in cohering the utterance(s) in question with antecedents or consequents.

THE CONSEQUENCES OF BEING FOREIGN

Given principles of specific interpretation, and the checks-and-balances method they support of attributing meanings to alien utterances and behaviors, communication even under conditions of maximum difference is both feasible and (in principle) systematic. This account also predicts an increasing reliance on nonverbals, and an increasing focus on illocutionary acts, as the degree of difference becomes greater. And it predicts that as the degree of difference between communicator and interpreter becomes greater, what can be communicated is limited to what is required to transact business in certain conventional settings.

All of this entails that the production of utterances and behaviors will be progressively more effortful as the degree of difference becomes greater. First, communicators are not likely to be able to express themselves either implicitly through conversational implicatures, or through nonverbal attributions of qualities to certain antecedents, given that it risks misunderstanding to do so in conditions of moderate difference, and is not feasible in conditions of maximum difference. The consequence is a substantial loss of economy and efficiency of expression. In addition, as the degree of difference increases, communicators have to be progressively more deliberate and self-conscious about what they intend to communicate, and how to do so. Second, as the degree of difference between communicator and interpreter increases, there is a hyperbolic increase in the effort needed to communicate anything besides what is required to transact business in the public setting at hand.

At the same time, as the degree of difference becomes greater, interpreters have to make progressively more adjustments and readjustments of specific interpretations of utterances and behaviors against each other, and exercise progressively more vigilance, to detect and remedy misunderstandings. The cognitive work involved is obviously magnified if at the same time the interpreter attempts to infer rules and conventions of expression, and background knowledge relied on in the alien community.

Part IV

A Theory of Strategic Communication and Its Application in Studies of Conversation and Persuasion

In formulating utterances and nonverbal displays, it is not only of strategic importance how they will be understood, but also what subsequent utterances or nonverbal displays will come to be relevant, and thus possible. For example, in formulating an apology, it is strategically important not only whether one's utterance will be focused on as an apology, but whether the apology would make possible (relevant) additional recriminations, and if so, whether it would at least make such recriminations improbable because they would warrant undesirable inductions about the respondent.

Chapter 8 transforms principles of relevance into forecasting principles which are the foundation of a decision-theoretic account of the selection among options of content, style, and delivery at particular junctures of an unfolding discourse or dialogue. Some attention is also given to the basis communicators have for estimating the relative probabilities of consequences that are subsequently possible (relevant) in discourses and dialogues.

Chapters 9 and 10 show that facts about conversation and persuasion, respectively, can be explained in terms of the ability of communicators to make cost-benefit estimates about the projected consequences of contemplated utterances and nonverbal displays.

The focus in Chapter 9 is on the fact that disorder in turn-taking and topic development does occur in conversations without being a source of confusion and breakdown. This fact contradicts basic ideas that have developed in conversation analysis about the normative, or at least procedural, importance of orderliness and turn-taking. On the other hand, the strategic utility of disorder as well as order, and the ability to avoid being confused by disorder, can be accounted for in terms of a decision-theoretic account of strategic communication where the relative probability of an utterance or nonverbal display depends on its projected costs and benefits.

Attention is given in Chapter 10 to conflicting data that have accrued in studies of persuasion. The chapter is intended in part to further show the utility of a decision-theoretic account of strategic communication in light of problematic facts. But it is also intended to show that the account applies only in interpersonal situations. Some data about persuasion indicate that messages will influence what people subsequently say, but not what they subsequently do. This finding is consistent with a decision-theoretic account of strategic communication.

However, there are data to the contrary that reveal a strong effect by messages on overt behavior. It is shown that the latter findings result from statistical changes in the distribution of behaviors within social aggregates across finite options, not necessarily from systematic changes in the particular behaviors of individuals at particular junctures. This justifies making a fruitful distinction between the effects of messages in interpersonal settings and the effects of messages on social aggregates.

CHAPTER 8

The Strategic Formulation of Utterances and Nonverbals: Projecting Possible and Probable Consequences

The objective in this chapter is to make explicit a decision-theoretic account of strategic communication. By definition a communicator engages in strategic communication whenever his/her entries in a discourse or dialogue are fomulated so as to achieve (or avoid) some social consequence (as opposed to being formulated so as to state true propositions or to communicate salient cognitions or feelings).

Strategic communication is thus contingent on, and explained by, the capacity to estimate the utility of contemplated utterances and behaviors in bringing about some consequence. The cognitive basis for this capacity can be represented as a set of principles for modeling the connection between alternative contemplated entries at a given decision point and the possibilities and probabilities of entries subsequent to that point.

Let us define the consequences of an entry in a discourse or dialogue as being the utterances and behaviors subsequently entered in the same sequence. This definition extends to utterances and behaviors that are fostered by (entries in) the discourse or dialogue, but made 'afterwards,' at other places and times. Insofar as such later responses have a substantive relationship to the antecedent discourse or dialogue, just as entries at the time do, they can be projected and strategically promoted or deterred on the same principles as subsequent entries at the time are. Hence, let us consider subsequent responses to completed discourses as functionally creating a dialogue in which the completed discourse is a single entry. Let us also consider that subsequent responses to a completed dialogue functionally resume and continue the dialogue.

THE CONNECTION BETWEEN CONTEMPLATED ENTRIES AND THEIR CONSEQUENCES

The thesis here is that the connection between contemplated entries and their consequences can be modeled in terms of the principles of specific interpretation made explicit above. In practical terms, this means that the way in which the contemplated entry is formulated will affect the specific interpretation of subsequent entries, and the possibilility and likelihood that particular entries will subsequently be made depends on what their specific interpretation would be.

Forecasting Principles

Given principles in Chapters 4 and 6 by which subsequent entries cohere with their antecedents on a specific interpretation, then for each entry in a sequence, there is an array of possible entries that can follow coherently. This results in a branching network of possible sequences that can follow the contemplated entry, E1, at a given juncture, as in [1] below.

Given the principle in Chapter 4 by which entries contribute to the progress of a discourse or dialogue (and given in addition extra-discursive factors), it is also possible to estimate the probability of those different possible sequences in [1]. Possible (relevant) entries are probable to the degree that they contribute to the present agenda, and also to the degree that they are normatively obligatory or proscribed, and consistent with the respondent's role, personality and other dispositional factors.

Of course, a decision-theoretic account of strategic communication does not entail that in practicing strategic communication, communicators project every possible subsequent entry, as in [1], and estimate its relative probability. Given that there is a principled basis for such projections, it is a separate consideration how those

[1]

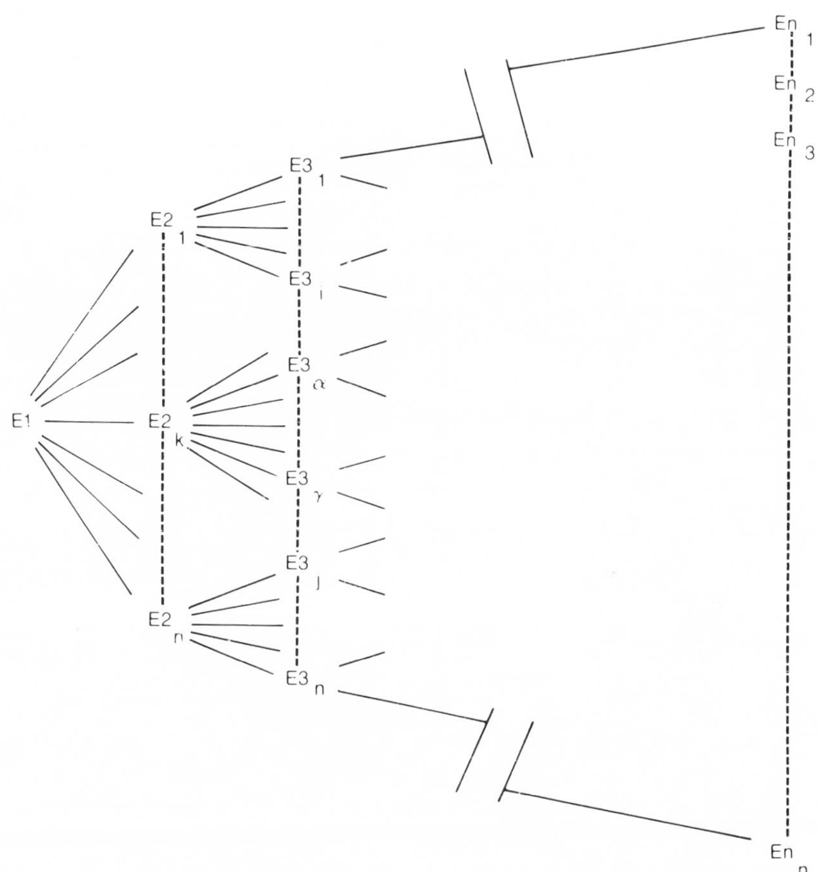

principles are utilized, if they are at all. This conceivably depends on whether there is a standardized procedure for achieving the goal, and on the communicator's particular needs and processing capabilities. However, the extent and thoroughness with which forecasting principles are utilized in practice—when they are utilized at all—falls on a continuum, along which we can distinguish the extremes and the middle ground.

Optimization Strategies

On one extreme, forecasting principles are utilized as in [1], to the degree that the communicator's processing capabilities permit. This is likeliest to happen when the communicator does not have a particular goal, but rather has the general goal of saying and doing whatever will promote his/her best interests in that situation, as substantive issues and possible outcomes develop in the unfolding discourse or dialogue. This would require evaluating each of an indefinitely large set of alternative formulations of the contemplated entry, so as to locate the options of content and style that provide maximum benefit and minimum risk with respect to: (1) what consequences are possible subsequent to the given juncture, and (2) what the resulting probabilities are of the various possible consequences.

Satisficing Strategies

The middle ground is when the communicator projects some, but not all of the possible sequences subsequent to that juncture, for just one or a few contemplated entries. This is likeliest when the communicator either has a particular agenda—desires to bring about or avoid a specific consequence—or is motivated to make an entry with a certain content and style, depending on its potential costliness. In that case, when it is desired to bring about some particular consequence, the communicator may project the consequences of different options of content and style just to the minimal extent required to locate options that make the desired consequence possible and sufficiently probable (or make the undesired consequence either not possible or sufficiently improbable). When it is intended to formulate the contemplated entry in a certain way unless its consequences are too costly, the communicator may project just the possibility and relative probability of particular undesired consequences.

Serendipity Strategies

At the other extreme, communicators do not utilize forecasting principles unless and until a ground of coherence emerges that has an unexpected effect on the specific interpretation of present entries, and thereby makes social consequences salient. This is likeliest when communicators rely on conventional procedures for achieving their objectives, or when communicators have personal, rather than social, motivations for the content and style of their entries (e.g., to state true propositions, or communicate salient thoughts or feelings). Such reactive utilizations of forecasting principles are likely to involve satisficing strategies, but only for the duration necessary to resolve the social or interpretive concerns that emerged in the discourse or dialogue.

The Empirical Reality of Forecasting Principles

The existence and utilization of this projective capability is often exhibited publicly. The most typical evidence of it is that communicators 'set the stage' for discourses and dialogues with introductory material that is formulated to warrant the desired specific interpretations of intended subsequent entries. This accounts for the formal introductions in scholarly works, the preliminary exchanges of social identifiers when people first meet, establishing shots and preliminary exposition in movies, etc. E's strategems in Conversation I (in Chapter 1) are a paradigm case: E evidently projected the possible consequences of F's self-disclosure, and from turn 57 to the end formulated her entries in a way she projected would avoid them.

Another evidence of the capacity to project the consequences of present entries is self-correction that is motivated by strategic considerations (the projected consequences). There is an example of this in Conversation II (Wiemann, 1977; a full transcript appears in the Appendix to this chapter).

Conversation II, like Conversation I, involves two undergraduate women suitemates, G and H, who were asked to have a conversation, and at some point to introduce and resolve any complaints they had about each other. At turn 69, G—who had maintained control over topic development throughout—terminated antecedent small talk and initiated the task of exchanging complaints by asking H if something was bothering her. However, G was not receptive to the complaint H made thereupon:

TURN

81 G: Okay [to H's complaint]. I . . . I don't really agree, but that's all right. Okay . . . //Uh

82 H: Well, wait. If you don't agree, then we should talk it all out.

83 G: No, no, okay, okay. I'll try to keep my stuff off your bed, but I don't do it on purpose. I don't use your bed as a . . . as a . . .

After this first complaint was resolved, G solicited further complaints in turn 87, despite her evident resistance to H's prior complaint. When H did make a second complaint, G balked in turn 89 and then reversed herself. It is this reversal that reflects G's projection of the consequence of her entry, and adjustment of its content to avoid that consequence:

87. G: Anything else?

88. H: Yeah, also, you know how last night the windows were open and it was 28 degrees out?

89. G: Aw, come on. Oh . . . okay. Go ahead.

G's evident ambivalence about having H complain probably results from the paradox that in order to preserve her control of the conversation, she had to surrender control (submit herself to H's complaints). It follows that at turn 89, G would be particularly disturbed at the prospect of having to contend with a second complaint against her. Yet for her to resist at that juncture would have the undesired consequence that H would then be unable to cohere G's antecedent invitations to complain except on the revised understanding that they were insincere and for the sole purpose of sustaining her dominant position. G's balk and immediate self-correction at turn 89, and the cessation of all further resistance, is evidence that she projected those consequences and adjusted the content of her entry so as to avoid them.

There is also some laboratory evidence that supports the thesis that entries in discourses and dialogues are fomulated at least so that they contribute to the ground of coherence (Clarke and Argyle, 1982: 162–165), which is the minimal way of constraining the subsequent progress of the sequence. Respondents were asked to construct, and other respondents to rate, sequences of differing orders of approximation. In zero-order approximations, each entry in a sequence was made by a different contributor, with each contributor ignorant of what the prior entries were. Entries in first-order approximations were made with knowledge of just the immediately prior entry in the sequence. Entries in second-order approximations were made knowing the immediately two prior entries, and so on. With reference to principles of specific interpretation and forecasting principles, as the number of prior entries known to contibutors increases, the basis for formulating entries that add to the ground of coherence of the sequence also increases. This predicts that sequences of a higher order of approximation will be rated as more 'natural' and plausible than sequences of lower orders of approximation. That was the result.

It should be noted, however, that the data indicate an upper limit to the processing that people engage in when formulating entries. The rated plausibility of third-order approximations was equivalent to that of actual sequences. Fourth-order approximations were rated as more plausible than actual sequences, and there was no gain in plausibility from any higher order of approximation.

The Theoretical Contribution of Principles of Specific Interpretation

There are of course factors other than interpretive consequences that influence estimates of the effects of contemplated entries. These correspond to the factors cited in Chapters 4 and 6 that influence interpreters' judgments of an entry's specific interpretation:

1. Knowledge about subsequent contributors sufficient to project what they will be disposed to say or do under the task or interpersonal conditions fostered by the contemplated entry.
2. One's knowledge of conventional or normative obligations that the contemplated entry will place (or contribute to placing) on subsequent contributors.
3. One's estimate of the effect of the contemplated entry on the ground of coherence in the dialogue or discourse, and thus its effect on the attributed meanings and specific interpretations of the contemplated entry, and of antecedent and possible subsequent entries.

For similar reasons as given in Chapter 4, 3 above is the more general and theoretically important of those factors. But this point can be supported more cogently in terms of present concerns. If projections of subsequent entries were made on the basis of 1 and

2 alone, strategic communication could theoretically occur and be accounted for only when communicators and respondents have knowledge of each other, and/or in circumstances where conduct is routinized by conventions and norms. However, 1 and 2 are not prerequisites for making such projections, although projections of the effects of contemplated entries obviously have a greater probability of being correct when the respondent is known and/or conduct is routinized.

Projections of the effect of contemplated entries can be and are made systematically even when the respondent is unknown (as in the drafting of policies and contracts, or in social interactions with strangers) and/or when conduct is not routinized (as during collaborative work on a novel task or problem, or during crises in personal relationships). Projections of the effect of contemplated entries in such circumstances are feasible just insofar as there are constraints on subsequent entries that are more theoretically basic than the dispositions of individuals and the routines practiced within communities and institutions.

With respect to principles for cohering entries in a sequence, factor 3 above enables a projection as in [1] of what is possible (relevant) following E1. And in addition, factor 3 enables estimates of probability along each pathway in [1] even in ignorance of the respondent's dispositions and in the absence of normative requirements, based on which possible subsequent entries would contribute to progress towards the desired resolution of the agenda (or away from undesired resolutions). In contrast, 1 and 2 only support estimates of probability along the branching pathways of [1], with reference to the disposition of contributors towards entries on their specific interpretations, and the conventional and normative obligations towards or away from entries on their specific interpretations. In that case, 1 and 2 are narrower and less general than 3.

The decision-theoretic account here based on 3 makes considerable headway on two core problems in work on strategic communication. First, of particular importance, it explains why details of style are as important or more important than details of content in the strategic formulation of entries in discourses and dialogues (Sanders, 1984). Details of phrasing, syntax and nonverbal behavior affect the specific interpretation of entries, and thus what can coherently be entered subsequently.

Second, given a principled basis for projecting different possible progressions in a sequence from the present juncture to some resolution, the decision-theoretic account here explains the capacity of communicators to be adaptive, and even innovative if necessary, in formulating entries so as to improve the chances of bringing about some consequence.

The primary concern below is to make explicit the principles that project the possible (relevant and coherent) consequences of a contemplated entry. Within the parameters of such forecasting principles, it is then possible to specify the basis for estimating the probabilities of those possible subsequent entries in such networks.

DECISION THEORY VERSUS GAME THEORY

It is important before continuing to justify the focus here on decision theory to the exclusion of game theory. The principal difference between the two is that decision theory concerns the maximization of gains (or minimization of costs) when the only 'adversary' standing between one's choices and their consequences is (the characteristics of) the physical or social environment. Game theory in contrast applies in cases where the pay-offs resulting from one's choices are contingent not just on the nature of the environment, but also on the choices others make in seeking to advance their own interests.

The critical difference between game theory and decision theory is that game theory assumes that the competing agents have to share the same finite pool of resources in pursuing their own interests. In that case, insofar as choices are made by individuals independently and simultaneously, the consequence of each choice is a function of their combined use of the available resources. This entails that to optimize the outcome of their individual choices, each individual's choices be predicated on judgments of what the other's choices will be.

This seems to make game theory applicable to dialogues, where the endpoint reached is contingent on others' entries as well as one's own. However, in dialogues the utterances and behaviors made by contributors are not drawn from a shared pool of resources, and they are sequential, not functionally simultaneous. At any juncture, each knows what the other has done, and can project its consequences before making the next decision.

Outcomes in dialogues therefore depend not on the combined effect of simultaneous choices, but on sequences of choices, as in multi-stage decision problems. Any choice among the alternatives at each juncture of a dialogue, precisely as at each juncture of a discourse, has to be based on the projection of outcomes in a potentially transient environment, with the object of successive decisions being to increasingly narrow subsequent possibilities toward (or away from) specific outcomes.

Hence, the same principles apply to projecting what is subsequently possible (relevant) at each juncture of a dialogue as at each juncture of a single-authored discourse. In that case, the contributors to a dialogue are operationally independent choice-makers each of whom alternately changes the environment in which the other(s) subsequently make choices in seeking a preferred outcome.

Formulating entries in dialogues and discourses alike thus closely approximates what is presumed in studies of complex-decision problems, where the environment is dynamic rather than static, and the full set of alternatives and contingencies cannot be known at a decision point. This motivates incremental decision strategies, which Radford (1977: 12) describes as follows:

> . . . the decision maker rejects the possibility of constructing a comprehensive decision model of the decision situation and concentrates on courses of action that are designed to bring about only an incremental change in the present circumstances. He selects a course of action that he considers will lead to improvements in the present situation, implements it cautiously, and reevaluates his decision as soon as information about the effects of his actions is available. The reevaluation includes a process by which both the means to achieve objectives and the objectives themselves can be altered if this is judged to be desirable in the light of the new information that has become available.

PROJECTING POSSIBLE ENTRIES SUBSEQUENT TO CONTEMPLATED ONES

Forecasting principles that will yield such structures as [1] are related to principles of specific interpretation as follows. At any given juncture, one can project what the specific interpretation of a contemplated entry will be relative to its antecedents if it comprises particular content, phrasing, syntax, and/or nonverbals. The possibility and probability of subsequent utterances and behaviors depends on whether they have a meaning that it would be warranted to focus on subsequent to the contemplated entry, and whether it would be desirable for that meaning to be focused on, given community standards and/or the respondent's known interests and dispositions. Communicators can either project the intended meanings that subsequent entries will possibly and probably have (without regard for what particular utterances or behaviors would actually be entered), or they can project what particular utterances and behaviors will possibly and probably be entered subsequently, on the basis of what meanings, if any, they have that it would be warranted to focus on.

Given an entry, E1, at some juncture of a discourse or dialogue, then on its specific interpretation an array of subsequent entries can be enumerated that have meanings that cohere with—are relevant to—E1. For each such projected entry, a similar array of entries subsequent to it can be projected, and so on. Successive repetitions of this procedure result in a branching network of alternative possible sequences.

The forecasting principles made explicit below are reciprocals of principles for the specific interpretation of utterances, as given in Chapter 4, and of principles for the specific interpretation of nonverbals, as given in Chapter 6. The principles in Chapter 4 will be transformed to principles for projecting what can subsequently be entered, with what specific interpretation, when the contemplated entry has specific utterance meanings. The principles in Chapter 6 will be transformed to principles for projecting discrete nonverbals that are possible subsequent to a contemplated entry with a specific utterance meaning, and also to principles for projecting what entries are possible subsequent to a contemplated behavior.

Subsequent Entries Relevant to the Content of the Contemplated Entry

By the principles in Chapter 4, entries on each of the possible types of utterance meaning follow relevantly from antecedents where the focus is on propositional content. Hence, subsequent entries follow that have propositional content about the same state of affairs as the content of one's contemplated entry. Subsequent entries also follow if they implicate propositions predicated on subjective states cited or expressed in one's contemplated entry. And subsequent entries follow if they count as acts that one's contemplated entry requests, or for which it cites or expresses felicity conditions.

However, while the content of a relevant implicated proposition can be projected, the fact that it was implicated rather then explicit—that the cooperative principle was breached—does not follow from the content of the contemplated entry, regardless of whether the contemplated entry expresses subjective states on which a subsequent implicature could be predicated. Hence, there is no principled basis (nor any strategic need) for projecting subsequent entries that cohere on their interpretation as implicatures, distinct from entries that cohere on the basis of their propositional content.

Subsequent Entries with Relevant Content

Given the principles in Chapter 4, the propositional content of an utterance is relevant to other constituents of the sequence if features of its content are included in the ground of coherence. If it is warranted to focus on the propositional content of an entry at some juncture, then features of that content must be included in the ground of coherence. Therefore, any subsequent entry is relevant that has content with those same features. If we denote such commonalities of content as P-REL, then the forecasting principle here can be expressed as follows:

> If the specific interpretation of a contemplated entry were its propositional content, members of the set of relevant subsequent entries would be such that their propositional content has those features in common with the content of the contemplated entry that are included in the antecedently established ground of coherence.

[2] $(SI_{ce} = PC_{ce}) \Rightarrow \{se \mid PC_{se} \cap PC_{ce} = \text{P-REL}\}$

where SI_{ce} = the specific interpretation of the contemplated entry
PC_{ce} = the propositional content of the contemplated entry
se = possible subsequent entries

PC_{se} = the propositional content of a subsequent entry
P-REL = the ground of coherence among the propositional contents of antecedent entries

The practical consequences of [2] are as follows. Let us represent the truth-conditional content of an utterance as a set of existential propositions, with each lexical item in the uttered expression being respectively the predicate of one of those propositions. Thus, the expression [3a] entails the truth of each proposition in [4]; the negative expression, [3b], entails the falsity of at least one proposition in [4]:

[3] a. The bookseller sold obscene materials to minors.
b. The bookseller didn't sell obscene materials to minors.

[4] a. The one who effected the transfer of property was some definite bookseller.
b. The method of transferring the property was by selling it (not lending or giving it).
c. The recipients of the transferred property were some indefinite minors.
d. The property transferred was materials.
e. The materials had obscene components.

In that case, given [2] above, both [3a] and [3b] are relevantly followed by entries with content that affirms, denies, or adds or seeks information regarding any proposition, or combination of propositions, in [4]. Of course, within an unfolding discourse or dialogue, entries relevant subsequently will involve just that subset of propositions in [4] that is included in the ground of coherence at that juncture. This is consistent with Tracy's (1982) findings that subsequent entries are rated as more "competent" if they stick to the "issue" in a sequence and not some incidental topic (an "issue" being the ground of coherence, though in some of her test materials an "issue" was the "communicative point" of an utterance, as in Chapter 3).

In any case, given a contemplated entry where the specific interpretation will involve propositional content, phrasing has a critically important effect on what can relevantly be entered subsequently. For example, the phrasing in [5a] below—"I was hurt," and "you stood me up"—makes relevant subsequent entries by either speaker or hearer about relational expectations and obligations. The phrasing of [5b] does not:

[5] **a.** I was hurt that you stood me up for lunch.
b. It's too bad we missed each other at lunch.

Subsequent Entries that Count as Relevant Acts

Principles in Chapter 4 entail that contemplated entries with certain propositional content can also be followed relevantly by illocutionary acts. The principle here is as follows:

> Given that the specific interpretation of a contemplated entry is its propositional content, members of the set of relevant subsequent entries would be any that count as an illocutionary act that the contemplated entry either requests, or for which it creates felicity conditions.

[6] $(SI_{ce} = PC_{ce}) \Rightarrow \{se \mid A_{se} \cdot (PC_{ce} \cap (R/I{:}A_{se} \vee FC{:}A_{se}) \neq \varnothing)\}$

where A = some illocutionary act
R/I:A = a request or imperative that the act be performed
FC:A = felicity conditions for performing the act

The practical consequences of [6] are as follows. The content of entries that request an act, or cite or express felicity conditions for the act, have a common denominator. Requests or imperatives to perform an act are predicated on there being certain features of the personal or interpersonal status quo that make it feasible, desirable or obligatory for the actor to have and undertake to fulfill the indicated social purpose. Similarly, felicity conditions are features of the personal or interpersonal status quo that warrant the adoption of some social purpose and/or the utility of certain utterances and behaviors in fulfilling it.

Because requests and imperatives explicitly name as relevant a subsequent act, it follows straightforwardly which acts it is possible will be entered subsequently: the requested act, a refusal to comply, a challenge to the legitimacy of the request, an excuse, or (from a hostile respondent) acts contrary to the requested one (threat instead of promise, warning instead of advice, reprimand instead of forgiveness).

Relevant subsequent acts follow in a more complicated way from the content of an entry that creates their felicity conditions. Given [6], when the content of an entry explicitly states the communicator's needs, desires or intentions, then subsequent acts are possible for which such needs, desires or intentions are felicity conditions. However, entries with (approximately) the same content, but phrased differently, can create felicity conditions in addition for different indirect speech acts if the alternate phrasings implicate (on pragmatic grounds) different perceptions of the personal or interpersonal status quo. This is illustrated by [7a] and [7b]:

[7] a. I hope none of you will object if I have a cigarette with my coffee.
b. I'm going to have a cigarette with my coffee; would anyone else like one?

The content of both [7a] and [7b] express the communicator's intention to be gratified at the potential expense of others. On that basis, both [7a] and [7b] create felicity conditions for the acts of objecting or consenting to the communicator's smoking, and also acts of advice or admonition about smoking in general, and smoking in the company of others. But the phrasings of [7a] and [7b] implicate different perceptions of the respective rights of the communicator and others, and those different perceptions are felicity conditions for different indirect speech acts. This is considered further in the following section regarding implicatures.

Subsequent Entries Relevant to a Contemplated Conversational Implicature

By the principles in Chapter 4, it is warranted to focus on a conversational implicature if the ground of coherence involves subjective states on which the implicature is predicated. Therefore, if the contemplated entry implicates a proposition predicated on some subjective state, subsequent entries relevant to that subjective state are possible. Subsequent entries can thus be projected that have content that is about that subjective state (i.e., content about the belief, perception, desire or feeling on which the implicature was predicated). Further, if that subjective state is a felicity condition for one or more illocutionary acts, then those acts can be projected as possible subsequent entries. However, for the same reasons as above, subsequent implicatures that cohere with the contemplated one cannot be projected on any basis distinct from the one for projecting the explicit content of subsequent entries.

Subsequent Entries with Relevant Content

As noted, a contemplated entry which implicates some proposition can be relevantly followed by entries with certain propositional content. The principle here can be expressed as follows:

> Given that the specific interpretation of the contemplated entry is an implicature, members of the set of subsequent entries would be any whose propositional content has features in common with the subjective state on which the implicated proposition is predicated.

[8] $((SI_{ce} = Imp_{ce}) \cdot SS{:}Imp_{ce}) \Rightarrow \{se \mid PC_{se} \cap SS{:}Imp_{ce} \neq \emptyset\}$

where Imp_{ce} = the contemplated implicature.
$SS{:}Imp_{ce}$ = the subjective state on which the contemplated implicature is predicated.

The practical consequence of [8] is as follows. Given an utterance (and accompanying nonverbals), it is a function of shared cognitive schema (as in Chapter 3) whether the entry breaches a conversational maxim, and if it does, what subjective state the implicature is construed as being predicated on. The subjective state on which the implicature is predicated depends on which maxim the contemplated entry breaches.

For example, one can implicate a disinclination for an activity in response to someone's endorsement by breaching either the maxim of manner (as H_1 does), or, by commenting vaguely, the maxim of quality (as H_2 does):

[9] S: Now that I've learned to ski I can't get enough of it.
H_1: Yeah, hurtling out of control off precipices is a rare treat.
H_2: Yes, skiing certainly stands apart among winter sports.

The implicature derived from breaching the maxim of manner is predicated on H_1's having definite beliefs and attitudes about skiing contrary to the ones stated, so that a number of subsequent entries are possible with content about e.g. H_1's beliefs about what skiers do, the conditions on ski trails, the physical experience; and H_1's attitudes about exertion, creature comforts and adventure. The implicature derived from breaching the maxim of quality, in contrast, is predicated on a subjective state such that H_2 is either unable or unwilling to be more precise (given the analysis in Chapter 3). The equivocality of that subjective state limits the subsequent content that can relevantly be entered about H_2.

In addition, subsequent content is contingent on whether the contemplated implicature is prefaced by a disclaimer of the subjective state it is in fact predicated on (e.g., "I'm sorry to interrupt, but . . . ," "I don't want to worry you, but . . . ," "I'd love to ask you in, but . . . "). Such disclaimers have the practical consequence of making subsequent entries with content about that subjective state redundant or adversarial, and therefore less probable (see the section below on estimating probabilities).

Subsequent Entries that are Relevant Acts

The subjective state on which an implicature is predicated may be a felicity condition for an illocutionary act. The forecasting principle that results is embedded in [6], and is expressed as follows:

> Given that the specific interpretation of the contemplated entry is an implicature, members of the set of subsequent entries would be any that count as an illocutionary act for which felicity conditions are created by the subjective state that the contemplated implicature is predicated on.

[10] $((SI_{ce} = Imp_{ce}) \cdot SS{:}Imp_{ce}) \Rightarrow \{se \mid A_{se} \cdot (SS{:}Imp_{ce} \cap FC{:}A_{se} \neq \varnothing)\}$

Given that the felicity conditions created by an implicature involve the subjective state it is predicated on, then the acts that can follow the contemplated implicature depend, as above, on what maxim is breached, and whether the contemplated entry is prefaced by a disclaimer.

The practical consequence of this is that entries with (approximately) the same content, but phrased differently, will create felicity conditions for different indirect speech acts if the alternate phrasings conventionally or conversationally implicate different perceptions of the personal or interpersonal status quo. This was illustrated above by [7], which is repeated below:

[7] a. I hope none of you will object if I have a cigarette with my coffee.
b. I'm going to have a cigarette with my coffee; would anyone else like one?

The phrasing of [7a], where *smoking* is embedded in a conditional, implies that the communicator perceives smoking as a departure from the status quo, to which others have the right to object. This creates felicity conditions such that the act of consenting to smoking is also an indirect speech act of conferring a benefit on the communicator. Conversely, the phrasing of [7b], where smoking is the unqualified intent and others are directed to cope, implies that the habit of smoking is the status quo to which others do not have the right to object. This creates felicity conditions such that objecting to smoking is an indirect speech act of confrontation. The different indirect speech acts that are relevant subsequent to the alternate phrasings in [7a] and [7b] may affect the probability that others will consent or object to the communicator's smoking (see the section below on estimating probabilities).

Subsequent Entries Relevant to a Contemplated Act

By the principles in Chapter 4 and as dealt with above, it is warranted to focus on an entry interpreted as an act if the act was requested, or if its felicity conditions are created. The forecasting principles derived from that have been given in [6] and [10]. But in addition, it is warranted to focus on an entry interpreted as an act if it is the conventional reciprocal of an antecedent act. The forecasting principle that follows from that is thus for any contemplated entry that counts as an act, entries that count as acts that reciprocate the contemplated one are subsequently possible. Precisely what the reciprocal(s) of a given act are is largely contingent on conventions in the speech community, as in adjacency pairs (e.g., Schegloff, 1972; Schegloff & Sacks, 1974). Acts can of course also be reciprocated by being duplicated (as in compliment-compliment, threat-threat, advice-advice, and other such pairs). The principle here is expressed as follows:

> Given that the specific interpretation of the contemplated entry is an illocutionary act, members of the set of subsequent entries would be any that count as an illocutionary act that duplicates or conventionally reciprocates the contemplated one.

[11] $(SI_{ce} = A_{ce}) \Rightarrow \{se \mid A_{se} \vee A^{-1}{}_{se}\}$

Where A = some illocutionary act.
A^{-1} = that act's conventional reciprocal.

The practical consequence of [11] is as follows. The act one's entry counts as is contingent on a number of factors (as in Chapter 3). First, it is contingent on the constitutive rules being borne out by the content of the entry, and on the personal and interpersonal status quo at that juncture. Second, it is contingent on there being a structural need for the act at that juncture. And third, it is contingent on the actor having dispositions consistent with the social purpose of the act.

While the personal and interpersonal status quo, structural need, and the actor's dispositions may have been established to some degree antecedently, communicators have discretion (through the content, phrasing and nonverbal aspects of the contemplated entry) about what act they are construed as performing, and thus what acts are subsequently possible. For example, [12] below could count as any of several acts (advice, an insult, an excuse), depending on its antecedents and on its nonverbal accompaniments. However, the communicator can influence the interpretation, and therefore what act(s) are subsequently possible, by formulating the entry so that his/her social purpose is explicit. For example, each of the expressions in [13] is an expansion of [12] that makes the actor's social purpose explicit (and thus disambiguates the act), and constrains what acts are subsequently possible.

[12] Your shirt is stained.

[13] **a.** You should change that stained shirt before the customers see you.
b. It shows what a slob you are that your shirt is stained.
c. I don't want to stop in to visit anyone because the shirt you're wearing is stained.

Subsequent Nonverbals Relevant to the Contemplated Entry

Subsequent Nonverbal Signals of Interior Conditions

By the principles in Chapter 6, a nonverbal display that signals some interior condition is relevant to an antecedent that is a sufficient cause of that interior condition. It was also noted that an entry in a discourse or dialogue can be a sufficient cause of an interior condition whether its content is focused on, its illocutionary force, or its implicature(s). Whether a subsequent nonverbal signal of an interior condition is possible thus depends less on the specific interpretation of the contemplated entry than on such extra-discursive factors as the applicable conventions of display and the respondent's dispositions.

In that case, the forecasting principle here, unlike the ones above, is not a transformation of some principle of specific interpretation. Rather, projecting the consequences of the contemplated entry is contingent on prior, extra-discursive knowledge of the possible effects on the respondent's interior condition of providing certain information, predicating an implicature on certain subjective states, or performing some act. The basis for such knowledge is of course prior experience with the respondent, and/or community understandings about the sufficient causes of particular interior conditions.

But principles of specific interpretation do play a secondary role here. Let us consider that the strategic problem at some junctures is: (1) to formulate an entry so that it has features sufficient to cause some interior condition, and that also has a specific interpretation by which it contributes to the unfolding sequence, or (2) to formulate an entry so that it has the intended meaning but does not also have features sufficient to cause some interior condition. Given extra-discursive knowledge about what features an entry must have to foster some interior condition, and thus make possible certain nonverbal displays, principles of interpretation apply to formulating entries so that they both have the intended meaning (or at least are relevant) and also do or do not have features sufficient to cause some interior condition.

First, whether an entry's propositional content is a sufficient cause of some interior condition generally depends on which features of the indicated state of affairs it makes explicit, not just on its indication that that state of affairs exists. Hence, phrasing plays a critical role in the subsequent possibility of certain interior conditions and the subsequent display of nonverbals that signal them:

[14] **a.** You're being highly irritating. You'd better leave.
b. I'm feeling highly irritable. I'd be better off alone.

Second, as noted above, the subjective state on which an implicature is predicated depends on which maxim the entry breaches. Thus, in [15] below, both H_1 and H_2 implicate dissatisfaction with S's proposal, but H_1 predicates that implicature on a subjective state that is evaluative of S's proposal whereas H_2's subjective state is evaluatively equivocal. Thus, H_1 is more likely than H_2 to be a sufficient cause of an effect on S's interior condition.

[15] S: I propose that to reduce our inventory we increase our advertising.
H_1: We'd better adjourn until somebody comes up with a sensible idea.
H_2: That's something to think about.

H_1 breaches the maxim of relation: in the absence of any aspects of the states of affairs identified by S and H_1 that bridge the substantive gap between their utterances, the implicated inadequacy of S's proposal is predicated on H_1 not perceiving any (productive) basis for further discussion in S's proposal. This subjective state is obviously evaluative of S's proposal. In contrast, H_2 breaches the maxim of quantity, so that the implicated inadequacy of S's idea is predicated on H_2's inability or unwillingness to say more about it. In contrast to H_1's subjective state, this inability or unwillingness to say more is not necessarily evaluative of S's proposal. It could result just as well from H_2 having his/her own agenda, or could result from situational constraints.

Third, similarly, alternative ways of performing some illocutionary act affect the sufficiency of the entry to cause some interior condition. For example, felicity conditions for the acts of giving advice and giving warning are that the hearer's welfare is in jeopardy, but such jeopardy can result from either shortcomings in the environment or shortcomings in the hearer. Hence, the same advice or the same warning can be given with different effects likely on the hearer's interior condition and subsequent nonverbal displays, depending on whether or not the jeopardy is attributed to shortcomings in the hearer:

[16] **a.** The car's brakes and steering are too sluggish to go this fast through these curves.
b. Your reflexes are too sluggish to drive this fast through these curves.

Subsequent Nonverbals that are Conventional in some Practice or Institution

By the principles in Chapter 6, nonverbals that have conventional signal-values in certain practices or institutions are relevantly displayed subsequent to entries that bring such practices or institutions into effect. Entries can bring such practices or institutions into effect, and thus make such conventional nonverbals possible, with regard to either their propositional content or to the illocutionary act they count as. Of course, as above, projections of such nonverbals are contingent on extra-discursive knowledge, particularly of the conventions involved in some practice or institution, and the sufficiency of some entry to bring that practice or institution into effect. But also as above, principles of specific interpretation do play a role in projecting the display of such nonverbals.

With regard to the content of entries, the same practice or institution can be brought into effect by entries that differ with regard to whether the display of certain constituent nonverbals is suspended or obligatory. For example, the content of each of [17a–c] below brings into effect the institutions and practices engaged in by physicians, but each differs with regard to the possibility (relevance) of the hearer's subsequently disrobing, and the doctor's subsequently touching and palpating parts of the hearer's body.

[17] **a.** The doctor will see you now
b. The doctor will speak with you now.
c. The doctor will examine you now.

However, in the case of illocutionary acts, it is the act itself that brings some practice or institution into effect, regardless of the various possible ways in which the same act can be performed. For example, there are ways of varying both the content and style with which the constituent illocutionary acts of a wedding ceremony are performed, but those differences do not alter the conventions of weddings and the nonverbal displays they involve. The projection of such nonverbals subsequent to certain acts is therefore entirely a function of extra-discursive knowledge.

Subsequent Entries Relevant to a Contemplated Behavior

By the principles in Chapter 6, any nonverbal is a signal that certain states or conditions exist. These can be interior conditions. They can be the location or qualities of objects, situations, or events. Or they can be states and conditions constitutive of certain practices or institutions. The display of any such nonverbal thus makes possible (relevant) subsequent entries whose specific interpretation is content about the signaled state or condition, or is an act whose felicity conditions have been signaled by the contemplated behavior.

The Content of Entries Subsequent to a Behavior

The display of nonverbals that signal certain interior conditions makes relevant subsequent entries with content about the indicated interior condition. The display of deictic or mimetic nonverbals makes relevant subsequent entries with content about the indicated extrinsic object, situation, or event. And the display of a conventional nonverbal make relevant subsequent entries with content about the indicated practice or institution. The principle here can be expressed as follows:

> Given that the contemplated entry is a nonverbal display whose specific interpretation is that it signals some condition of the actor, the objective environment, or within an institution, members of the set of subsequent entries can be any that have propositional content with features in common with features of the signaled condition.

[18] $(SI_{ce} = [NV_{ce}]S{:}C_j) \Rightarrow \{se \mid PC_{se} \cap C_j \neq \emptyset\}$

where $[NV_{ce}]S{:}C_j$ = the signal-value of the contemplated behavior.
C_j = the condition(s) signaled by the nonverbal display.

The practical applications of [18] involve deictic and mimetic nonverbals, and particularly, nonverbal signals of interior conditions. It is of course precisely the utility of deictic and mimetic nonverbals that they constrain the content of subsequent entries. Given a ground of coherence based on features of some state of affairs, deictic and mimetic nonverbals narrow that ground of coherence by specifying particular components, or the qualities of components, of that state of affairs.

More importantly with regard to strategic communication, the display of nonverbals that signal the actor's interior condition makes possible subsequent entries about the signaled interior conditions (beliefs, attitudes or feelings), and about the antecedents that are arguably the sufficient causes of those interior conditions. The content of such entries generalizes to propositions about the actor's character and traits.

In either case, one cannot vary the display of a contemplated behavior so as to change the subsequent entries that are possible (except by not displaying the behavior at all). But one can vary the way in which the behavior is 'staged' (the way it is prefaced, accompanied, or followed by other behaviors and utterances) so as to create a ground of coherence that warrants focusing on a specific signal–value. This can be generalized to account for the strategic aspects of other types of public behavior, especially consumer behavior and face–work in general.

Subsequent Acts Relevant to a Contemplated Behavior

The display of a nonverbal which signals some interior condition can create felicity conditions that make subsequent entries of certain illocutionary acts relevant. And the display of nonverbals which are conventional in a given practice or institution also make relevant the subsequent entry of acts which are conventional in that same practice or institution. In either case, the way others are entitled (or obligated) to treat the communicator and to act in the situation—the subsequent acts that are relevant—can be varied by the communicator's nonverbal displays. The forecasting principle involved is expressed as follows:

> Given that the contemplated entry is a nonverbal display whose specific interpretation is a signal that some condition exists, members of the set

of subsequent entries can be any illocutionary act for which the signaled conditions are felicity conditions.

[19] $(SI_{ce} = [NV_{ce}]S{:}C_j) \Rightarrow \{se \mid A_{se} \cdot (FC{:}A_{se} \cap C_j \neq \varnothing\}$

where A_{se} =an illocutionary act which the subsequent entry counts as
$FC{:}A_{se}$ = the felicity conditions for the subsequent act

The practical consequences of [19], as in the case of [18] above, do not involve alternative ways of displaying nonverbals. Rather, they involve alternative ways of staging nonverbals so as to warrant a specific interpretation to which certain subsequent acts and not others are relevant.

ESTIMATES OF THE RELATIVE PROBABILITY OF POSSIBLE SUBSEQUENT ENTRIES

As was noted above, there are three basic grounds for estimating the relative probability of a possible subsequent entry. First, possible entries that contribute to progress toward the resolution of the (presumed) agenda are more probable than entries that do not. Second, entries that fulfill normative or conventional obligations are more probable than entries that do not. Third, entries towards which the communicator is disposed (by belief, attitude, and/or role) are more probable than entries towards which the communicator is not disposed.

Let us suppose that the relative probabilities of subsequent entries are "averages" of the probabilities on each of the grounds above (insofar as each applies and is known). The relative probabilities of two possible entries, E_i and E_j, would be estimated as follows:

1. E_i
- **a.** Would not contribute to resolving the agenda (improbable).
- **b.** Is not normatively obligated (improbable).
- **c.** Conforms to the communicator's dispositions (probable).

2. E_j
- **a.** Would contribute to resolving the agenda (probable).

b. Is normatively obligated (probable).
c. Is opposed to the communicator's dispositions (improbable).

3. By simple averaging, E_j is relatively more probable than E_i.

Of course, the estimate of their relative probability will vary if those factors are given unequal weights.

The general logic here closely resembles Fishbein and Ajzen's (1975: 301) view that people act in part as a function of personal dispositions towards particular acts, and in part as a function of what the communal valuation of those acts is:

[20] $B \sim I = (A_B)w_1 + (SN)w_2$

where B = a behavior.
I = an intention to perform B, usually a verbalization.
A_B = the attitude toward performing B.
SN = the subjective norm(s) (communal valuations) regarding the performance of B.
w = an empirically determined weight.

The object of strategic communication is to formulate entries that affect the probability as well as the possibility of certain subsequent entries. The thesis here is that the probability of a subsequent entry is contingent on its specific interpretation. In that case, given that the specific interpretation of subsequent entries is contingent on their antecedents, the probability of subsequent entries is contingent on the way in which communicators formulate present entries. Furthermore, the effect of a contemplated entry on the relative probability of subsequent entries can be estimated on the basis of the forecasting principles above, given that they enable projections of the effect of the contemplated entry on the specific interpretation of subsequent entries.

In more detail, given that the relative probability of an entry is higher if it contributes to resolving the (presumed) agenda, it depends on the specific interpretation of the entry whether it so contributes. In Conversation I (in Chapter 1), E's difficulty in resolving the agenda of stating and resolving complaints was that she could not be sure that the content of any complaint she entered would be focused on, as necessary for the complaint to be resolved.

F's antecedent self-disclosure about her insecurity created a felicity condition such that it would be warranted to focus on the act of complaining, not the content. That would make the entry of undesirable acts possible subsequently, as well as interfere with resolving the agenda. Hence, in affecting the specific interpretation of subsequent entries intended as complaints, F's self-disclosure reduced the probability of E's complaining subsequently.

Similarly, whether entries are normatively or conventionally obligatory depends on what their specific interpretation is. Suppose, for example, that a salaried white-collar worker is asked to take on additional responsibilities without additional compensation. The possible subsequent entries for the employee obviously include consenting or refusing. Suppose further that the worker's supervisor has antecedently complained about 'unprofessional' attitudes in others, and the importance of being a 'team player,' in such a way that acting professionally and being a team player are normative obligations. The supervisor's antecedent entries create felicity conditions such that it would be warranted to focus on the illocutionary act, not the content, involved in the employee's subsequent expression of willingness or unwillingness to take on those additional responsibilities—the acts involved being, respectively, cooperation and obstruction. On that basis, expressing a willingness to take on those additional responsibilities acquires a specific interpretation that would make that response normatively obligatory, and thus relatively more probable.

Finally, it is necessarily contingent on the specific interpretation of a possible entry what the subsequent communicator's disposition is towards making it. The disposition of a subsequent communicator towards or against an entry because of beliefs regarding its content is contingent on there being a warrant for focusing on the content at that juncture. A disposition towards or against a subsequent entry because of attitudes regarding the act it can count as (regarding the social purpose and/or the entry as a means of fulfilling it) is contingent on there being a warrant for focusing on that act. A disposition that results because it fulfills the subsequent communicator's role to enter certain content or perform certain acts is contingent on there being a warrant for focusing on the role-fulfilling interpretation. Consequently, the relative probability of subsequent entries is increased (or diminished) by creating a ground of coherence that warrants focusing on the type of interpretation toward which the communicator is favorably disposed by virture of his/her beliefs, attitudes, and/or role.

COMPETENCE AND PERFORMANCE

The competence to undertake strategic communication does not entail the practice. Despite having the cognitive basis for it, communicators are not constantly strategic, actively calculating at each juncture the effects of contemplated ways of formulating entries. Rather, a considerable amount of communication undeniably is undertaken in routinized discourses and dialogues, where it is standardized what to communicate and how to communicate it in response to antecedent entries and/or in order to bring about certain consequences. In addition, communicators may speak and act egocentrically, out of conviction or out of narcissism, rather than for social purposes.

But let us take as axiomatic that communicators are competent to formulate their entries in discourses and dialogues strategically, and that they actively do so at least sometimes—when the stakes are sufficiently high, or the present situation is sufficiently novel or problematic.

In that case, strategic communication must be considered paradigmatic, with standardized communication the special case (even though standardized communication is probably more commonplace). Given a principled basis for strategic communication, and the fact that individuals do at least sometimes practice it, then standardized communication represents "artificial simplicity," where the cognitive work in producting utterances and behaviors can be substantially reduced without a corresponding reduction in effectiveness—as long as all parties share knowledge of the conventional procedures used.

At the same time, strategic communication is practiced more commonly than one might think, and surfaces in ways that have not generally been appreciated. The following chapters on ordinary conversation and on persuasion are each intended to make explicit the ways in which strategic communication surfaces, and to be suggestive about the extent to which strategic communication is practiced.

APPENDIX: CONVERSATION II

(Simultaneous speech is marked by double slashes (//) and underlining)

1. G: Have you been up to the apartments there?
2. H: No, but I just talked to Cheryl today.
3. G: And what did she tell you?
4. H: She told me to take [?] over there Saturday.
5. G: What's going on Saturday? Oh, spring fest. Spring fest is Saturday.
6. H: Oh, well, she was . . . she was in the middle of studying, so she just said, well listen, I'll call you Saturday and you can come over, so I didn't know there was something going on.
7. G: Yeah, spring fest. //with the
   H: What is
   G: in October, you, Octoberfest . . . the . . . the
8. H: Oh, with the beer?
9. G: Yeah, but this time it's a spring fest instead of Octoberfest.
10. H: Oh.
11. G: Yeah, I wasn't invited.
12. H: You weren't invited?
13. G: Yeah, I noticed that. [pause] Hummmmmm.
14. H: That is such a weird situation.
15. G: You're not kidding, 'cause I feel really uncomfortable.
16. H: When was the last time you looked at it?
17. G: Wednesday night. No, last night, last night, yeah, Wednesday night. That's right. I saw his rabbit. It's cute.
18. H: What rabbit? He has a rabbit?
19. G: No, Dennis has a rabbit.
20. H: Dennis has a . . . *(laughs)*—Dennis Snots?
21. G: Yes, Dennis has a rabbit. That big. And it's gray and it's cute. //It really is . . .
22. H: Oh, uh, is it a baby?
23. G: I assume so.
24. H: Awwwww.
25. G: Awwwww. It seems like I gave it to him. You know, that . . . that we . . . you know, when we talked—crew cut, ROTC—he, uh, he told him that I gave it to him. //[garble]
26. H: You mean he just kind of found it there?
27. G: //Yes.
28. H: Just . it was, just //all of a sudden
29. G: It was in Colgate's desk.

30. H: Oh.
31. G: Yeah.
32. H: That's a nice thing to give someone.
33. G: Yeah, I wish I had one of my own. I really do.
34. H: What—a rabbit?
35. G: Anything—parakeet, rabbit, dog.
36. H: Well, you were going to get one.
37. G: //Parakeet.
38. H: How come you didn't?
39. G: Can't afford it.
40. H: Oh, that's a good reason. Why not get a gerbil?
41. G: I don't like gerbils. //They're like rats.
42. H: That's a good reason. //I don't either.
43. G: You like rats?
44. H: You don't like Guinea pigs?
45. G: No.
45. H: You don't like fish?
47. G: Fish are OK.
48. H: I really like goldfish.
49. G: OK.
50. H: Or a silverfish.
51. G: Yeah?
52. H: I have a silverfish.
53. G: You don't have a pet silverfish.
54. H: I do so. It's a goldfish, but it's silver. It's at home.
55. G: There's a difference between a pet goldfish that's silver and a silverfish.
56. H: *(laughs)*
57. G: Silverfish are these ugly things that crawl out of the wall and eat books.
58. H: Do they eat paper?
59. G: Sure they do; it agrees with them.
60. H: Really? Oh, that's neat.
61. G: I have a whole bunch in my closet right now. You want one?
62. H: No.
63. G: Two?
64. H: No.
65. G: Three?
66. H: No.
67. G: I don't want them either.
68. H: You don't want them?
69. G: No. [pause] Is something bothering //you?

70\. H: It's something. Linda.
71\. G: I can tell. I can really tell. What's the problem.
72\. H: Well, I feel really dumb.
73\. G: Why?
74\. H: Well, do you think . . . I think that maybe we should make a couple of compromises with stuff. You know how . . . you know how your stuff, your junk is always on my bed? [pause]
75\. G: Okay.
76\. H: Well, I was wondering, do you think you could keep your junk on your side of the room? And I keep my junk on my side of the room? [pause] Do you think that's a fair compromise? [long pause]
77\. G: That was not worded very nicely.
78\. H: Why not?
79\. G: Well, I don't know why; I don't know why you think my stuff is always on your side of the room.
80\. H: Because my bed is my side of the room, you know [pause] and your bed is your side of the room and my bed is my side of the room. [pause]
81\. G: I . . . don't really agree, but that's all right. Okay . . . //Uh
82\. H: Well, wait. If you don't agree, then we should talk it all out.
83\. G: No, no, okay, okay. I'll try to keep my stuff off you bed, but I don't do it on purpose. I don't use your bed as a . . . as a . . .
84\. H: Oh, I know you don't. It's just like, you know, I'll come in to sit down on my bed and there will be all this junk on it. [pause] And it's just that I don't know where to put it 'cause it's not mine. And I don't know where it belongs so [pause] it's, you know [pause] . . . if you could just keep it on your side of the room.
85\. G: Okay, Susan. *(laughs)* Okay.
86\. H: *(laughs)*
87\. G: Anything else?
88\. H: Yeah, also, you know how last night the windows were open and it was 28 degrees out?
89\. G: Aw, come on. Oh . . . okay. Go ahead.
90\. H: Well.
91\. G: Yeah.
92\. H: Do you think it would be possible to leave the windows like just half open or something?
93\. G: I don't think I leave them open that much. You know I can't

always sleep without at least some air in the room. Like I get claustrophobic. //You know

94. H: Well, maybe we should rearrange the room then.
95. G: That is a //great idea. I mean
96. H: Yeah
97. G: Like put me //nearer the window.
98. H: Yeah. Yeah, because we are both near a window now. If you're near all the windows and I'm away from all the windows . . .
99. G: Then I'll get all the air and you won't get any of it.
100. H: Yeah.
101. G: Great . . . fine, great, okay.

CHAPTER 9

Orderliness, Disorder and Strategy in Ordinary Conversation

The purpose of this chapter is to show that numerous features of ordinary conversation are strategic. Of course, to a degree this follows directly from the preceding chapters—much that is strategic in conversation involves details of content, style, and sequencing to control understandings and constrain subsequent entries, as in Conversation I and Conversation II (Wiemann, 1977). But in addition, turn-taking, and topic development and topic change, can be strategic—not only when turns and topic management are coordinated, but when they are not.

Conversation has been an object of study in sociology, cognitive science, language studies, and communication. The singular achievement of this work is its demonstration that in addition to being socially important, ordinary conversation is unexpectedly complicated. Conversants have options of utterance and behavior to select from that facilitate (or undermine) the orderliness and coordination of turn-taking and topic development, in addition to options of content and style that they take to bring about desired interpretive consequences (e.g., Goffman, 1959; Garfinkel, 1967; Sacks, Schegloff and Jefferson, 1974; Nofsinger, 1975; Pearce, 1976; Schank and Abelson, 1977; Labov and Fanshel, 1977; Reichman, 1978; Duncan, Brunner and Fiske, 1979; Psathas, 1979; Goodwin, 1981; Hopper, 1981; Keller, 1981; Gumperz, 1982a; Tracy, 1982; Crow, 1983; Goldberg, 1983; Jacobs and Jackson, 1983a, 1983b; Levinson, 1983: 284-370; Sanders, 1983, 1984).

However, two strikingly different pictures of conversation have developed. One view has at its center Sacks, Schegloff and Jefferson's (1974) analysis of turn-taking. Conversation is regarded as an intricate and complicated social activity, where (1) participants have to alternate and coordinate their respective contributions, and (2) there are specific devices and protocols that conversants employ to achieve this. It is an activity which is possible because there are shared rules, at minimum procedural rules, that conversants rely on to achieve coordination:

> [T]he existence of organized turn–taking is something that the data of conversation have made increasingly plain. It has become obvious that, overwhelmingly, one party talks at a time, though speakers change, and though the size of turns and ordering of turns vary; that transitions are finely coordinated; that techniques are used for allocating turns, whose characterization would be part of any model for describing turn–taking materials; and that there are techniques for the construction of utterances relevant to their turn status, which bear on the coordination of transfer and on the allocation of speakership. (p. 699)

This point of departure has fostered an atomistic examination of conversational means and ends which has been extremely fruitful, particularly in bringing to the surface that micro-features of utterance and behavior elaborately orchestrate the collaborative aspects of conversation (e.g., Sacks, Schegloff and Jefferson, 1974; Reichman, 1978; Duncan, Brunner and Fiske, 1979; Craig and Tracy, 1983; Atkinson and Heritage, 1984). These data reveal strategic utilities in much finer details of utterance and behavior than had previously been recognized, and consequently they are suggestive of the level at which people are able, when necessary, to monitor themselves and others.

But there are studies of conversation which reveal a far less orchestrated and finely–tuned social activity. More importantly, they reveal what was otherwise missed—the subtle and complex ways in which differences in the background knowledge, social norms and conventions, and personal attitudes of conversants influence the way in which they participate in conversation.

Edelsky (1981) and Erickson (1982) have provided transcripts and analysis of conversations which comprise interruptions, simultaneous speech, uncompleted turns, side comments, different simultaneous topics, and rapid topic changes. Edelsky (1981) in particular found that her data created fundamental questions about what the objective reality of a "turn at speech" is, and found herself forced to attempt a distinction between "having a turn at speech" and "taking the floor" in order to explain certain functional differences among utterances.

Further, Tannen (1984) has provided a transcript and analysis of an extended dinner–table conversation which reveals that the six conversants had markedly different, personalized ways of participating. While each relied on certain linguistic and nonverbal devices to regulate and coordinate participation, there were enough differences among them about these devices, as well as in their respective agenda, to have created a certain amount of uncoordination and misunderstandings as well as different levels of participation and control.

When there are data that support two contrasting pictures of the same phenomenon, then there must almost certainly be a valid way to transcend the apparent contradiction and accept both pictures. The principles of specific interpretation in Chapters 4 and 6, and the forecasting principles in Chapter 8, can be applied to integrating the disparate pictures we have about conversation. In particular, applying these principles to conversation analysis makes it possible to achieve the following objectives:

1. An explanation of the fact that conversants can and do make contributions in disregard of requirements for order and coordination, without engendering confusion and conversational breakdown.
2. A correct representation of the power of regulatory devices and protocols as constraining, rather than "necessitating" or "dictating," the alternation of turns and the development of topics.
3. The generalization that the use and force of regulatory devices and protocols depends, just as the selection of "substantive" options of utterance and behavior does, on projections of what is required at a given juncture to bring about desired consequences, or at least avoid undesired ones.

Work following Sacks, Schegloff and Jefferson (1974) has focused on the observable devices and protocols that conversants utilize to achieve order and coordination. However, it is implausible that order and coordination (and disorder and uncoordination) depend entirely on such regulatory signals. Details of utterance and behavior that are regulatory of turns and topics can occur incidentally, or mistakenly, or be equivocal, or be overlooked. If such signals are the sole basis for order and coordination in turn–taking and topic management, it should be the case that any error in providing or apprehending a regulatory signal will necessarily result in a failure of coordination, and conversely, that failures of coordination necessarily follow from such errors. This has not been investigated directly, but the available data obviously do not support it.

A more important limitation of such studies of turn–taking and topic development is that they take for granted that it is a practical necessity to achieve orderliness and coordination. The assumption is that conversants could not otherwise ensure mutual understanding and progress towards shared goals. Again, this entails that disorder and uncoordination must be consequences of communicator inability, error, or excitation, and will necessarily produce confusion and breakdown. Again, this is contrary to the data.

In that case, for people to converse with any reasonable chance of being heard, let alone achieving something, conversants must have an additional, cognitive basis for identifying the transition boundaries within turns and topics, distinguishing between entries intended to be contributions and spurious ones, and organizing contributions into coherent wholes (e.g., episodes). The existence of such cognitive underpinnings is certainly consistent with such data as Edelsky's (1981), Erickson's (1982), and Tannen's (1984).

However, even though some of these data suggest it, none of this entails the conclusion that conversants can and do independently pursue their own goals, and say and do whatever they want, whenever they want to. Except for very young children, people generally have conversations to achieve an exchange of some kind with others, not to unilaterally express themselves. To have an exchange, conversants have to limit what they say and do, have to be constrained by the projected consequences in taking and yielding the floor, managing topics, taking turns, and being orderly or disorderly. Conversants thus are strategic, not necessarily to achieve certain results, but at least to the extent of avoiding incoherence, and not making possible (i.e., relevant) undesired topics or undesired outcomes.

The strategic aspects of conversation are bound to be overlooked whether one assumes that conversants have their separate methods and goals and make unilateral contributions, or assumes that there are shared rules for ordering and coordinating turns and topics. And if the strategic aspects of conversation are overlooked, the generalization is lost that both orderliness and disorder are options, not a necessity or necessarily a dysfunction, respectively.

There are times when there is social utility in disorder, in interruptions and other struggles for the floor, as well as jumping abruptly from one topic to another, or dragging out a single topic *ad nauseum* (e.g., when conversants have interpersonal agenda or conflicting purposes). It depends on the conversants' goals, and what those require that conversants do to foster (1) desired (re)interpretations of antecedents or (2) the possibility and probability of desired subsequent entries.

If conversational disorder can result from the exercise of strategic options—not necessarily from error, inability, or excitation—then achieving order and coordination must also result from the exercise of strategic options, not out of practical necessity. Granted, the option of utilizing available devices and protocols to coordinate turns and topics is probably taken for the sake of expediency much of the time, to minimize the cognitive burden of formulating and understanding entries, or out of politeness to show respect for the other. But there are times when orderly turn-taking and topic development have great utility, and interruptions, topic changes and the like would be dysfunctional (e.g., when co-workers collaborate on performing some task or solving some problem). In addition, coordination on turns and topics is an option that can be taken for other, more subtle strategic purposes, in particular to disguise interpersonal attitudes and agenda (e.g., Sanders, 1983, and below).

The account of strategic communication in conversation which is developed in the following sections makes explicit the dependence of turn-taking and topic development on projections of others' intended contributions and agenda. In the section immediately following, it is shown that when turn-taking is disorderly, intrusions in another's turn may nonetheless be harmless or even facilitative insofar as the offending conversant has projected what the entry in progress is intended to contribute. Following that, it is shown that the way topics are defined, developed and changed depends on what the conversant(s)' agenda are presumed to be, and that agenda in turn are inferred on the basis of the way entries are sequenced, turns taken, and topics managed. Finally, a strategic interdependence is show between agenda, topic development, and turn-taking in an excerpt from a televised talk/interview program, the *Donahue* show.

TURNS AT SPEAKING AND INTENDED CONTRIBUTIONS

Sacks, Schegloff, and Jefferson's (1974) analysis of turn–taking implies that when people interrupt each other and/or talk at the same time, it represents a failure to correctly employ the rules and techniques of turn-taking. In some cases, uncoordination about turns at talk does result from such errors and conversants respond to it accordingly.

For example, Gumperz (1982a: 145–47) describes a conversation among several graduate students, one of them an Indian woman, where the Indian commits more interruptions than the others (yet protested afterwards she had not intended to interrupt), and was interrupted more by the others (who said afterwards they thought in each instance she had finished her turn). To explain this, Gumperz cites cross-cultural differences in the nonverbal cues used to coordinate turn-taking.

But Gumperz gives a specific example of this uncoordination which involves more than that. The Indian (IW) interrupts a black woman (BW) as she is summing up her previously stated thesis about the relationship between specializations in her field:

[1] BW: It's like all parts of the hand. The fingers operate independently, but they have the same–
IW: What I would like to say is . . .

Gumperz does not attribute this interruption simply to IW's misreadings of nonverbal cues, but rather to IW's ignorance of the formula in BW's speech community of making (and completing) extended similes in summation. This formula warrants redundancy at certain junctures. IW's interruption interfered with that formulaic redundancy, but not with the contribution BW evidently intended to make to the coherence and progress of the sequence. IW took the floor just at the point where BW had functionally effected that contribution.

Gumerpz' remarks imply that IW would not necessarily have erred by taking the floor 'early'—before BW signaled that she was yielding—were it not for the convention/norm by which BW's redundancy was warranted.

The point at which IW took the floor away from BW indicates

that she had an independent basis for projecting what contribution BW intended her entry to make. There is of course strategic utility in projecting the contributions intended by the other. First, such projections enable the current speaker to estimate the interpretive consequences of yielding the floor at a given juncture. Second, they enable conversants to avoid substantively interfering with each other, while minimizing their dependence on the current speaker's readiness to yield the floor in a timely and equitable way. Third, they enable conversants to take the floor before it has been surrendered in order to help each other formulate entries so as to make the intended contribution. These predict that not all interruptions are interruptions.

Let us distinguish between the BRUTE FACT of an INTERRUPTION$_1$ (a physical event where one speaker begins making an entry while another speaker still has the floor) and the INSTITUTIONAL FACT of an INTERRUPTION$_2$ (an interference with the contribution that the conversant intends). It is evident from the data below in [2]–[4] that while speakers can and do unilaterally attempt to signal at transition boundaries whether they are ending or continuing their turns, those signals may not be waited for, or may be missed or disregarded. This could of course result in an interruption$_2$, but it often results just in an interruption$_1$. Mere interruptions$_1$ may be rude, as BW evidently considered IW's was in [1]. But they are often harmless, as in [2], and sometimes (intended to be) facilitative, as in [3]:

[2] Traffic Court (Pollner, 1979: 233)

Judge: Well, I don't know—car in fron' of yuh I, don't know thetchud' be guilty, why don't yuh plead not guilty en set it down fer trial.
Defendant: Well, it's a matter of uh, (pause) of,
Judge: //Of econom
Defendant: time en
Judge: ics?
Defendant: inconvenience sir. (clears throat) (pause)

[3] From Conversation III (Wiemann, 1977)

26. B. Oh, good. We can do it [try out B's kite] here one day.
27. A: Yeah, bring it down to the . . . the field by Morray Gym. //Where the, uh
28. B: At the tennis . . .?
29. A: No, uh, uh. We could do it there,

> too, but it's not as large. The field where they practice golf over, like there's Hickman and there's the walkover bridge and here's Loree Gym.

In order for a conversant to interrupt$_1$, without interrupting$_2$, and to interrupt$_1$ in ways that are either harmless or facilitative, it is necessary for him/her to have projected correctly what contribution the other intended to make. The grounds that conversants have for such projections have been identified previously.

1. What the other conversant would be disposed to contribute, given his/her cognitions, personality, role.
2. What it is conventional or normative within the social practice or institution in effect to contribute at that juncture.
3. The features that the specific interpretation of the next entry would need for it to contribute to the ground of coherence and agenda at that juncture.

In addition, given the ability to project the contribution currently intended, then the 'victims' of both interruptions$_1$ and interruptions$_2$ can induce whether they are accidental, or are intended to make some particular contribution to the coherence and progress of the sequence. In that case, victims will generally be able to cope with interruptions, and can optionally allow, disregard, or object to them. The fragment of conversation in [4] below strongly supports this. That fragment includes three interruptions (and three changes of topic) in the space of thirteen turns, but these do not result in any evident confusion:

[4] From Conversation III (Wiemann, 1977)

35. A: That's terrible. That's really terrible. (clears throat) I didn't get pixied today.
36. B: You didn't? Well, Nancy got pixied. She got this big plant. //So I took it in the room . . .
37. A: Got this big what?
38. B: Plant.
39. A: I thought you said "clam." (laughs) What would Nancy do with a clam? (Long pause) Uh, that's really str . . . Were you outside when it rained today? At, oh, like 12 o'clock or so? I heard there was this real thunderstorm.

//Not just a calm
40. B: I was in class.
41. A: thundershower. I was in the commons eating lunch. I was at the commons for a long time today . . .
42. B: Yeah.
43. A: Uh (pause) and I . . . it . . . it was wet out when I came out and I heard it had been thundering and lightning and everything and everyone loved it.
44. B: I was in class. I //was looking out
45. A: Oh, that's right.
46. B: the window.
47. A: Did you have that exam . . . no, you didn't have that exam today?

A's interruption of B's turn 36 came just at the juncture where B had not articulated clearly her reference to Nancy's purchase. The interruption to request clarification was motivated insofar as A had projected that it would make a substantial difference in the content and quality of the subsequent narrative what that particular referent was—a *big clam* (novel but implausible) or something else. That this was the motivation, and that B had inferred it, is borne out by the fact that B did not continue the narrative after clarifying the referent, but yielded the floor, thus giving the informed A the option of endorsing continuation of the narrative, or making a substitution (as she did).

In contrast, B's interruption of A's turn 39 came at a juncture where A had begun elaborating a question, and thus it could be considered the result of a failure by A to clearly signal that she was continuing her turn at speaking. However, B's effort to answer the question at that juncture could have been motivated regardless of A's turn-taking cues insofar as she had projected that it would make a difference to A's agenda that B had not been outside during the storm. A's interruption of B's turn 44 bears this out. The interruption comes just at the juncture that B restates her earlier talked-over answer. The motivation for A's interruption at turn 44 is conceivably identical to B's motivation for having intruded that answer earlier, a projection that B could not usefully contribute on the topic of the thundershower if she had been indoors. Note that A's interruption at that juncture uses B's answer to introduce a new topic.

TOPICS AND AGENDA

It has been recognized that conversants are able to conduct conversations with fairly high levels of disorder in terms of topic management as well as turn-taking (Erickson, 1982). However, the question remains how this is possible.

Identifying the Topic of Conversation

The operationalization of 'topic' is problematic. The common sense notion of 'the topic of conversation' in the terms developed above is that it is the ground of coherence across the content of a contiguous sequence of entries—(features of) a person, object, situation, act or event that the content of entries in the sequence are commonly about. But this will not work.

When entries in a sequence cohere on the basis of their content, that ground of coherence can be equated with the topic of conversation, but the reverse is not necessarily the case. Topics can develop in sequences that do not cohere in terms of the content of their constituents. For example, a conversation on the topic of promoting a nuclear freeze could relevantly include entries that are about the indebtedness of individual members of Congress to defense industries. While the content of such entries is not about the promotion of a nuclear freeze, those entries are likely to implicate propositions about the motivations of opponents of a nuclear freeze, and thus to have a connection to the topic.

An alternative operationalization of 'topic' is to identify it with the script (or some such knowledge structure) that comprises all of the various states of affairs that the specific interpretations of constituent entries are about, implicate or enact (Schank and Abelson, 1977). However, if topics are identified with knowledge structures, so that the content of each entry on the topic represents some segment of the knowledge structure(s) in use, it is difficult to explain how conversants are able to introduce new information without being perceived to have entered a non sequitur or to have changed the topic. The introduction of new information on a topic without such consequences would only be possible if conversants take it as a given that all contributions are about components of the given knowledge structure. Then, whenever information is provided that is not already included in that knowledge structure, conversants would have to presume it to be 'new information' on the topic to be incorporated into the knowledge structure. But in that case, there is no objective basis for distinguishing non sequiturs and entries that change the topic from entries on the topic that provide new information.

With reference to the objective record, the parameters of a topic are in fact elusive in just that way. Derber (1979: 29–30) gives the following conversation as an example of the way an egoist (Bill) manipulates the topic so that he will remain the center of attention. However, to construe Bill's agenda as egocentric, one has to define the topic(s) of that conversation in a certain way, and there is no objective basis for doing so:

[5] Cars and Bikes

Jim: You know, I've been wanting to get a car for so long.
Bill: Yeah.
Jim: Maybe when I get the job this summer, I'll finally buy one. But they're so expensive.
Bill: I was just thinking about how much I spend on my car. I think over $1500 a year. You know I had to lay out over $750 for insurance. And $250 for that fender job.
Jim: Yeah, It's absurd.
Bill: I'm sick of cars. I've been thinking of getting a bicycle and getting around in a healthy way. I saw a great red racer up in that bike shop on Parkhurst Ave.
Jim: I love bikes. But I'm just really feeling a need for a car now. I just want to be able to drive up the coast whenever I want.
Bill: Uh huh . . .
Jim: I could really get into a convertible.
Bill: Oh, you can go anywhere on a bike. I'm going to borrow John's bike and go way up north next weekend. You know, a couple of weekends ago Sue and I rented bikes and rode down toward the Cape . . .

If the original topic in [5] is defined as Jim's desire for a car, then Derber is justified in characterizing Bill's entries as egocentric. Bill's introduction of talk about bikes and about his recent weekend with Sue would represent topic changes that are unmotivated unless Bill's agenda is to keep talk focused on himself. But suppose we define the original topic as the pros and cons of owning a car, not Jim's desire for a car. Bill's introduction of talk about bikes and biking excursions then is not a change of topic, but is support for his position that Jim is not worse off for being without a car. In that case, it would be unjustified to consider Bill's entries as egocentric; to the contrary, they would have to be considered other-directed.

Although there are limits on what the topic of conversation can be construed as being, given the content and grounds of coherence of entries in the sequence, there is little objective basis for any particular definition of the topic (even when the notion of the basis for definition includes knowledge structures). Rather, let us take the issue raised by [5] as paradigmatic and postulate the following:

> Within the topical parameters created by the content and ground of coherence in a segment of conversation:
>
> 1. Definitions of topic depend on what the conversants' agenda are construed as being.
> 2. Construals of the conversants' agenda depend on the way topics are defined.

Conversational Agenda

The various agenda that conversants can have are reducible to two types. There are INFORMATIONAL agenda, where conversants talk for such purposes as obtaining or providing information, reconciling conflicting beliefs, and coordinating work on some task. And there are INTERPERSONAL agenda, where conversants talk for various purposes related to face-work, definition of the situation, or the creation, definition or dissolution of their relationship to each other or to third parties.

Informational Agenda

Given any such agenda, the problem for conversants would be to ensure common understandings of what the subject matter at hand is, and to develop and sustain talk about it until information has been exchanged as needed, agreement has been reached, work on the task has been coordinated, etc. The study of topic management from this point of view presumes that it is a practical necessity for topic development and topic change to be orderly and coordinated, and that the problem for conversants is to ensure a shared understanding of what subject matter is at issue, and of marking which aspect of that subject matter each new entry is about, and what its intended contribution is (e.g., Halliday and Hasan, 1976; Dascal, 1977; Reichman, 1978; Grimes, 1982; Tracy, 1982; van Dijk, 1982).

Given the postulate above, however, it also follows that insofar as topics are initiated, developed and changed in an explicit and orderly way, the conversants' agenda must be informational. This can have strategic utility.

For example, in a casual conversation between two women transcribed by Craig and Tracy (1983: 299–320), there is an exceptional degree of orderliness. Most of the entries are semantically chained, and there are few interruptions and talk-overs. Given the postulate above, this warrants construing the agenda of the women as having to do with information exchange. However, there is reason to consider that their orderliness was strategic, to conceal their interpersonal agenda (Sanders, 1983).

The women were sufficiently different in age, social class, experience, attitudes and values that there was a potential for competition or antagonism between them. In addition, the content of their entries was primarily about autobiographical details that accentuated the differences between them. Moreover, there was a recurrent pattern in the development and change of topics that resembles a series of interpersonal skirmishes, with one of the women seeking to establish herself as having higher status than the other, while her partner sought to keep an equal footing. Topics (defined on the basis of common features across the content of entries) were developed by first identifying a dimension along which the women could compare themselves. The entries of one woman—the older, more cosmopolitan one—accentuated her social advantages over her partner or minimized her own disadvantages; the entries of the younger woman were generally reactive counters to her partner's representations of social advantage. Topics were changed each time differences in their representations of relative worth on some dimension were resolved, which happens to always have been in favor of the older conversant.

The orderliness of the conversation had the strategic utility of preventing these skirmishes from coming to the surface. This resulted first because such orderliness warrants construals of informational rather than interpersonal agenda. Second, the ground of coherence involved in that orderly progression warranted a focus on propositional content, rather than on the implicated judgments and acts of condescension and self-aggrandisement that fueled their conflict.

Interpersonal Agenda

Talk on a topic might not be undertaken for its own sake, but because it is projected as being instrumental to effecting some change in the interpersonal status quo, (e.g., Shuy, 1982). Given such an agenda (such as self-concept verification, role differentiation, negotiating power relations, interpersonal bonding or distancing), there is unlikely to be much regard for topical continuity or for many regulatory cues because topics are initiated, developed and dropped as called for by each conversant's agenda. It is consistent with this that Crow (1983) observed topic shifts on the average of one every 48 seconds in the respective conversations of five couples.

In that case, given the postulate above, insofar as topics are developed in a disorderly and uncoordinated way, it will be construed that the conversants' agenda are interpersonal in nature. Being disorderly in this respect can therefore have strategic utility.

For example, DeVito (1983: 430–431) constructed the conversation from which [6] below is excerpted to illustrate the way family relations surface in their communication with each other. DeVito's object was to exhibit family tensions and antagonisms. He achieved this in part by the way he formulated individual entries, particularly by the use of abusive language, slurs and threats. But of importance to the postulate here, he also achieved this by the development of topics in a sufficiently disordered and uncoordinated way to warrant the construal of interpersonal rather than informational agenda.

[6] Family Conflict

Mother: O.K. Dinner's almost ready. Come on. Wash up and sit down.

(at table)

Daughter: Mom, I'm going to the shore for the weekend with some friends from work.

Mother: O.K. When will you be leaving?
Daughter: Friday afternoon, right after work.
Father: Like hell you're going. No more going to the shore with that group.
Mother: Fred, they're nice people. Why shouldn't she go?
Father: Because I said so, O.K.? Finished. Closed.
Daughter: (mumbling): I'm 22 years old and he gives me problems. You make me feel like a kid, like some stupid little kid.
Father: Get married and then you can tell your husband what to do.
Daughter: I wish I could.
Son: But nobody'll ask her.
Mother: Why should she get married? She's got a good life—good job, nice friends, good home. Listen, I was talking with Elizabeth and Cara this morning and they both feel they've just wasted their lives. They raised a family and what have they got? They got nothing. (To daughter): And don't think sex is so great either; it isn't, believe me.
Father: Well, they're idiots.
Mother: They're idiots? (snidely) Yeah, I guess they are.
Daughter: Joanne's getting married.
Mother: Who's Joanne?
Son: That creature who lives with that guy Michael.
Father: Watch your mouth wise-ass. Don't be disrespectful to your mother or I'll teach you how to act right.
Mother: Well, how do you like the dinner?
(prolonged silence)
Daughter: Do you think I should be in the wedding party if Joanne asks me? I think she will; we always said we'd be in each other's wedding.
Mother: Sure, why not. It'll be nice.
Father: I'm not going to no wedding; no matter who's in it.
Son: Me neither.
Daughter: I hope you'll both feel that way when I get married.
Son: By then I'll be too old to remember I got a sister.

STRATEGIC TURN-TAKING AND TOPIC MANAGEMENT

Whether conversants are engaged in some task or are just chatting, there is a potential for them to face possible outcomes which they are disposed to promote or avoid. Such outcomes of conversation can be the satisfactory completion of the task and/or changes e.g., in interpersonal distance, in cognitive similarity (in held information, beliefs, or dispositions), and in sociological cohesion (in roles, norms, and conventions). Thus, there are strategic considerations even in non–task oriented conversations. Topic development and turn–taking have the following connection to those strategic considerations.

What the topic is and the way it develops, and the opportunity to have regular turns at talk, are critical to ensuring that the unfolding conversation will provide each communicator with the opportunity to make entries that warrant desired interpretations of subsequent messages he/she intends to produce, or constrain what it would be coherent and productive for others to say or do subsequently.

The conversation in [7] below is excerpted from the *Donahue* Show (Transcript #10132, given to me by W.B. Pearce). The *Donahue* show often features representatives of the opposing sides of a social controversy and serves as a forum in which their differences can be aired and debated. This is a relatively unusual conversational setting, but it is nonetheless a rich source of data for present purposes, given the high incentive in this situation to engage in strategic communication. The conversation in [7] is about the moral and social dimensions of homosexuality. In addition to Donahue, the participants are Jerry Falwell and columnist Cal Thomas, opponents of gay rights who then represented The Moral Majority, and Virginia Apuzzo and Dan Bradley, advocates of gay rights who then represented the Human Rights Campaign Fund.

[7] On the Agenda for Debating Gay Rights (Transcript pp. 9–13)

1. Thomas (to Apuzzo): I want to know if there is anything sexually that you believe is wrong.
2. Apuzzo: I will tell you something: we are concerned with the Constitution of the United States–
3. Thomas: Is there anything sexual that you believe is wrong? Anything!
4. Apuzzo: What I believe is–
5. Thomas: Trees, dogs, whatever–
6. Donahue: Can I try and answer him? I'm good about talking about sex things that are wrong. That's my area.
7. Falwell: By the way, can I go along as a chaplin on your Paris trip?

8. Donahue: Let me answer you. Intimate activity which involves the exploitation of another person, involves another person against his or her will, injures the other person, hurts the other person with evidence that it is wrong.
9. Thomas: You don't think homosexuals have been hurt.
10. Apuzzo: I've been hurt. I think we've been hurt and you've hurt us.
11. Bradley: We've been hurt because of the fear–
12. Thomas: Adulterers.
13. Bradley: –the discrimination that people like you and my good friend Reverend Falwell preach in the pulpit.
14. Thomas: What I'm trying to get at without letting you slip away from this, I'm asking you if there is any standard in America for right and wrong and based on what?
15. Apuzzo: The Constitution.
16. Thomas: The Constitution?
17. Falwell: What about the Judeo-Christian ethic? You mentioned you had a Baptist upbringing. Do you believe the Bible is the Word of God?
18. Donahue: Here we go now. We're going to need a four hour show here.
19. Thomas: We're trying to find out what their standards are, if they have any standards.
20. Bradley: The standards are—and see, the problem with Reverend Falwell and the other–
21. Falwell: I read the Bible is my problem.
22. Bradley: –preachers of condemnation, the preachers of hate, the preachers of not forgiveness, the preachers not of love—I mean what they are trying to do is reduce what we're talking about as a simple question of basic common decency, fairness, legality.
23. Falwell: We are talking about common decency.
24. Bradley: Fairness. Black people are not going to sit on the back of the bus any longer. Women are not going to stay in the kitchen any more. And gay people are not going to stay in the closet any longer.
25. Donahue: I'll tell you what I've noticed. I've noticed a lowering of the venom and the accusatory nature of statements from religious figures. Obviously they're not getting a standing ovation within the fundamentalist Christian community. But I think–

26. Falwell: Or the Orthodox Jewish Community, or the Roman Catholic Community. Excuse me, go ahead.
27. Donahue: Okay, you have a point. But I think that there is a growing awareness that maybe we had better not be too harsh on this. These folks got a lot of votes or these people are present in greater numbers than we heretofore ever realized.

The concern here is to identify the strategic utility and principled basis for the way in which these conversants took turns and developed topics. Of particular importance theoretically, there is as much strategic utility involved in instances where topic development and turn-taking were disordered, as when they were ordered.

There are a number of instances in [7] which (on the surface) involve disorder and uncoordination:

There are uncoordinated turn transitions at turns 3, 5, 8, 12, and 21 (5 turns out of the total 27).

There are shifts in the ground of coherence or applicable knowledge structure—the topic—at turns 7–8, 12–13, 14, 17, 18, 19, 20, and 25 (10 of 27 turns).

However, it should be recognized that to a degree the conversation's disorder was compensated for by explicit statements of intent and overt markers of the ground of coherence across apparent topic changes:

Explicit statements of conversational agenda at turns 1, 14, and 19.

Semantic chaining between distinct knowledge structures at turns 8–10, and 19–20.

Explicit statements of what particular entries were intended to contribute at turns 6, 8, 14, and 25—most by Donahue, likely more necessary for him to do than the others because of the equivocal basis of his right to the floor, sometimes as host and moderator, sometimes as a partisan discussant.

To account for the features of this conversation listed above it will be helpful to make the conversational 'problem' explicit that was involved.

The agenda announced by Thomas at turn 1 was to elicit,

presumably so he could challenge and renounce, a statement from Apuzzo and Bradley of the sexual morality they endorsed. However, Apuzzo and Bradley had a different agenda, implied particularly by Apuzzo's entries—to show that gay rights involve constitutional protections, moral reservations notwithstanding. This conflict over setting the conversational agenda was strategically critical. Apuzzo and Bradley could not have made a substantial case for gay rights in the context of a debate about Judaeo–Christian strictures regarding sexual conduct. Thomas and Falwell in turn could not have made a substantial case against the social acceptance of homosexuality in the context of a debate about personal liberties that are protected by the Constitution. In addition, this conflict over agenda was not in Donahue's interest because as long as it continued, it prevented anyone from engaging substantively in the kind of debate that attracts Donahue's audience.

The interruptions and topic changes that occur in this conversation thus make good strategic sense. In turns 1–5, Apuzzo could not easily have put her agenda on the table and discounted Thomas' except by not responding to Thomas' requests for information and by introducing an entirely different topic. Thomas in turn could not easily have avoided discussing Apuzzo's agenda in stating his objections to it except by interrupting her and reiterating his own. Note that Apuzzo's introduction of a distinct topic in turn 2 must have been predicated on her projecting the strategic consequences of replying to Thomas, and that Thomas' subsequent interruptions must have been predicated on his projecting the strategic consequences of giving Apuzzo an opening to advocate her preferred agenda.

Donahue's effort at that point to break the impasse also can be attributed to his projecting the strategic consequences of letting Thomas and Apuzzo continue. For his mediation to succeed, Donahue had to provide a solution that served the interests of both parties. He evidently sought to do this by proposing the adoption of Thomas' agenda, but in terms of ethical criteria that conceivably would have enabled Apuzzo and Bradley to justify their focus on constitutional guarantees of individual liberties.

Donahue's solution was not adopted, indicating that the others projected it was not in their interest. This left the conversants without an agenda, and thus with no basis for saying anything substantive at that point about gay rights. In that case, they had little alternative to the exchange of ad hominem attacks that followed.

When Thomas reintroduced his agenda in turn 14, Apuzzo this time stated her contrary agenda as a relevant answer to Thomas' question. Thomas evidently had not projected that that was possible, and taken by surprise, he only echoed her answer. This made it relevant—coherent and productive—for Apuzzo to explain and develop her agenda. Falwell's taking the floor at that point before Apuzzo could claim it indicates that he projected what was going to follow. He further offset Apuzzo's advantage at that point by confronting her with personal questions that put Thomas' agenda back on the table.

Hence, the same impasse was reached in turn 17 that had been reached in turns 4–5. Donahue's taking the floor at that point indicates he projected this. However, in contrast with his previous effort to mediate, his change of topic in turn 18 implicated his dissatisfaction with the direction the conversation would likely take following Thomas' and Falwell's agenda.

Thomas' restatement of his preference for that agenda in turn 19 left the conversants in the same position they were in after Donahue's previous intrusion. There was no shared agenda, and thus no basis for making substantive contributions. There was little alternative in that case to Bradley's commenting on the impasse itself, blaming it on Thomas' and Falwell's rigidity and hostility. But Falwell countered Bradley's attack by stating that their concern was also 'common decency', something that Bradley had attributed to himself and Apuzzo. This blurred the lines of difference and deflected Bradley's attack. Bradley was left with little he could relevantly say that would not risk further confusing the issue. He thus did not reply to Falwell, and instead brought Apuzzo's agenda back up by citing the insistence on their civil rights of historically disenfranchised constituencies.

This deepening of the impasse over the agenda at that juncture is evidently what led Donahue to make his third effort to transcend it, this time by introducing an entirely new topic—the political/pragmatic dimensions of gay rights.

The conversation in [7] thus provides substantial evidence that a decision-theoretic account of strategic communication applies even to topic development and turn-taking. The interruptions and frequent changes of topic in [7], their placement, and the fact that they did not result in any evident confusion or breakdown in coordination, all indicate that entries were constrained by projections of their interpretive consequences.

THE UTILITY OF ORDERLINESS AND DISORDER

Conversational disorder does not entail confusion and breakdown insofar as it is strategic rather than accidental. Further, strategic considerations can foster a substantial disregard of orderliness and coordination. The theoretical question in that case is not so much how do conversants achieve orderly and coordinated conversations, but why do they?

Order and coordination in conversations, like any other form of etiquette, is not a practical necessity, but a general defensive strategy, all else being equal.

First, as noted above, orderly turn-taking and topic development is an expedient because it enables a high degree of predictability and a corresponding minimization of cognitive work. Second, orderliness and coordination generally depend on adopting conventional roles and practices, and thus the effort to coordinate reaffirms the basic social contract of the family, group or community.

Third, pertaining directly to strategic communication, it was considered above that proceeding in an orderly and coordinated way reduces the degree to which one can be perceived as having an interpersonal agenda. More importantly, conversing in an orderly way reduces the degree to which one can be perceived as exercising options in the formulation of utterances and behaviors, and thus reduces the basis others have for inductions about one's character and traits.

Given that conversants are able to project the contribution which the current entry is intended to make, and what consequences of the current entry are possible and probable, forecasting principles (and underlying principles of specific interpretation) have utility in accounting for the following:

1. Conversants can and do make contributions in disregard of requirements for order and coordination, without engendering confusion and conversational breakdown.

2. Regulatory devices and protocols constrain, rather than "necessitate" or "dictate," the alternation of turns and the development of topics.
3. The use and force of regulatory devices and protocols depends, just as the selection of "substantive" options of utterance and behavior does, on projection of what is required at a given junctive to bring about desired consequences, or at least avoid undesired ones.

CHAPTER 10

Persuasion: Constraining Individuals and Changing Social Aggregates

This chapter has been written to achieve two goals, and is correspondingly divided into two parts. The primary goal is to show that strategic communication is involved in persuasion to a greater degree and in a different way than is generally acknowledged. While persuasive discourse is strategic by definition, its strategic aspects have been conceived narrowly as having to do primarily with what information the discourse provides and how its presentation is ordered (e.g., Marwell and Schmitt, 1967; Burgoon and Bettinghaus, 1980; Woelfel and Fink, 1980). The importance of linguistic form and phrasing, and of nonverbals, have gotten only sporadic attention (e.g., Pearce and Conklin, 1971; Sandell, 1977) and been considered as mainly having an effect on inductions about the communicator.

Further, it has not been seriously considered that individuals' responses to persuasive discourse are themselves strategic. It is a methodological concern in both laboratory and field research that respondents are often strategic about reporting their reactions to persuasive appeals (i.e., they are responsive to social-demand characteristics in the reporting situation, which I equate with being constrained by the interpretive consequences of what they report). But these strategic reports have been viewed as covering up the real effects of such appeals on the cognitions of respondents. This obviously overlooks the possibility that the practical effects of such appeals are precisely that they alter what individuals consider it strategic to report or publicly display in reaction.

These considerations, and a basis for pursuing them, follow from the core idea in this book that entries in discourses and dialogues can affect the meanings and do affect the specific interpretations of what is said and done subsequently, and thus constrain communicators and their respondents in the way they formulate their utterances and behaviors.

The secondary goal here is to conclude this book by putting in context the account of strategic communication it provides. The description above of the strategic aspects of persuasion contrasts with the widespread view that persuasive discourse affects individuals' conduct by inducing real changes in their beliefs or attitudes. That view presupposes that people generally act out of convictions they have about objects and situations—out of what they regard as true and false, right and wrong, desirable and undesirable about them—rather than out of concern for the social consequences of what they say and do.

Of course, neither view can be preferred to the other on a priori grounds. In the abstract most public conduct has both practical (material) consequences and social (interpretive) consequences. This raises the key question for studies of public conduct in general and communication in particular. Are actors prone to organize their social lives around the symbolic needs or benefits for what they say and do? Or do actors generally organize their social lives around their beliefs and attitudes about what it would be (most) correct or practically necessary to say or do?

It has been controversial which of these views of the organizing basis for public conduct is correct, and thus how to account for the effects of persuasive discourse (e.g., Blumer, 1955; Goffman, 1959; Garfinkel, 1967; Fishbein, 1967; Ajzen, et al. 1970; Larson and Sanders, 1975; Steinfatt and Infante, 1976; Cushman and McPhee, 1980). Moreover, there are conflicting data about which view is valid (e.g., Deutscher, 1973; Roloff and Miller, 1980). Intuitively, those two conceptions of the organizing basis of social conduct are not mutually exclusive, although they are treated as being so in the controversy surrounding them. This makes it possible below to reconcile the conflicting data in a way that entails that each of those contrasting motives for public conduct makes a difference in social life, but on different levels of analysis.

Numerous data indicate that it is at an interpersonal level, in the dealings of individuals with each other, that what actors say and do tends to be organized around symbolic needs and benefits. The data that indicate that people act out of conviction can be accounted for by premising that it is in the public conduct of social masses that behavior is correlated with aggregate beliefs and attitudes about the relative practicality or correctness of each option among a fixed set of possible utterances and behaviors. This way of reconciling the data puts the account of persuasion here, and more broadly the account of strategic communication in this book, in proper perspective.

PERSUASION AND THE INTERPRETIVE CONSEQUENCES OF PUBLIC CONDUCT

Let us define persuasive discourse as that species which is formulated so as to increase (maximize) the probability that respondents will subsequently make particular utterances or behaviors (in contrast to other goals of strategic communication, such as ensuring that it will be relevant in the desired way to make certain utterances or behaviors of one's own subsequently, or ensuring that undesired utterances and behaviors are irrelevant or minimally probable). In that case, given the principles in Chapter 8, discourses and entries in dialogues will be persuasive insofar as:

1. They establish a ground of coherence that warrants subsequently focusing on a specific interpretation of the desired utterances and behaviors.
2. It is more probable on that specific interpretation that respondents will make the desired utterances and behaviors because:
    a. they contribute to a resolution of the agenda,
    b. they are normatively obligated,
    c. the respondent is disposed towards them by belief, attitude, and/or role.

In every case, then, the strategic problem is to ensure that the desired utterances and behaviors will have a specific interpretation such that they contribute to the resolution of the present agenda, are normatively obligated, and/or conform to the respondent's dispositions.

Persuasive Appeals in Dialogues

For reasons detailed in the second part of this chapter, persuasive discourse that has its effect by influencing the interpretive consequences of subsequent conduct is most likely at the level of personal appeals by one individual to another. An instance is given in a dialogue elicited by Edmondson, (1981). Edmondson had respondents adopt specified roles in a defined situation and improvise dialogues. The following dialogue (Edmondson, 1981: 175–178) involves a situation where X is doing work in a university library, and returns to where she had been sitting to find that Y had moved her books and papers aside and taken her seat. No other work spaces are available. (Edmondson's transcript has been altered here by the addition of punctuation and the deletion of his notations of vocal inflections.):

1. X: Excuse me, I—I don't know you, do I?
2. Y: I don't think so, no.
3. X: Well, er, I'm terribly sorry but, er, I'm afraid you're in my seat. You've moved //my books
4. Y: Oh dear
5. X: and papers. You must have realised somebody was here.
6. Y: Oh, that's, er, well I looked around and there wasn't anybody else, any, any other space and er //I waited a little
7. X: Well I'm awfully sorry
8. Y: while and nobody came. I'm sorry if I've taken your place but there doesn't seem to be anywhere else and I—I thought you'd gone away for a long time. People do and er
9. X: Well, honestly, I left my books here and my bag; surely you could see it was my place. I'm //awfully busy
10. Y: I did wait a little while to see if anybody was coming back, if you'd just been to the ladies or something, but it—time went on, I thought you must have gone out. But er okay I'll move. I //don't want to
11. X: Well I'm terribly sorry about this, but you know, I know we're supposed to speak quietly in here but I simply must get on, I've got all this work to do and it's Friday afternoon. I haven't worked well all morning.
12. Y: mmmm, I know
13. X: You know I just have to get on so if you //wouldn't mind getting out
14. Y: (has started collecting her papers) Well I've got er I've got to read this article, I've got to get my essay finished too, erm, could I possibly share your desk?

15. X: (now back in her place) Well do you think you can find another chair, I mean //you can't share my chair.
16. I think I'll find another chair.
17. X: Okay, okay, I'll move over.
18. Y: That would be very kind, I won't get in your way then.
19. X: Right, hm hm (moves over)
20. Y: Okay, right, well thanks very much, I'll go look for another chair.
21. X: Not a bit.

X's goal is to get Y voluntarily to relinquish the seat she has taken. Note that it is contrary to Y's practical needs to relinquish the seat, and that X gives Y no information likely to change Y's beliefs and attitudes about the practical utility of having that seat, or the practical advantage of relinquishing it. Further, while X does implicate that it would be correct for Y to yield the seat and incorrect that she has it, both of those appear to involve information Y already possessed.

But given the principles above, X's strategic problem is not to change Y's understanding of the practicality or correctness of yielding her seat—it is to establish what the specific interpretation will be of keeping or relinquishing the seat in such a way as to maximize the probability that Y will surrender it. This requires that X's entries warrant a specific interpretation of 'relinquishing the seat' which will maximize the probability of Y's doing so. To influence the specific interpretation of the target behavior (relinquishing the seat), it is necessary that X create a ground of coherence to which that target behavior is relevant in regard to one of its possible meanings. X does this as follows.

X's entries in turns 1, 3, 5, 7 and 9 have as their content the stipulation that Y's having taken X's seat in the first place counts as a usurpation, a normatively proscribed seizure of territory. The content of Y's responses in turns 6, 8 and 10 identifies states of affairs that excuse her having violated the 'rule' X has cited to defend her claim of right to the seat—that a library workspace marked by one's papers and books and other such personal materials is reserved in perpetuity. But none of Y's excuses void the applicability of this rule, and in fact, she tacitly acknowledges it by trying to excuse her breach.

Given that X's entries restrospectively assign Y's possession of the seat the specific interpretation of an act with the force of a usurpation, then X's citations of the applicable rule and its violation is relevant to that act as acts also, of grievance and petition. Given that ground of coherence, which was created by X's entries, Y's retention of the seat or its surrender will also be relevant as acts—respectively as acts of belligerence or the redress of X's grievance. Given that an act of belligerence is normatively proscribed, and with the further possibility that it is contrary to Y's attitudes and role definition as a fellow scholar, X's entries will have minimized the likelihood that Y would retain the seat.

Persuasive Appeals in Public Discourse

Again, for the reasons given in the second part of this chapter, persuasive discourse addressed to an aggregate is less likely than appeals on a personal level to have its effect by influencing the interpretive consequences of the target utterances or behaviors. The exception to this is when the target utterances or behaviors will have to be undertaken in interpersonal settings, so that their interpretive consequences in those settings may systematically constrain respondents.

A case in point involves the "Checkers Speech," given on national television in 1952 by Richard Nixon. Nixon was then a candidate for Vice-President, running with General Eisenhower. Nixon's political credibility and place on the ticket were put in jeopardy when news stories began to appear that private businesspeople had contributed $18,000 to a private fund for his use while he was a U.S. Senator. Nixon's speech was made to defend himself against the appearance of wrongdoing. At the end he placed his political future in the hands of the audience, asking the viewers to convey to the Republican National Committee their desire either for his retention on the ticket or resignation from it.

It would generally be visible to friends and intimates of respondents whether they spoke in Nixon's behalf or against him, or remained silent. This makes it likely that Nixon's audience would be constrained by the interpretive consequences of their reactions to his speech, particularly given that prior to Nixon's speech, endorsing his candidacy would have warranted the specific interpretation of being an act of blind faith, or of such acts as tolerating or forgiving political corruption. In that case, it was a practical imperative for Nixon to create a warrant for focusing on specific interpretations of endorsing him and opposing him across a majority of those interpersonal settings that would maximize the probability of endorsements.

It is thus significant that a relatively small proportion of the content of Nixon's speech provides information regarding beliefs and attitudes about the practical need for and correctness of the slush fund in question. Of 118 paragraphs, the content of only 15 paragraphs (approximately 15% of the text) is devoted explicitly to the fund and Nixon's use of it. Paragraphs 6–9 specify criteria for a judgment of wrongdoing and paragraphs 10–15 comprise assertions that none of the money was used for personal expenses, and that none of the contributors received special favors. In addition, paragraphs 41–45 cite an independent audit that confirms the first of those two assertions, that none of the money was used for personal expenses. This raises the question of what the strategic need was for (the bulk of) the other 103 paragraphs.

The content of much of Nixon's speech is a description of his biography, his affairs and his motives that represents him as a public servant and family man with the highest scruples and integrity, devoted to traditional American values and dedicated to the fight against Communist subversion. However, given the account of strategic communication in this book, this in itself would theoretically be insufficient to influence respondents: it would not have any particular influence on the specific interpretation of respondents' endorsements (or repudiation) of his candidacy. It does not establish a ground of coherence and an agenda to which such endorsements (or repudiations) would be relevant.

However, Nixon's characterization of himself was presented in the form of a chronological sequence of acts and events. Within that sequence, the current entry comprised his being forced to bare his soul on national television. That made the next entry in that sequence be the cumulative endorsements (or repudiations) communicated to the Republican National Committee by his respondents. This is theoretically the key.

In this narrative reconstruction, Nixon represented himself as the blameless victim of political adversaries whose ethics and patriotism, and thus whose motives, were suspect:

> Now, let me say this: I know that this is not the last of the smears. In spite of my explanation tonight, other smears will be made. Others have been made in the past. And the purpose of the smears, I know, is this, to silence me, to make me let up.
>
> Well they just don't know who they are dealing with. I'm going to tell you this: I remember, in the dark days of the Hiss trial [involving an alleged spy for the Soviets whom Nixon was instrumental in prosecuting], some of the same columnists, some of the same radio commentators who are attacking me now and misrepresenting my position, were violently opposing me at the time I was after Alger Hiss. (paragraphs 88–89)

The ground of coherence in that narrative is the combative features of a series of acts in which attacks made by the foes of the righteous, anti-Communist Nixon are fearlessly countered by him. In that case, respondents' endorsement or repudiation of Nixon's candidacy would not be publicly interpretable as sanctioning, tolerating, or forgiving his slush fund. Endorsements and repudiations would warrant the specific interpretation of being one more of those combative acts, either to help him in his fight for American ideals or to help his enemies pressure him to let up. Given those specific interpretations warranted by Nixon's speech, the probability of endorsements is maximized, given that: (1) they contribute to a successful resolution of Nixon's anti-Communist agenda, (2) they are normatively obligatory for any patriotic citizen, and (3) they would be consistent with the political dispositions of many of the respondents who perceived themselves as having a vested interest in the affairs of the Republican Party.

Empirical Support

There are numerous data that support the premise that people profess beliefs and attitudes and adopt certain behaviors on the basis of their interpretive consequences. Individuals' reports of their beliefs and attitudes often do not predict their public behaviors, and it is not unusual for individuals to profess beliefs and attitudes that are directly opposed to what they actually do in public, or at least in the company of intimates (Deutscher, 1973).

The first and most prominent of studies with this finding is LaPiere's (1935), whose concern was about the adequacy of the methodological shortcut of finding out what the social attitudes (behavioral tendencies) of individuals and communities are by querying respondents about them. The substance of his concern was not just that opinion questionnaires are inherently too simple to capture the complexity of a social attitude. He also indicated that people take different factors into account—factors that involve the interpretive consequences of one's public conduct—in responding to a questionnaire, as compared with actually exhibiting some behavior publicly:

> The technique is simple. Thus from a hundred or a thousand responses to the question "Would you get up to give an Armenian woman your seat in a street car?" the investigator derives the "attitude" of non-Armenian males towards Armenian females. Now the question may be constructed with elaborate skill and hidden with consummate cunning in a maze of supplementary or even irrelevant questions, yet all that has been obtained is a symbolic response to a symbolic situation. The words "Armenian woman" do not constitute an Armenian woman of flesh and blood, who might be tall or squat, fat or thin, old or young, well or poorly dressed—who might in fact be a goddess or just another old and dirty hag. And the questionnaire response, whether it be "yes" or "no," is but a verbal reaction and this does not involve rising from the seat or stolidly avoiding the hurt eyes of the hypothetical woman and the derogatory stares of other street-car occupants. (LaPiere, 1935: 230)

The methodological flaws in LaPiere's study are well known (in particular, that not all of his questionnaires were completed and returned, and that the people who completed the questionnaires were not necessarily the same ones whose behavior had been observed previously). But considering how decisive the trends are, these problems do not warrant discarding the data, only caution about its extremity. LaPiere compared the treatment experienced by a Chinese couple at hotels and restaurants with subsequent written statements by representatives of those establishments about whether they would accommodate Chinese. The Chinese alone were accommodated without difficulty at 11 of the 12 hotels they visited, and in LaPiere's company, at 50 of 55 hotels. Yet among the 47 of those hotels from which replies were obtained, 91% stated that Chinese would not be accommodated there. Similarly, the Chinese alone were served without difficulty at 18 of 19 restaurants they visited, and in LaPiere's company, at 160 out of 165 restaurants. But of the 81 of those restaurants from which replies were obtained, 93% stated that Chinese would not be served.

These discrepancies between professed beliefs and attitudes and overt behavior within and across social situations should not occur if public conduct is organized around actual beliefs and attitudes. But precisely such discrepancies are to be expected if the first consideration of actors is the interpretive consequences in each instance of professing certain beliefs and attitudes, and independently, the interpretive consequences of exhibiting certain behaviors.

Inconsistencies between professed beliefs and attitudes and overt behavior in other studies have explicitly been attributed to the concerns of respondents with the interpretive consequences of what they say and do.

Warriner (1958) found substantial discrepancies between the official morality about drinking alcoholic beverages that was publicly endorsed by respondents in a rural Kansas town, and the professed beliefs and attitudes, and actual behavior of those same respondents in private (in the company of intimates). He attributed these to the different social functions (i.e., specific interpretations and their consequences) of endorsements of community standards, and more personal, unofficial, utterances and behaviors.

Defleur and Westie (1958) and Linn (1965) conducted more rigorous studies of the relationship between professed racial attitudes and overt behavior. DeFleuer and Westie first obtained measures of their White respondents' attitudes towards Blacks, and subsequently asked them to commit themselves to participating in a project supportive of improved race relations by being photographed in friendly conversation with a Black. While they did find a significant positive relationship between measured racial attitudes and willingness to sign a release for the photographic session, they were concerned that 14 of 46 respondents had acted contrary to their stated attitudes:

> The lack of a straight-line relationship between verbal attitudes and overt behavior more likely may be explained in terms of some sort of social involvement of the subject in a system of social constraints, preventing him from acting (overtly) in the direction of his

> convictions, or otherwise 'legitimizing' certain behavioral patterns. (DeFleur and Westie, 1958: 672)

Linn's (1965) replication of DeFleur and Westie's (1958) study refined the measures of racial attitude, and strengthened the behavioral demand on respondents. The overall result was a weaker relationship between professed attitudes and behavior than DeFleur and Westie found (except in the case of respondents who professed racial prejudices). Linn provides excerpts from post-experimental interviews that are generally supportive of the view here that individuals speak and act out of concern for the interpretive consequences:

> I didn't know if I should sign (the release for a photograph) or not. *I really couldn't visualize the consequences.* Yes, I was aware of the fact that there was a Negro present. I couldn't look at him but only at you (White E) when I told you I wouldn't sign the releases. It was really a very embarrassing type of situation. *What could he* (the Negro E) *be thinking of me?* (italics added)
>
> In the questionnaire I wasn't faced with the real thing. It (the signing of the releases) *should* be done, but I can't. Those were my desires, but I couldn't do them. *I had to think of my parents and my hometown.* (italics added)
>
> At that time (time of the questionnaire) I was thinking of what I *should* do, but when confronted with the situation, I thought more deeply about participating. *I was worried about other people and what they would think.* (italics added) I was not worried for myself.
>
> On the questionnaire it seemed all right but when it came to the *real* thing, it seemed "scary." It wouldn't have been so bad for a large group picture. *Did anybody else do what I did?* (italics added)

PERSUASION AND CHANGES IN COGNITIONS AND CONDUCT IN THE AGGREGATE

There are numerous data that are contrary to the theoretical account and related findings above. Techniques of political opinion polling have developed that substantially correctly detect changes and changeability in voter preference over time, and more importantly, predict voter behavior (i.e., candidates' shares of the total vote). More particularly, Woelfel and Fink's (1980) Galileo method for measuring cognitions has been applied to problems in marketing, and Woelfel (personal communication) has reported that his measures of cognitions about different product brands are very highly correlated with buyer behavior (i.e., each brand's respective market share).

Woelfel and Fink (1980) stress that their measures of cognition and predictions of conduct are valid for social aggregates, ideally very large aggregates, not for individuals. This is the key. Data that show a strong relationship between cognitions and conduct have involved large aggregates; data that show an inconsistent relationship between cognition and communication involve individuals and small groups. Hence, the conflicting data involve different levels of analysis, and are not necessarily irreconcilable.

But to reconcile those data, we are obligated to explain how it is possible that individuals strategically express their cognitions and behave in situational and variable ways, while at the same time aggregates comprising those individuals have stable collective beliefs and attitudes that generally and consistently predict behaviors in the aggregate.

Cognitions

Measures of beliefs and attitudes generally involve calling on individuals to make utterances (or mark positions on rating scales or the like) in a structured progression that expresses propositions across a restricted set of objects or situations of experience. Let us suppose that individuals' responses to specific questionnaire items are affected by the three major factors noted in previous chapters—most basically and generally by the interpretive consequences, and in addition, normative and conventional obligations, their role requirements and their actual beliefs and dispostions. In addition, responses to questionnaire items in a structured progression are also likely to be influenced by a concern with being internally consistent across those items. This requires respondents to make a trade-off between expressing their actual beliefs and attitudes, preserving their (public) consistency, and satisfying their personal and strategic goals.

In that case, as the number of respondents increases, individual differences regarding that trade–off will tend to cancel each other out, so that they will account for increasingly less of the variance in the proportional distribution of responses in the aggregate. That proportional distribution of responses to questionnaire items will thus increasingly be a product of common denominators among respondents—for the most part, of those actual beliefs and attitudes that they have in common that produce conceptual interrelationships among the questionnaire items.

Therefore, beliefs and attitudes in the aggregate do not entail that any individual respondent will have certain cognitions in fact, nor that any individual respondent will profess those beliefs and attitudes or be consistent in his/her professions of belief and attitude. Conversely, if individual professions of belief and attitude are situational and variable, that does not preclude the stability of surveyed beliefs and attitudes in an aggregate.

Behavior

Behaviors in the aggregate are recorded as a proportional distribution of behaviors across a fixed set of alternatives (e.g., the proportional distribution of votes across the alternative candidates, or of purchases across alternative product brands). As above, individual members of the aggregate, if they exhibit any of the alternative behaviors at all, may do so for strategic reasons, because of conventional or normative obligations, because of role requirements or because it is called for by their beliefs and attitudes. These individual differences will affect whether any of the alternate behaviors is exhibited, and under what circumstances (if there is a choice). However, as above, such individual differences will be canceled out as the number of recorded instances increases. The proportional distribution of behaviors among the alternatives in the aggregate is thus a product of common denominators in the population, which in this case must involve the relative—not the absolute—desirability of each alternative.

In that case, there is no reason to expect that the distribution of behaviors in the aggregate will predict the behavior of any individual respondent. Further, even given a stable distribution of behaviors in the aggregate, when behaviors can be repeated (e.g., the purchase of product brands), individuals may nonetheless be variable and situational about which alternative behavior they exhibit, if any at all.

The Correlation between Cognition and Behavior

By definition, there will be a high correlation between two measures insofar as the same variables influence what each measure records. Behaviors in the aggregate are a product of some set of variables that influences their proportional distribution, or relative desirability, across the alternatives. Those same variables will therefore influence measures of relevant cognitions in the aggregate insofar as the questionnaire items involve comparisons of those behavioral alternatives or their constituent features (as opposed to items about each behavioral alternative in its own right). Such comparative questionnaire items are of course characteristic of political polls in general, and are a key aspect of Woelfel and Fink's (1980) Galileo method.

Correlations between cognitions and conduct in the aggregate, then, involve those actual beliefs and attitudes shared in the population about the relative desirability among a set of behavioral alternatives, and the proportional distribution of behaviors among those alternatives. Such correlations therefore do not necessitate that there will be any comparable degree of relationship between the actual cognitions, professed beliefs and attitudes, and behaviors of individuals.

The Effects of Persuasive Discourse on Cognition and Conduct

It is given above that the proportional distribution of aggregate responses on a set of questionnaire items corresponds to just those actual beliefs and attitudes about the relative desirability of the behavioral alternatives that are shared among the respondents. In that case, persuasive discourse is unlikely to foster changes in cognitions in the aggregate unless it is widely distributed. If each member of the aggregate encounters a different persuasive appeal and each changes his/her actual beliefs and attitudes in a different way, it is not necessary that cognitions in the aggregate will be significantly changed. Second, it is given above that measures of belief and attitude will correlate with behaviors in the aggregate insofar as the questionnaire items interrelate the behavioral alternatives (or their constituent features). In that case, persuasive discourse is only likely to be effective in fostering changes in cognitions and behavior in the aggregate when (1) it is distributed to all members of the aggregate, and (2) it provides new or newly integrated information about the interrelationship among behavioral alternatives.

On that basis, it is not necessarily the case that persuasive discourse that is effective in the aggregate will have a corresponding influence on the actual and professed cognitions of individual members, or their behaviors. Further, as noted above, it will not necessarily be the case that persuasive discourse that effects change in the public conduct of individuals will have any effect on cognitions and conduct in the aggregate.

For the purpose of effecting changes in a social aggregate, then, it is true that details of linguistic form and phrasing and nonverbals are strategically unimportant (except for inductions about the communicator, and for attention-getting) as long as the new or newly integrated information required is distributed in a uniform and undistorted way in the aggregate. But this does not entail that such details are strategically unimportant for the purpose of effecting changes in the professed beliefs and attitudes and behaviors of individuals.

CONTROLLING UNDERSTANDINGS IN EVERYDAY LIFE

It was asserted at the beginning of this book that the first consideration in formulating utterances and behaviors is to control the way in which one is understood. This is entailed by the fact that adhering to the rules and conventions of expression does not in itself guarantee that one will be understood in the intended or desired way, and thus that one will be responded to in a way that serves one's best interests under the circumstances. Hence, the postulate that controlling understandings is the first consideration involves a practical necessity, not a metaphysical priority.

This has been put in proper perspective in this chapter. Given that the first consideration for individuals is to control understandings, that does not entail that it is theoretically unimportant that people have beliefs and attitudes about what it is practical or correct to say and do. But the force of those beliefs and attitudes is most pronounced in aggregates, not in the situated utterances and behaviors of individuals. The problem of communicating so as to maximize the probability that the desired utterances or behaviors will be made is thus substantially different when the goal is to influence social aggregates than when the goal is to influence individuals in particular situations. Persuasive appeals to aggregates do depend primarily on what information is presented and in what order (as has been mistakenly assumed to be the key for persuasion in general).

The exception is when the utterances or behaviors desired in the aggregate have to be undertaken in interpersonal situations. This is borne out strikingly by the difficulties reported by Rogers (Rogers with Shoemaker, 1971; Rogers, 1976) in fostering the adoption of innovations that have interpretive consequences at the interpersonal level, such as family planning. Efforts to foster such innovations by the mass distribution of information about their practical utility and correctness generally do not succeed; efforts made by supplementing such mass distributions of information with persuasive appeals at the interpersonal level were far more effective.

The strategic problem involved in persuasion on the interpersonal level has the same theoretical roots as the strategic problem in communication in general at that level. The key is to establish a ground of coherence that influences the specific interpretation of targeted utterances and behaviors so that they are constrained in the desired way. This entails what every practicing communicator knows, but what we have previously been unable to explain. It is not just *what* one says or does that matters, but *how* it is said or done. How utterances are formed and phrased, how nonverbals are displayed, and at what juncture those utterances and behaviors are entered in the unfolding discourse or dialogue are all critically important in producing an effect.

This entails that the means of communication strongly limit the social goals that a person can reasonably have at any juncture. Only some of the indefinitely large number of utterances and behaviors an individual is able to produce will be relevant (and thus interpretable) at each juncture. A much smaller number of those utterances and behaviors will have a specific interpretation that: (1) is desirable in its own right, and (2) increases the probability that the sequence will subsequently progress towards desired outcomes (or away from undesired ones). On those grounds, indefinitely many outcomes cannot be coherently reached by continuing the present discourse or dialogue as it has unfolded at that juncture, and some outcomes cannot be coherently avoided.

The practice of communication is thus properly represented in terms of a dialectic between an individual's social purpose(s), the principles of specific interpretation and forecasting principles made explicit here, and the way in which the discourse or dialogue has unfolded. This entails that formulating utterances and exhibiting behaviors is potentially a complex, decision-making activity, in which individuals engage themselves to varying degrees, and at which they are varyingly proficient.

We can at last rid ourselves of the myth that the linguistic and other means we have of communicating are neutral conduits that can be bent to serve any social purpose we might have. A person cannot say and do anything he/she wants or needs to do at any juncture, at least not without risking severe penalties, despite the fact that people have the means to express any and every one of their observations, thoughts, feelings and desires. It is a minimal requirement of an adequate theory of human communication that it account for this.

Endword

ON THE COMPETENCE TO PRODUCE CALCULATED SPEECH

The account of strategic communication I have developed here grew out of an interest in the fact that individuals usually manage to avoid problems in calculating what to say and do in their everyday lives. This is no small feat, considering the potential for problems to emerge no matter how routinized the unfolding discourse or dialogue is. Clerks in stores may introduce a personal element into a routine transaction; casual remarks can unpredictably hurt or offend a child. Further, the relatively low incidence of prolonged social dysfunctions and conflict indicates that when communication problems do arise, people have considerable ability to solve them (or at least to devise an intelligent solution, as E did in Conversation I).

Explaining such facts improves our understanding of the practices and effects of communication among people in general, from one culture to the next, from one institutional context to the next, from one social purpose to the next.

ON PRACTICING STRATEGIC COMMUNICATION

The principles that were formulated in Chapters 4, 6 and 8 also apply directly to the practice of communication in various professional situations. There are a number of professions and institutions in which the core activity is the formulation and production of discourses and dialogues. A partial list includes management, politics, teaching, counseling and psychotherapy, diplomacy, negotiations and bargaining, journalism, marketing, and law. In every case, the first consideration is to formulate messages in a way that makes intended understandings or desired responses probable (or undesired ones improbable).

The principles formulated here can thus be applied by theorists to account for what is characteristically done in such professions or institutions, and what the result is. By the same token, practitioners can apply them to evaluate before the fact, and perhaps to some degree to formulate, the messages and message strategies they contemplate producing. It will be helpful to illustrate this with brief characterizations of the communication problem in selected professional situations.

Teaching

The goals of teachers are generally either of the following: for students to become more able to perform effectively, or for students to have greater mastery of their subject matter. It is common sense to conceive of either goal as contingent on the student's acquisition of the cognitions necessary to produce certain behaviors with the desired qualities or speech with the desired content. However, more has to be involved in this than imparting information and prescribing exercises. Students exposed to the same information and conditions of practice do not progress equally well. Given that the teacher is knowledgable, and has communicated accurately and clearly, the tendency is to put the blame for student deficiencies on their differing abilities to learn and perform.

However, the theoretical propositions developed here entail that more is required of teachers than being knowledgable and expressing themselves clearly. It does little violence to the common-sense view of teaching if we identify the goal in every case as being to enable students to subsequently recognize what the "correct" or "preferred" options of content, style and delivery would be in new circumstances. In that case, the teaching problem is not just to instruct students about what to do, or to provide them with the information they need. In addition, the teaching problem is to control understandings of the new behaviors or information sufficiently to constrain in the desired way what students subsequently do and say.

The principles here entail that this can be done systematically both through lecture and discussion before the fact, and through feedback to students about their subsequent mastery of new behaviors or information. In either case, teachers have to make explicit the antecedents (in personal, social or intellectual experience) of new behaviors or information, and the ground of coherence among them. They also entail that subsequent speech and behavior are more likely to be constrained in the desired way if it is made explicit what the ground of coherence is between what is being taught and prototypes of desired responses.

A failure to do either only ensures an ability to reproduce mechanically what was taught, but not to transform and apply it in formulating original speech and behavior as necessary in new situations. Of course, this does not preclude some students from independently seeking out and forming their own understandings of at least the ground of coherence between what is being taught and prototypical responses. These understandings will make the students either more or less proficient, depending on whether the construed ground of coherence is correct.

Politics

The willingness of citizens to support individual politicians and to support particular social policies depends on the understandings they form of those politicians or those policies. It also depends on how citizens project that others would understand them (or project the self-understanding they would have) if they publicly supported or opposed some politician or policy. The principles here entail that political communication thus make explicit the relevance a politician or policy has to particular antecedents, or the relevance that desired public response would have to particular antecedents. This is what Hitler achieved in his reconstruction of German history in *Mein Kampf,* and what Reagan has achieved by linking his persona and policies to fundamental American myths about heroism and achievement in the old West.

This is also what Carter tried to do by linking himself and his policies with the morality and goals of our agrarian past. However, the focus on those antecedents was a strategic mistake. Among other things, the ground of coherence among such antecedents gave Carter and his policies meanings that made equivocal their relevance to problems facing our neo-industrial society, and thus Carter's policies were subject to diverse and fluid interpretations. That fluidity of understandings over time about Carter and his policies fostered inductions that it was he who vascillated and was ineffectual.

Management

Managers of units within business, manufacturing and government organizations have as their primary goal the maintenance of cooperation and coordination among subordinates required to perform the unit's tasks. There are diverse theoretical accounts of how this should be done. For example, from a systems perspective, it requires the allocation of responsibility, the regularization of task requirements and procedures, and the creation of ways to control product quality by monitoring and regulating operations. From a human-relations perspective, it requires the creation of a social environment that supports interpersonal cooperation, particularly in regard to task requirements and procedures.

Of course, from the perspective here, the goal of unit managers is to constrain the speech and behavior of subordinates so it is probable they will achieve the coordination and cooperation needed to perform tasks. This can be achieved first by controlling understandings of the unit's major tasks and sub-tasks by making explicit their relevance to each other, to the work of other units, and to the organization's overall operation. The major avenues for such communication are during the training and socialization process that new workers experience, and in feedback about job performance. This requires that managers make explicit the antecedents of defined tasks, of their creation and assignment, and also the ground of coherence among them so as to foster desired understandings. It further requires that managers make explicit the relevance of prototypical speech and behavior to the task and its antecedents.

Such communication practices are consistent both with a systems approach and a human-relations approach. They provide workers an independent basis for judging the consequences for coordination and cooperation of contemplated speech or behavior, and the consequences for fulfilling task requirements. Without this, the functioning of the system would be in constant jeopardy, and come to depend almost entirely on the unit manager's ability to oversee and regulate all facets of the unit's operation. Similarly, the creation of social environments that foster interpersonal coordination and cooperation depend on there being a shared knowledge of antecedents of e.g., contributions to productive working relationships that warrant a desirable interpretation of such contributions, and thus make them more probable.

Counseling and Psychotherapy

I will assume that a line can be drawn between psychopathologies that often necessitate hospitalizing patients for treatment, and emotional and behavioral patterns that are dysfunctional but not pathological. I intend the following generalizations to apply only to treatment of the latter.

From the perspective here, when individuals routinely speak or act in a socially dysfunctional way, there are two basic explanations. One is that the individual has acquired a heightened sensitivity to certain (types of) occurrences, or a heightened dependence on achieving certain goals. Given such occurrences or goals, the individual would form dispositions of sufficient intensity to become likely to speak and act in particular ways regardless of constraints in the discourse or dialogue. However, these heightened sensitivities are often pathological, and thus their treatment is beyond the scope of the theory.

The other explanation of dysfunctional utterances or nonverbals is that the individual came to interpret and cohere certain antecedent acts and events in an idosyncratic way, and was able to perpetuate that idiosyncratic ground of coherence over time in a wide range of subsequent discourses and dialogues. As a result he/she would tend to make incorrect projections of the consequences of any contemplated utterance or nonverbal display perceived relevant to those antecedents, fostering unintended inductions about him/herself and unexpected understandings and reactions from others. Any of his/her utterances and nonverbal displays that he/she perceives relevant to those antecedents would be constrained in a discourse or dialogue in a different way from those of other communicators.

In such cases, the theory here entails that the first goal for a therapist is to reveal to the patient what the problem is by making evident the alternative possible understandings of his/her dysfunctional utterances or nonverbals. The next goal is to work backward through as many discourses and dialogues as possible to reveal alternative ways of interpreting and cohering their components. This can in time help the patient learn different, more standard, ways of interpreting and cohering speech and behavior, thus enabling him/her to engage more productively in formulating entries in discourses and dialogues.

ON THEORY AND PRACTICE

It is difficult to conceive of communicating as an activity that is ever undertaken for its own sake, rather than as a means to some end. Because of its inherently practical aspect, communication is rarely studied apart from the social institutions and social purposes that depend on it. The way we distinguish topics of research testifies to this: interpersonal communication, group communication, persuasion, organizational communication, intercultural communication, mass communication, political communication, and so on.

But without denying the achievements and advantages that have resulted from this orientation to communication, the concern in this book has been to reveal generalizations that have otherwise been obscured about how and why people communicate in general as they do, achieving the results they do, encountering the problems they do. Such generalizations are not only important for their own sake, but they also can have the utility of helping focus and cohere our studies of communication in particular institutions, in particular cultures, for particular purposes.

References

Abelson, R. 1981. Psychological status of the script concept. *American Psychologist, 36,* 715–729.

Ajzen, I., Darroch, R.K., Fishbein, M. and Hornik, J.A. 1970. Looking back revisited: A reply to Deutscher. *American Sociologist, 5,* 267–272.

Atkinson, J.M. and Heritage, J. (Eds.). 1984. *Structures of Social Action: Studies in Conversation Analysis.* Cambridge: Cambridge University Press.

Austin, J. 1962. *How To Do Things with Words.* New York: Oxford University Press.

Bach, K. and Harnish, R.M. 1979. *Linguistic Communication and Speech Acts.* Cambridge, MA: MIT Press.

Bailey, C.-J.N. 1981. Theory, description and differences among linguists (or, what keeps linguistics from becoming a science). *Language and Communication, 1,* 39–66.

Begg, I. and Harris, G. 1982. On the interpretation of syllogisms. *Journal of Verbal Learning and Verbal Behavior, 21,* 595–620.

Birdwhistell, R. 1970. *Kinesics and Context: Essays on Body Motion and Communication.* Philadelphia: University of Pennsylvania Press.

Blumer, H. 1955. Attitudes and the social act. *Social Problems, 3,* 59–65.

Bolinger, D. 1965. The atomization of meaning. *Language, 41,* 555–573.

Bradac, J.J., Martin, L.W., Elliott, N.D. and Tardy, C.H. 1980. On the neglected side of linguistic science: Multivariate studies of sentence judgment. *Linguistics, 18,* 967–995.

Brown, G., Currie, K.L. and Kenworthy, J. 1980. *Questions of Intonation.* London: Croom Helm.

Brown, P. and Levinson, S.L. 1978. Universals in language usage: Politeness phenomena. In Goody, E.N. (Ed.), *Questions and Politeness: Strategies in Social Interaction,* pp. 56–289. Cambridge: Cambridge University Press.

Buck, R. 1982. Spontaneous and symbolic nonverbal behavior and the ontogeny of communication. In Feldman, R. (Ed.), *Development of Nonverbal Behavior in Children,* pp. 29–62. New York: Springer-Verlag.

Bugental, D.E., Henker, B. and Whalen, C.K. 1976. Attributional antecedents of verbal and vocal assertiveness. *Journal of Personality and Social Psychology, 34,* 405–411.

Bugental, D.E., Kaswan, J.W. and Love, L.R. 1970. Perception of contradictory meanings conveyed by verbal and nonverbal channels. *Journal of Personality and Social Psychology, 16,* 647–655.

Burgoon, M. and Bettinghaus, E.P. 1980. Persuasive message strategies. In Roloff, M. and Miller, G. (Eds.), *Persuasion: New Directions in Theory and Research,* pp. 141–169. Beverly Hills, CA: Sage.

Carpenter, P.A. and Daneman, M. 1981. Lexical retrieval and error recovery in reading: A model based on eye fixations. *Journal of Verbal Learning and Verbal Behavior, 20,* 137–160.

Chomsky, N. 1957. *Syntactic Structures.* The Hague: Mouton.

——— 1965. *Aspects of the Theory of Syntax.* Cambridge, MA: MIT Press.

——— 1972. *Studies on Semantics in Generative Grammar.* The Hague: Mouton.

Chun, A.E., Day, R.R., Chenoweth, N.A., and Luppescu, S. 1982. Errors, interaction, and correction: A study of native-nonnative conversations. *TESOL Quarterly, 16,* 537–547.

Clarke, D.C. and Argyle, M. 1982. Conversation sequences. In Fraser, C. and Scherer, K. (Eds.), *Advances in the Social Psychology of Language,* pp. 159–204. Cambridge: Cambridge University Press.

Cole, P. (Ed.). 1981. *Radical Pragmatics.* New York: Academic Press.

Coulmas, F. (Ed). 1981. *Conversational Routine: Explorations in Standardized Communication Situations and Prepatterned Speech.* The Hague: Mouton.

Coulthard, M. and Brazil, D. 1982. The place of intonation in the description of interaction. In Tannen, D. (Ed.), *Analyzing Discourse: Text and Talk,* pp. 94–112. Georgetown University Roundtable on Languages and linguistics. Washington, D.C.: Georgetown University Press.

Crow, B.K. 1983. Topic shifts in couples' conversations. In Craig, R.T. and Tracy, K. (Eds.), *Conversational Coherence: Form, Structure, and Strategy,* pp. 136–156. Beverly Hills: Sage.

Craig, R.T. and Tracy, K. (Eds.). 1983. *Conversation and Coherence: Form, Structure, and Strategy.* Beverly Hills, CA.: Sage.

Cushman, D.P. and McPhee, R.D. (Eds.). 1980. *Message-Attitude-Behavior Relationship: Theory, Methodology and Application.* New York: Academic Press.

Dascal, M. 1977. Conversational relevance. *Journal of Pragmatics, 1,* 309–328.

DeFleur, M.L. and Westie, F.R. 1958. Verbal attitudes and overt acts: An experiment on the salience of attitudes. *American Sociological Review, 23,* 667–673.

Derber, C. 1979. *The Pursuit of Attention: Power and Individualism in Everyday Life.* Boston: G.K. Hall.

Deutscher, I. (Ed.) 1973. *What We Say/What We Do: Sentiments & Acts.* Glenview, IL: Scott, Foresman.

DeVito, J.A. 1983. *The Interpersonal Communication Book,* 3rd ed. New York: Harper & Row.

Duncan, S. Jr., Brunner, L.J. and Fiske, D.W. 1979. Strategy signals in face-to-face interaction. *Journal of Personality and Social Psychology, 37,* 301–313.

Edelsky, C. 1981. Who's got the floor? *Language in Society, 10,* 383–421.

Edmondson, W. 1981. *Spoken Discourse: A Model For Analysis.* London: Longman.

Ekman, P. and Friesen, W.V. 1969. The repertoire of nonverbal behavior: Categories, origins, usage, and coding. *Semiotica, 1,* 49–98.

——— 1972. Hand movements. *Journal of communication, 22,* 353–374.

——— 1975. *Unmasking the Face.* Englewood Cliffs, N.J.: Prentice Hall.

Ekman, P., Friesen, W.V. and Ellsworth, P.C. 1972. *Emotion in the Human Face: Guidelines for Research and an Integration of Findings.* New York: Pergamon.

Erickson, F. 1982. Money tree, lasagna bush, salt and pepper: Social construction of topical cohesion in a conversation among Italian-Americans. In Tannen, D. (Ed.), *Analyzing Discourse: Text and Talk,* pp. 43–70. Georgetown University Roundtable on Languages and linguistics. Washington, D.C.: Georgetown University Press.

Festinger, L. 1957. *A Theory of Cognitive Dissonance.* Stanford: Stanford University Press.

Fishbein, M. 1967. Attitude and the prediction of behavior. In Fishbein, M. (Ed.), *Readings in Attitude Theory and Measurement*, pp. 477–490. New York: Wiley.

Fishbein, M. and Ajzen, I. 1975. *Belief, Attitude, Intention and Behavior: An Introduction to Theory and Research.* Reading, MA: Addison-Wesley.

Friedman, H.S. 1982. The modification of word meaning by nonverbal cues. In Key, M. (Ed.), *Nonverbal Communication Today: Current Research*, pp. 57–67. Berlin: Mouton.

Frijda, N.H. 1958. Facial expression and situational cues. *Journal of Abnormal and Social Psychology, 57,* 149–154.

Galin, D. and Ornstein, R. 1974. Individual differences in cognitive style—I. Reflective eye movements. *Neuropsychologia, 12,* 367–376.

Garfinkel, H. 1967. *Studies in Ethnomethodology.* Englewood Cliffs, NJ: Prentice-Hall.

Gass, S.M. and Varonis, E.M. 1985. Variation in native speaker speech modification to non-native speakers. *Studies in Second Language Acquisition, 7,* 37–58.

Gazdar, G. 1979. *Pragmatics: Implicature, Presupposition and Logical Form.* New York: Academic Press.

Goffman, E. 1959. *The Presentation of Self in Everyday Life.* Garden City, NY: Doubleday.

Goldberg, J. 1983. A move toward describing conversational coherence. In Craig, R.T. and Tracy, K. (Eds.), *Conversational Coherence: Form, Structure, and Strategy,* pp. 25–46. Beverly Hills: Sage.

Goodwin, C. 1981. *Conversational Organization: Interaction between Speakers and Hearers.* New York: Academic Press.

Gordon, D. and Lakoff, G. 1975. Conversational postulates. In Cole, P. and Morgan, J.L. (Eds.), *Syntax and Semantics 3: Speech Acts,* pp. 83–106. New York: Academic Press.

Green, G.M. and Morgan, J.L. 1981. Pragmatics, grammar, and discourse. In Cole, P. (Ed.), *Radical Pragmatics,* pp. 167–181. New York: Academic Press.

Grice, H.P. 1957. Meaning. *Philosophical Review, 66,* 377–388.

——— 1967. Logic and conversation. Mimeo. William James Lectures. Cambridge, MA: Harvard University.

——— 1975. Logic and conversation. In Cole, P. and Morgan, J.L. (Eds.), *Syntax and Semantics 3: Speech Acts,* pp. 41–58. New York: Academic Press.

——— 1978. Further notes on logic and conversation. In Cole, P. (Ed.), *Syntax and Semantics 9: Pragmatics,* pp. 113–128. New York: Academic Press.

Grimes, J.E. 1982. Topics within topics. In Tannen, D. (Ed.), *Analyzing Discourse: Text and Talk,* pp. 164–176. Georgetown University Roundtable on Languages and linguistics. Washington, D.C.: Georgetown University Press.

Gumperz, J.J. 1977. Sociocultural knowledge in conversational inference. In Saville-Troike, M. (Ed.), *Twenty-eighth Annual Roundtable Monographs on languages and Linguistics,* pp. 191–211. Washington, D.C.: Georgetown University Press.

——— 1982a. *Discourse Strategies.* Cambridge: Cambridge University Press.

——— 1982b. The linguistic bases of communicative competence. In Tannen, D. (Ed.), *Analyzing Discourse: Text and Talk,* pp. 323–334. Georgetown University Roundtable on Languages and linguistics. Washington, D.C.: Georgetown University Press.

Halliday, M.A.K. 1967. Notes on transitivity and theme in English, part 2. *Journal of Linguistics, 3,* 199–244.

Halliday, M.A.K. and Hasan, R. 1976. *Cohesion in English.* London: Longman.

Harper, R.G., Wiens, A.N. and Matarazzo, J.D. 1978. *Nonverbal Communication: The State of the Art.* New York: John Wiley & Sons.

Hart, R.J. and Brown, B.L. 1974. Interpersonal information conveyed by the content and vocal aspects of speech. *Speech Monographs, 41,* 371–380.

Harris, R.J. and Monaco, G. 1978. Psychology of pragmatic implication: Information processing between the lines. *Journal of Experimental Psychology, 107,* 1–22.

Hofstadter, D. 1979. *Gödel, Escher, Bach: An Eternal Golden Braid.* New York: Basic Books.

Holloway, C.A. 1979. *Decision Making under Uncertainty: Models and Choices.* Englewood Cliffs, NJ: Prentice-Hall.

Hopper, R. 1981. The taken-for-granted. *Human Communication Research, 7,* 195–211.

Horn, L. 1972. On the semantic properties of logical operators in English. Mimeo. Bloomington: Indiana University Linguistics Club.

Hymes, D. 1964. Formal discussion. In Bellugi, U. and Brown, R. (Eds.), *The Acquisition of Language.* Monographs of the Society for Research in Child Development, *29* (no. 1; serial no. 92), 110–112.

Jacobs, S. and Jackson, S. 1983a. Strategy and structure in conversational influence attempts. *Communication Monographs, 50,* 285–304.

——— 1983b. Speech act structure in conversation: Rational aspects of pragmatic coherence. In Craig, R.T. and Tracy, K. (Eds.), *Conversational Coherence: Form, Structure, and Strategy,* pp. 47–66. Beverly Hills: Sage.

Kartunnen, L. and Peters, S. 1979. Conventional implicature. In Oh, C.-K. & Dinneen, D. A. *Syntax and Semantics 11: Presupposition,* pp. 1–56. New York: Academic Press.

Katz, J.J. 1977. *Propositional Structure and Illocutionary Force.* New York: Crowell.

Katz, J.J. and Fodor, J. 1963. The structure of a semantic theory. *Language, 39,* 170–210.

Kaufer, D. 1979. The competence/performance distinction in linguistic theory. *Philosophy of the Social Sciences, 9,* 257–275.

Keenan, J.M. and Kintsch, W. 1974. The identification of explicitly and implicitly presented information. In Kintsch, W. (Ed.), *The Representation of Meaning in Memory,* pp. 153–166. Hillsdale, NJ: Lawrence Erlbaum.

Keller, E. 1981. Gambits. Conversational strategy signals. In Coulmas, F. (Ed.), *Conversational Routine: Explorations in Standardized Communication Situations and Prepatterned Speech,* pp. 93–114. The Hague: Mouton.

Kempson, R. 1977. *Semantic Theory.* Cambridge: Cambridge University Press.

Kochman, T. 1973. *Rappin' and Stylin' Out: Communication in Urban Black America.* Champaign-Urbana: University of Illinois Press.

Kreckel, M. 1981. Where do constitutive rules for speech acts come from? *Language and Communication, 1,* 73–88.

Kuleshov, L. 1974. *Kuleshov on Film: Writings of Lev Kuleshov.* Selected, translated, and edited by R. Levaco. Berkeley: University of California Press.

Labov, W. 1967. *The Social Stratification of English in New York City.* Washington, D.C.: Center for Applied Linguistics.

——— 1972. *Language in the inner city.* Philadelphia: University of Pennsylvania Press.

Labov, W. and Fanshel, D. 1977. *Therapeutic Discourse: Psychotherapy as Conversation.* New York: Academic Press.

Lachman, R., Lachman, J. and Butterfield, E. 1976. *Cognitive Psychology and Information Processing: An Introduction.* Hillsdale, NJ: Lawrence Erlbaum.

Ladd, R.D. 1980. *Intonational Meaning.* Bloomington: Indiana University Press.

Lakoff, G. 1971. Presupposition and relative well-formedness. In D. Steinberg and Jakobovits, L. (Eds.), *Semantics: An Interdisciplinary Reader in Philosophy, Linguistics, and Psychology,* pp. 328–340. Cambridge: Cambridge University Press.

LaPiere, R. 1935. Attitudes vs. actions. *Social Forces, 13,* 230–237.

Larson, C. U. and Sanders, R. E. 1975. Faith, mystery, and data: An analysis of 'scientific' studies of persuasion. *Quarterly Journal of Speech, 61,* 178–194.

Levinson, S.C. 1983. *Pragmatics.* Cambridge: Cambridge University Press.

Lewis, D. 1979. Scorekeeping in a language game. *Journal of Philosophical Logic, 8,* 339–359.

Linn, L.S. 1965. Verbal attitudes and overt behavior: A study of racial discrimination. *Social Forces, 43,* 353–364.

Loewenberg, I. 1975. Identifying metaphor. *Foundations of Language, 12,* 315–338.

Long, M. 1983. Linguistic and conversational adjustments to nonnative speakers. *Studies in Second Language Acquisition, 5,* 177–193.

Longacre, R.E. 1983. *Grammar of Discourse.* New York: Plenum Press.

Lowenthal, F. 1982. Examples of auxiliary formalisms to help the development of children's logical thinking. In Lowenthal, F., Vandamme, F. and Cordier, J. (Eds.), *Language and Language Acquisition,* pp. 113–121. New York: Plenum Press.

——— 1984. Non-verbal communication devices in language acquisition. Paper read at the 7th World Congress of Applied Linguistics, Brussels.

Malandro, L.A. and Barker, L. 1983. *Nonverbal Communication.* Reading, MA: Addison-Wesley.

Marwell, G. and Schmitt, D. 1967. Dimensions of compliance-gaining behavior: An empirical analysis. *Sociometry, 30,* 350–364.

Mehrabian, A. 1972. *Nonverbal Communication.* Chicago: Aldine and Atherton.

Mehrabian, A. and Ferris, S. 1967. Inference of attitudes from nonverbal communication in two channels. *Journal of Consulting Psychology, 31,* 248–252.

Mehrabian, A. and Wiener, M. 1967. Decoding of inconsistent communications. *Journal of Personality and Social Psychology, 6,* 109–114.

Munn, N.L. 1940. The effect of knowledge of the situation upon judgment of emotion from facial expressions. *Journal of Abnormal and Social Psychology, 35,* 324–338.

Nofsinger, R.E. 1975. The demand ticket: A conversational device for getting the floor. *Speech Monographs, 42,* 1–9.

Novitz, D. 1977. *Pictures and their Use in Communication: A Philosophical Essay.* The Hague: Martinus Nijhoff.

Partee, B. (Ed.). 1976. *Montague Grammar.* New York: Academic Press.

Pearce, W.B. 1976. The coordinated management of meaning: A rules-based theory of interpersonal communication. In Miller, G.R. (Ed.), *Explorations in Interpersonal Communication,* pp. 17–35 Beverly Hills: Sage.

Pearce, W.B. and Conklin, F. 1971. Nonverbal vocalic communication and perception of a speaker. *Communication Monographs, 38,* 235–241.

Philipsen, G. 1975. Speaking 'like a man' in Teamsterville: Cultural patterns of role-enactment in an urban neighborhood. *Quarterly Journal of Speech, 62,* 13–22.

——— 1984. Deep perplexity, cultures, and ethnography. Paper read at the Speech Communication Association convention, Chicago.

Pollner, M. 1979. Explicative transactions: Making and managing meaning in a traffic court. In Psathas, G. (Ed.), *Everyday Language: Studies in Ethnomethodology,* pp. 227–256. New York: Irvington.

Posner, R. 1980. Semantics and pragmatics of sentence connectives in natural language. In Searle, J., Kiefer, F., and Bierwisch, M. (Eds.), *Speech Act Theory and Pragmatics,* pp. 169–204. Dordrecht: Reidel.

Potoker, S. 1982. The interpretation of discourse. Unpublished M.A. Thesis, State University of New York, Albany.

Poyatos, F. 1983. *New Perspectives in Nonverbal Communication.* Oxford: Pergamon.

Psathas, G. (Ed.). 1979. *Everyday Language: Studies in Ethnomethodology.* New York: Irvington.

Radford, K.J. 1977. *Complex Decision Problems: An Integrated Strategy for Resolution.* Reston, VA: Reston Publishing.

Raskin, V. 1985. *Semantic Mechanisms of Humor.* Dordrecht: Reidel.

Reichman, R. 1978. Conversational coherency. *Cognitive Science, 2,* 283–327.

Rogers, E. 1976. Communication and development: The passing of the dominant paradigm. *Communication Research, 3,* 121–133.

Rogers, E. with Shoemaker, F. L. 1971. *Communication of Innovations: A Cross-cultural Approach.* New York: Free Press.

Roloff, M. and Miller, G. (Eds.). 1980. *Persuasion: New Directions in Theory and Research.* Beverly Hills, CA: Sage.

Ross, J.R. 1970. On declarative sentences. In Jacobs, R. A. and Rosenbaum, P.S. (Eds.), *Readings in English Transformational Grammar,* pp. 222–272. Waltham, MA: Ginn.

Ruben, B. (Ed.). 1979. *Communication Yearbook III.* New Brunswick, NJ: Transaction Press.

Rumelhart, D. 1975. Notes on a schema for stories. In Bobrow, D. and Collins, A. (Eds.), *Representation and Understanding: Studies in Cognitive Science,* pp. 211–236. New York: Academic Press.

Sacks, H., Schegloff, E. A., and Jefferson, G. 1974. A simplest systematics for the organization of turn-taking for conversation. *Language, 50,* 696–735.

Sadock, J. 1974. *Toward a Linguistic Theory of Speech Acts.* New York: Academic Press.

Sandell, R. 1977. *Linguistic Style and Persuasion.* London: Academic Press.

Sanders, R.E. 1973. Aspects of figurative language. *Linguistics,* #96, 56–100.

——— 1980. Principles of relevance: A theory of the relationship between language and communication. *Communication and Cognition, 13,* 77–95.

——— 1981. The interpretation of discourse. *Communication Quarterly, 29,* 209–217.

——— 1983. Tools for cohering discourse and their strategic utilization: Markers of structural connections and meaning relations. In Craig, R. T. and Tracy, K. (Eds.), *Conversational Coherence: Form, Structure, and Strategy,* pp. 67–80. Beverly Hills, CA: Sage.

——— 1984. Style, meaning, and message effects. *Communication Monographs, 51,* 154–167.

——— 1985. The interpretation of nonverbals. *Semiotica, 55,* 195–216.

Schank, R. 1977. Rules and topics in conversation. *Cognitive Science, 1,* 421–441.

Schank, R.C. and Abelson, R.P. 1977. *Scripts, Plans, Goals, and Understanding: An Inquiry into Human Knowledge Structures.* Hillsdale, NJ: Lawrence Erlbaum.

Scheflen, A.E. 1972. *Body Language and the Social Order.* Englewood Cliffs, NJ: Prentice Hall.

Schegloff, E.A. 1972a. Sequencing in conversational openings. In Gumperz, J. J. and Hymes, D. (Eds.), *Directions in Sociolinguistics,* pp. 346–380. New York: Holt, Rinehart & Winston.

——— 1972b. Notes on a conversational practice: Formulating place. In Sudnow, D. (Ed.), *Studies in Social Interaction,* pp. 75–119. New York: Free Press.

——— 1982. Discourse as an interactional achievement: Some uses of 'uh huh' and other things that come between sentences. In Tannen, D. (Ed.) *Analyzing Discourse: Text and Talk,* pp. 71–93. Georgetown University Roundtable on languages and linguistics. Washington, D.C.: Georgetown University Press.

Schegloff, E.A., Jefferson, G., and Sacks, H. 1977. The preference for self-correction in the organization of repair in conversation. *Language, 53,* 361–382.

Schegloff, E.A. and Sacks, H. 1974. Opening up closings. In Turner, R. (Ed.), *Ethomethodology,* pp. 233–264. Harmondsworth, England: Penguin.

Schneider, D.J., Hastorf, A.H., and Ellsworth, P.C. 1979. *Person Perception,* 2nd Ed. Reading, MA: Addison-Wesley.

Searle, J.R. 1969. *Speech Acts: An Essay in the Philosophy of Language.* London: Cambridge University Press.

——— 1972. Chomsky's revolution in linguistics. *New York Review of Books,* June 29, *18,* 16–24.

——— 1979. *Expression and Meaning.* Cambridge: Cambridge University Press.

——— 1980. The background of meaning. In Searle, J., Kiefer, F. and Bierwisch, M. (Eds.), *Speech Act Theory and Pragmatics,* pp. 221–232. Dordrecht: Reidel.

Shuy, R.W. 1982. Topic as the unit of analysis in a criminal law case. In Tannen, D. (Ed.), *Analyzing Discourse: Text and Talk,* pp. 113–126. Georgetown University Roundtable on Languages and Linguistics. Washington, D.C.: Georgetown University Press.

Simon, H. 1965. *Administrative Behavior,* 2nd ed. New York: Free Press.

Sontag, S. 1977. *On Photography.* New York: Farrar, Straus, & Giroux.

Sousa-Poza, J.F. and Rohrberg, R. 1977. Body movement in relation to type of information (person- and non-person oriented) and cognitive style (field independence). *Human Communication Research, 4,* 19–29.

Sperber, D. and Wilson, D. 1982. Mutual knowledge and relevance in theories of comprehension. In Smith, N.V. (Ed.), *Mutual Knowledge,* 61–85. London: Academic Press.

——— 1986. *Relevance: Communication and Cognition.* Oxford: Basil Blackwell.

Stampe, D.W. 1975. Meaning and truth in the theory of speech acts. In Cole, P. & Morgan, J.L. (Eds.), *Syntax and Semantics 3: Speech Acts,* pp. 1–39. New York: Academic Press.

Steinfatt, T.M. and Infante, D.A. 1976. Attitude-behavior relationships in communication research. *Quarterly Journal of Speech, 62,* 267–278.

Tannen, D. 1981. New York Jewish conversational style. *International Journal of the Sociology of Language,* 30, 133–139.

——— 1984. *Conversational Style: Analyzing Talk among Friends.* Norwood, NJ: Ablex.

Taylor, T.J. 1984. Editing rules and understanding: The case against sentence-based syntax. *Language and Communication, 4,* 105–127.

Thomas, J. 1983. Crosscultural pragmatic failure. *Applied Linguistics, 4,* 91–112.

Tracy, K. 1982. On getting the point: Distinguishing "issues" from "events," an aspect of conversational coherence. In Burgoon, M. (Ed.), *Communication Yearbook 5,* pp. 279–301. New Brunswick, NJ: Transaction Press.

Townsend, D.J. and Bever, T.G. 1982. Natural units of representation interact during sentence comprehension. *Journal of Verbal Learning and Verbal Behavior, 21,* 688–703.

Van Dijk, T.A. 1972. *Some Aspects of Text Grammars.* The Hague: Mouton.

——— 1977. *Text and Context: Explorations in the Semantics and Pragmatics of Discourse.* New York: Longman Group.

——— 1980. *Macrostructures: An Interdisciplinary Study of Global Structures in Discourse, Interaction, and Cognition.* Hillsdale, NJ: Lawrence Erlbaum.

——— 1982. Episodes as units of discourse anlysis. In Tannen, D. (Ed.), *Analyzing Discourse: Text and Talk,* pp. 177–195. Georgetown University Roundtable on Languages and Linguistics. Washington, D.C.: Georgetown University Press.

Varonis, E.M. and Gass, S.M. 1985. Miscommunication in native/nonnative conversation. *Language in Society, 14,* 327–343.

Veltrusky, J. 1976. Some aspects of the pictorial sign. In Matejka, L. and Titunik, I. (Eds.), *Semiotics of Art,* pp. 245–264. Cambridge, MA: MIT Press.

Volkmar, F.R. and Siegel, A.E. 1982. Responses to consistent and discrepant social communications. In Feldman, R. (Ed.), *Development of Nonverbal Behavior in Children,* pp. 231–256. New York: Springer-Verlag.

Warriner, C.K. 1958. The nature and functions of official morality. *American Journal of Sociology, 64,* 165–168.

Werth, P. 1981. The concept of 'relevance' in conversational analysis. In Werth, P. (Ed.), *Conversation and Discourse: Structure and Interpretation,* pp. 129–154. London: Croom Heim.

Wiemann, J. 1977. Transcriptions of four conversations in dyads comprising undergraduate female suitemates. Mimeo, University of California, Santa Barbara.

Wilson, D. 1975. *Presuppositions and Non-truth-conditional Semantics.* New York: Academic Press.

Winograd, T. 1980. What does it mean to understand language? *Cognitive Science, 4,* 209–241.

Wittgenstein, L. 1953. *Philosophical Investigations.* Oxford: Blackwell.

Woelfel, J. and Fink, E. 1980. *The Measurement of Communication Processes: Galileo Theory and Method.* New York: Academic Press.

Zivin, G. 1982. Watching the sands shift: Conceptualizing development of nonverbal mastery. In Feldman, R. (Ed.), *Development of Nonverbal Behavior in Children,* pp. 63–98. New York: Springer-Verlag.

Subject Index

Page numbers for definitions are in italics

Agenda, 95–98, 149, 164, 165, 182, 199–200, 218–220, 224–226
Attributions, 37–38, 85–86, 136–137, 159–160

Background knowledge, 51–53, 60, 62–63, 73, 79–81, 130, 162–166, 167–168

Calculated speech
  examples of, 13–14, 17–21, 203–206, 222–224, 232–233, 234–236
  in conversation, 218–220
  in counseling and psychotherapy, 251
  in management, 250
  in politics, 249
  in teaching, 248
  to achieve goals, 12–13
  to constrain responses, 6–7, 17
  to control understandings, 6–7, 17
  to persuade, 232–239
Checks and balances on specific interpretations, 83–86, 137–139, 160–161
Cognition and meanings of nonverbal displays, 130, 133, 136–137
Cognition and utterance meaning
  conversational implicature, 62–67
  illocutionary acts, 73–74
  propositional content, 52–55
Cognitive foundations of specific interpretations. *See* Warrants for interpretive focus
Cognitive foundations of calculated speech, 8–9, 25, 30–31, 34–36
  in conversation, 225–227
  for estimating the probability of subsequent entries, 197–202
  for projections of subsequent nonverbal displays, 193–197
  for projections of subsequent utterances, 185–193, 197–199
Cognitive schemata, 34–36, 62–64, 66–67, 164, 167–170
Coherence, *84*
  and constraints on speech, 11–12, 17, 24, 35, 135, 176
  and relevance, 8, 82, 83, 98, 133
  and specific interpretations, 9, 83–86, 137–139, 160–161
  See also Grounds of coherence
Competence/performance distinction, 26–27
  and decision theory, 176–177
  and strategic communication, 30–31, 202, 247

criticisms of, 27–28
need for, 29–30
Constraint, 9, 10–12, *24–25,* 31–32, 135–136, 186–199, 231–236, 248–251
Conventional implicatures, 58–59
Conversation
agenda of participants, 218–220
coordination, 208–211
strategic communication, 224–228
topic, 216–218
turn-taking, 212–215
Conversational implicatures
and background knowledge, 62–63, 165–166
and illocutionary acts, 191–192
and nonverbal displays, 141–142, 144–145
and propositional content, 33, 48–49, 61, 64, 68, 81–82, 91–92, 190–191
and speaker's subjective state, 61, 64–65, 92–93
apprehension of, 61–67
generalized, 59–60
in intercultural communication, 165–166, 170, 171
relevance of, 91–94, 189–192
Conversational maxims, 61, 62–65

Decision theory, 34–36, 38, 175–179, 183–184
Dialogue, *4*
Discourse, *4*

Errors in performance, 30, 50, 67, 80–81, 154–155, 161–166, 210–211

Forecasting principles
and principles of specific interpretation, 181–182, 184–185
for entries subsequent to conversational implicatures, 180–182
for entries subsequent to illocutionary acts, 192–192
for entries subsequent to nonverbal displays, 197–199
for entries subsequent to propositional content, 185–189
for nonverbal displays subsequent to utterances, 194–197
in performance, 178–179
Fluidity of understandings, 9, 10, 12–13, 16, 25, 83–85, 86, 101–102

Grounds of coherence, *84*
and progression of entries in sequence, 99, 180–181, 216–218, 231–236, 244
in intercultural communication, 154, 160–170
of illocutionary acts, 88–91, 188–189, 192–193
of conversational implicatures, 91–94, 189–191
of nonverbal displays, 133–135, 194–199
of propositional content, 86–88, 186–189

Illocutionary acts
and conversational implicatures, 191–192
and nonverbal displays, 141–142, 145–146
and propositional content, 47–48, 75–76, 188–189
equivocality of, 69–71

identification of, 72–74
in intercultural communication, 164–166, 168–169
relevance of, 88–91, 188–189, 192–193, 198–199
Inference
of actor's traits, 37–38
of conversational implicatures, 61–67
of illocutionary act, 71–74
of intended nonverbal meaning, 133–137
of intended utterance meaning, 79–81
of interpretation errors, 154, 156–158
Implicature. *See* Conventional implicature; conversational implicature
Intercultural communication, 153–158, 160–161, 170–171
under conditions of maximum difference, 158–160, 167–170
under conditions of moderate difference, 161–167

Meanings
contrasted with specific interpretations, 4–5, 49–50, 98–99, 131
conversational implicature, 60–61, 64–67
illocutionary act, 69–73
of nonverbal displays, 130, 148–149
propositional content, 50–58
Meaning relations, 9–10
Media of communication, 146–151
Metaphor, 58
Metatheory. *See* Theory of strategic communication

Native-nonnative communication. *See* Intercultural communication
Nonverbal displays
combined with utterances, 137–140, 143–146
in intercultural communication, 154, 162–163, 167–168
meanings of, 130, 148–149
relevance of, 136–137, 140–143, 194–196
role in turn-taking, 209–210, 212
specific interpretation of, 133–137

Person perception, 37–38
Persuasion
and controlling understandings, 5–7, 231, 243–244
and strategic communication, 229, 243–244
in dialogues, 231–234
in discourse, 234–236
of individuals, 230–236
of social aggregates, 239–243
Pictures, 148–149
Pragmatics of utterance, 51–68
Principles of specific interpretation
and forecasting principles, 184–185, 194
empirical test of, 33–34, 102–109
explanatory power of, 31–32
for nonverbal displays, 135, 137
for utterances, 87, 90–91, 94, 96
Probability
and theory of strategic communication, 24–27, 33, 34, 39, 175
of specific interpretations, 87, 135–136, 154
See also Relative probability
Propositional content

and background knowledge, 51–55
and conversational implicatures, 33, 48–49, 61, 64, 68, 81–82, 91–92, 190–191
and illocutionary acts, 47–48, 75–76, 188–189
and nonverbal displays, 141–144
and pragmatics of utterance, 55–58
and truth conditions, 50–51
relevance of, 86–88, 185–189, 197–198
Public record, 8, 80, 151

Relative probability
and constraints on speech, 5–6, 24
of subsequent entries, 176, 178, 199–202, 231, 233–234, 236
Relevance of nonverbal displays
in mass media, 149–150
in sequences, 133–137, 194–197
to utterances, 140–143, 197–199
Relevance of utterances
alternative concepts of, 81–82, 86, 88–89
in terms of conversational implicature, 91–94, 189–192
in terms of illocutionary force, 88–91, 188–189, 192–193
in terms of propositional content, 86–88, 186–188
to goals, 94–97
to nonverbal displays, 143–146, 197–199

Scripts. *See* Cognitive schemata
Semantic theory, 51–58
Specific interpretations
contrasted with meanings, 4–5, 49–50, 98–99
fluidity of, 9, 83–86
influences on judgments of, 79–81, 133
of nonverbal displays, 135–137, 140–143
of utterances, 86–97, 143–146
Strategic communication
and decision theory, 35, 175–179, 183–184
and intelligent activity, 25–26
and projecting consequences, 3–7, 34–38, 185–199
in mass media, 150
See also Calculated speech
Structural relations, 10
Style, 178–179, 182, 187–188, 190–191, 194–196, 219

Theory of strategic communication, 23, 25–27, 29–31, 34–38, 39–42, 175, 183–185
Topic of conversation, 216–218
Turn-taking, 207–208, 209–210, 212–215

Utterance. *See* Conversational implicature; illocutionary act; pragmatics of utterance; propositional content

Warrants for interpretive focus
or conversational implicatures, 91–94
on illocutionary acts, 88–91
on particular utterance meanings, 95–96
on propositional content, 86–87
on single-values of nonverbal displays, 133–137

Index of Proper Names

Abelson, R., 35
Ajzen, I., et al., 230
Atkinson, J.M. and Heritage, J., 208
Austin, J., 8, 69

Bach, K. and Harnish, R.M., 70, 71
Bailey, C.-J.N., 27
Begg, I. and Harris, G., 101
Birdwhistell, R., 130, 145
Blumer, H., 230
Bolinger, D., 52
Bradac, J.J., et al., 27
Brown, G., Currie, K.L. and Kenworthy, J., 144
Brown, P. and Levinson, S.L., 32
Buck, R., 132
Bugental, D.E., Henker, B. and Whalen, C.K., 144, 165
Bugental, D.E., Kaswan, J.W. and Love, L.R., 138
Burgoon, M. and Bettinghaus, E.P., 229

Carpenter, P.A. and Daneman, M., 101
Chomsky, N., 27, 28, 56, 143
Chun, A.E., et al., 155, 156
Clarke, D.C. and Argyle, M., 180
Cole, P., 8
Coulmas, F., 153
Coulthard, M. and Brazil, D., 143
Crow, B.K., 207, 220
Craig, R.T. and Tracy, K., 208, 219
Cushman, D.P. and McPhee, R.D., 230

Dascal, M., 82, 91, 219
DeFleur, M.L. and Westie, F.R., 238, 239
Derber, C., 217
Deutscher, I., 230, 236
DeVito, J.A., 220
Duncan, S. Jr., Brunner, L.J. and Fiske, D.W., 207, 208

Edelsky, C., 208, 210
Edmondson, W., 10, 32, 70, 73, 74, 89, 95, 232
Ekman, P. and Friesen, W.V., 132, 133, 145, 153
Ekman, P., Friesen, W.V. and Ellsworth, P.C., 132
Erickson, F., 208, 210, 216

Fishbein, M., 230
Fishbein, M. and Ajzen, I., 200
Friedman, H.S., 129, 146

Frijda, N.H., 132

Galin, D. and Ornstein, R., 145, 165
Garfinkel, H., 35, 153, 207, 230
Gass, S.M. and Varonis, E.M., 155, 156
Gazdar, G., 8, 56
Goffman, E., 35, 207, 230
Goldberg, J., 207
Goodwin, C., 207
Gordon, D. and Lakoff, G., 51
Green, G.M. and Morgan, J.L., 70
Grice, H.P., 8, 48, 58, 59, 60, 61, 67, 81, 82, 92, 143, 144, 153
Grimes, J.E., 219
Gumperz, J.J., 153, 155, 207, 212

Halliday, M.A.K., 56
Halliday, M.A.K. and Hasan, R., 56, 219
Harper, R.G., Wiens, A.N. and Matarazzo, J.D., 130, 153
Hart, R.J. and Brown, B.L., 145, 165
Harris, R.J. and Monaco, G., 101
Hofstadter, D., 40
Holloway, C.A., 35
Hopper, R., 207
Horn, L., 59
Hymes, D., 12, 27, 153

Jacobs, S. and Jackson, S., 207

Kartunnen, L. and Peters, S., 86
Katz, J.J., 51
Katz, J.J. and Fodor, J., 51
Kaufer, D., 27
Keenan, J.M. and Kintsch, W., 101
Keller, E., 207
Kempson, R., 8, 51
Kochman, T., 153
Kreckel, M., 27
Kuleshov, L., 132, 134

Labov, W., 153
Labov, W. and Fanshel, D., 89, 207
Lachman, R., Lachman, J. and Butterfield, E., 101
Ladd, R.D., 153
Lakoff, G., 143
LaPiere, R., 236, 237
Larson, C.U. and Sanders, R.E., 230
Levinson, S.C., 8, 153, 207
Lewis, D., 12
Linn, L.S., 238, 239
Loewenberg, I., 58
Long, M., 155, 156
Longacre, R.E., 10
Lowenthal, F., 159

Malandro, L.A. and Barker, L., 130, 145
Marwell, G. and Schmitt, D., 229
Mehrabian, A., 129
Mehrabian, A. and Ferris, S., 138
Mehrabian, A. and Wiener, M., 138
Munn, N.L., 132

Nofsinger, R.E., 207
Norton, R., 129
Novitz, D., 148

Partee, B., 51
Pearce, W.B., 35, 207
Pearce, W.B. and Conklin, F., 229
Philipsen, G., 153, 166
Pollner, M., 213
Posner, R., 57
Potoker, S., 103, 104
Poyatos, F., 146, 153
Psathas, G., 207

Radford, K.J., 35, 184
Raskin, V., 52
Reichman, R., 56, 207, 208, 219
Rogers, E., 244
Roloff, M. and Miller, G., 230
Ross, J.R., 51
Rumelhart, D., 10

Sacks, H., Schegloff, E.A., and Jefferson, G., 207, 208, 209, 212
Sadock, J., 51
Sandell, R., 229
Sanders, R.E., 8, 9, 34, 58, 82, 131, 182, 207, 211, 219
Schank, R., 94
Schank, R.C. and Abelson, R.P., 35, 86, 153, 207, 216
Scheflen, A.E., 145
Schegloff, E.A., 74, 192
Schegloff, E.A., Jefferson, G., and Sacks, H., 10
Schegloff, E.A. and Sacks, H., 192
Schneider, D.J., Hastorf, A.H., and Ellsworth, P.C., 37
Searle, J.R., 8, 27, 47, 52, 69, 70, 75, 145, 153, 163
Shuy, R.W., 220
Simon, H., 36
Sontag, S., 149
Sousa-Poza, J.F. and Rohrberg, R., 145, 165–166
Sperber, D. and Wilson, D., 81, 82
Stampe, D.W., 70, 73
Steinfatt, T.M. and Infante, D.A., 230

Tannen, D., 153, 209, 210
Taylor, T.J., 27
Thomas, J., 155
Tracy, K., 94, 187, 207, 219
Townsend, D.J. and Bever, T.G., 101

Van Dijk, T.A., 10, 82, 86, 219
Varonis, E.M. and Gass, S.M., 155, 156
Veltrusky, J., 147
Volkmar, F.R. and Siegel, A.E., 132

Warriner, C.K., 238
Watzlawick, P., Beavin J., and Jackson, D., 129
Werth, P., 86
Wiemann, J., 13, 179, 213
Winograd, T., 35
Wittgenstein, L., 35, 153
Woelfel, J. and Fink, E., 229, 240, 242

Zivin, G., 132, 135